Charles Peirce on Ethi
and the Normative Sci

This book presents a comprehensive and systematic picture of Charles Peirce's ethics and esthetics, arguing that Peirce established a normative framework for the study of right conduct and good ends. It also connects Peirce's normative thought to contemporary debates in ethical theory.

Peirce sought to articulate the relation among logic as right thinking, ethics as good conduct and, in an unorthodox sense of esthetics, the pursuit of ends that are fine and worthy. Each plays an important role in ethical life. Once esthetics has determined what makes an end worthy and admirable, and ethics determines which are good and right to pursue, logical and scientific reasoning is employed to figure the most likely means to attain those ends. Ethics does the additional duty of ensuring that the means conform to ideals of conduct. In the process, Peirce develops an interesting theory of moral motivation, an account of moral reasoning, moral truth and a picture of what constitutes a moral community.

Charles Peirce on Ethics, Esthetics and the Normative Sciences will be of interest to scholars and students working on Peirce, pragmatism, American philosophy and metaethics.

James Jakób Liszka is a Senior Scholar at the Institute for Ethics in Public Life and Professor of Philosophy at The State University of New York, College at Plattsburgh. He is also Director of the Center for Interdisciplinary and Area Studies. He is Professor Emeritus at the University of Alaska Anchorage and was Visiting Professor at Beijing Language and Culture University and the China Youth University for Political Sciences in Beijing. He was Humanities Fellow at the University of Toronto, Scarborough College. He is the author of *Pragmatist Ethics: A Problem-Based Approach to What Matters* (2021), *Moral Competence* (2002), *A General Introduction to the Semeiotic of Charles S. Peirce* (1996) and *The Semiotic of Myth: A Critical Study of the Symbol* (1989). He has also published several articles on ethical theory, environmental ethics, pragmatism, semiotics and narrative theory.

Routledge Studies in American Philosophy
Edited by Willem deVries
University of New Hampshire, USA

Henry Jackman
York University, Canada

Pragmatic Perspectives
Constructivism beyond Truth and Realism
Robert Schwartz

Wilfrid Sellars and Twentieth-Century Philosophy
Edited by Stefan Brandt and Anke Breunig

Challenging the New Atheism
Pragmatic Confrontations in the Philosophy of Religion
Aaron Pratt Shepherd

John Dewey's Ethical Theory
The 1932 *Ethics*
Edited by Roberto Frega and Steven Levine

The Philosophy of Ralph Waldo Emmerson
Joseph Urbas

Pragmatism and Social Philosophy
Exploring a Stream of Ideas from America to Europe
Edited by Michael G. Festl

C. I. Lewis
The *A Priori* and the Given
Edited by Quentin Kammer, Jean-Philippe Narboux, and Henri Wagner

Charles Peirce on Ethics, Esthetics and the Normative Sciences
James Jakób Liszka

For more information about this series, please visit: www.routledge.com/Routledge-Studies-in-American-Philosophy/book-series/RSAP

Charles Peirce on Ethics, Esthetics and the Normative Sciences

James Jakób Liszka

NEW YORK AND LONDON

First published 2021
by Routledge
605 Third Avenue, New York, NY 10158

and by Routledge
2 Park Square, Milton Park, Abingdon, Oxon, OX14 4RN

Routledge is an imprint of the Taylor & Francis Group, an informa business

Library of Congress Cataloging-in-Publication Data
Names: Liszka, James Jakób, 1950– author.
Title: Charles Peirce on ethics, esthetics and the normative sciences / James Jakób Liszka.
Description: New York, NY : Routledge, 2021. | Series: Routledge studies in American philosophy | Includes bibliographical references and index.
Identifiers: LCCN 2021018296 (print) | LCCN 2021018297 (ebook)
Subjects: LCSH: Peirce, Charles S. (Charles Sanders), 1839–1914. | Ethics. | Aesthetics. | Normativity (Ethics)
Classification: LCC B945.P44 L57 2021 (print) | LCC B945.P44 (ebook) | DDC 170/.44—dc23
LC record available at https://lccn.loc.gov/2021018296
LC ebook record available at https://lccn.loc.gov/2021018297

ISBN: 978-0-367-74600-1 (hbk)
ISBN: 978-0-367-75086-2 (pbk)
ISBN: 978-1-003-16089-2 (ebk)

Typeset in Sabon
by Apex CoVantage, LLC

To my brother, Joseph Liszka

Where would we be without gratitude?
The loss of memory.
Of parents aside the sick-child bed,
The comfort of the hearth-warm home,
A brother's arm around the shoulder,
A sister's little mercies,
A teacher's inspiriting help.
They would never know.
At the end of life,
What did it all mean to you?
They would not be sure
If the path upon which their compass sent you,
Was the path of all your life's goods.
Thank you.

Contents

Acknowledgments

Any scholarly work is a product of a community of inquiry. I would like to thank the many colleagues who, in the give-and-take of criticism and response and through their scholarship, helped to refine this work. I am especially grateful to colleagues whose comments on papers related to this work helped to shape its core arguments. Among these are Nathan Houser, Vincent Colapietro, André De Tienne, Ivo Ibri and Cornellis de Waal. These included presentations at the Society for the Advancement of American Philosophy, the American Philosophy Association, the Charles S. Peirce Society and the Center for Pragmatism Studies at the Pontifical Catholic University of São Paulo. In addition, I would like to thank the reviewers of the manuscript whose reading improved the original. I'm especially beholden to Genie Babb for many long talks that helped to work out some of the more difficult arguments of the book. I would also like to thank Zachary Liszka and Caitlin Terry for some insightful conversations as well. Many thanks to Andrew Weckenmann, Philosophy Editor at Routledge/Taylor & Francis Group, for being so helpful in shepherding the manuscript to its publication.

I am grateful to the editors of *Cognitio*, Prof. Ivo Ibri, for permission to reprint extracts from the following: "Peirce's Convergence Theory of Truth Redux" (2019), "Peirce's Esthetics as a Science of Ideal Ends" (2018), "New Direction in Pragmatic Ethics" (2013) and "Rethinking the Pragmatic Theory of Meaning" (2009). Also, the book has excerpts from "Peirce's Idea of Ethics as a Normative Science," *Transactions of the Charles S. Peirce Society* (2014), "Community in Peirce: Science as a Means and as an End," *Transactions of the Charles S. Peirce Society* (1978) and *A General Introduction to the Semeiotic of Charles S. Peirce* (1996), published by Indiana University Press. There are also excerpts from "Charles Peirce on Ethics" in *The Normative Thought of Charles S. Peirce* (2012), Cornelis De Waal and Krzysztof Skowroński, editors and published by Fordham University Press.

Notes on In-Text Citations

All in-text citations follow APA style except the following:

Citations to the work of Charles Peirce are indicated as follows (dates are the dates of the original publication or manuscript):

(Date, CP volume. paragraph)
(1978). *The collected papers of Charles S. Peirce* (Charles Hartshorne, Paul Weiss and Arthur Burks, Eds.) (Vols. 1–8). Harvard University Press.

(Date, W, volume, page)
(1982–). *The writings of Charles S. Peirce* (Max Fisch, Edward Moore, Christian Kloesel, Nathan Houser, André De Tienne, et al., Eds.) (Vols. 1–6, 8). Indiana University Press.

(Date, EP, volume, page)
(1992). *The Essential Peirce* (Nathan Houser and Christian Kloesel, Eds.) (Vol. 1–2) Indiana University Press.

(Date, VC, page)
(1958). *Values in a universe of chance. Selected writings of Charles S. Peirce* (Philip Wiener, Ed.). Doubleday.

(Date, NEM, volume, page)
(1976). *The new elements of mathematics* (Carolyn Eisele, Ed.) (Vols. 1–4). Mouton.

(Date, CN, volume, page)
(1978). *Charles S. Peirce: Contributions to The Nation* (Kenneth Ketner and James Cook, Eds.) (Vols. 1–3). Texas Tech University Press.

(Date, LW, page)
(1977). *Semiotic and significs. The Correspondence between Charles S. Peirce and Victoria Lady Welby* (Charles Hardwick, Ed.). Indiana University Press.

(Date, RLT, page)
(1992). *Reasoning and the logic of things* (Kenneth Ketner, Ed.). Harvard University Press.

(Date, HL, page)
(1997). *Pragmatism as a principle and method of right thinking.: The 1903 Harvard lectures on pragmatism* (Patricia Turrisi, Ed.). State University of New York Press.

(Date, R, manuscript number, page)
Manuscript numbers as listed in Robin, Richard (1967). *Annotated catalogue of the papers of Charles S. Peirce*. University of Massachusetts Press.

Citations to Aristotle's work by **(title, standard Bekker numbers)**. Citations to Plato's work by **(title, standard Stephanus pagination)**. Because of the uncertainty of the dates of Plato's and Aristotle's works, in-text citations do not include dates.

Introduction

If philosophy is witness, there are three fundamental inquiries that have vexed thinkers over the years: How to distinguish the true from the false; what counts something as good and is beauty more than just a matter of taste? Like all great philosophers, Charles Peirce put his shoulder to the wheel in service to the "great movement" of the "true, beautiful and good" (1893, CP 6.292). They are a "trio of ideals which has been recognized since antiquity" (1902, R433, p. 1) and are "three fundamental categories of objects of desire" (1902, R433, p. 3).

Peirce, the logician and scientist, was mostly concerned with the matter of truth, and much of his academic life was devoted to developing the science of logic and the understanding of scientific methodology. These were key since he argued that truth would be the result of inquiries with right methodologies persisted sufficiently over time (1902, CP 2.781). A convergence of belief among such a community of inquirers would be a fallible indication of success. But starting sometime in the 1880s, Peirce saw an important interrelation between truth and goodness, logic and ethics—and eventually between ethics and esthetics, as he understood it. In a letter to William James in 1902, he writes:

> It was not until after that [the Cambridge Lectures in 1898] that I obtained the proof that logic must be founded on ethics, of which it is a higher development. Even then, I was for some time so stupid as not to see that ethics rests in the same manner on a foundation of esthetics,—by which, it is needless to say, I don't mean milk and water and sugar.
>
> (1902, CP 8.255)

As he elaborates in *The Minute Logic*,

> Before my logic was brought under the guidance of ethics, it was already a window through which much important truth could be seen, but dim with dust, distorting details by striae. Under the guidance of ethics, I took it and melted it down, reduced it to a fluid

> condition. I filtered it till it was clear. I cast it in the true mould; and when it had become solid, I spared no elbow-grease in polishing it. It is now a comparatively brilliant lens, showing much that was not discernible before.
>
> (1902, CP 2.198)

Peirce realized that reasoning needed to be directed toward good ends, and there had to be some account of why people should adopt the standards of reasoning to attain those ends. Otherwise, scientific reasoning in particular was in danger of becoming amorally instrumental. “A man,” Peirce says, “might be ever so great a rogue without being the worse reasoner for that” (1902, R432, p. 6). Moreover, if truth was the result of inquiries done right, inquirers had to have certain moral sentiments and virtues and communities of inquiry had to adopt certain norms for inquiries to be truth-apt. Logic and scientific methodology alone was not sufficient for such success. “The most vital factors in the method of modern science,” he says, “have not been the following of this or that logical prescription—although these have had their value too,” but “moral factors” (1902, CP 7.87).

His attempt to show an interrelation and coherence among the three fundamental norms of truth, beauty and goodness may have been inspired by one of Peirce’s favorites among the 18th-century moral sentimentalists—Shaftesbury. There may also have been some inspiration from Victor Cousin, whose *Lectures on the True, the Beautiful and the Good* (1853), brought the same issue to the fore in the 19th century. He was certainly a thinker with whom Peirce was quite familiar (1869, W2, p. 312; n.d. R 1573, pp. 10–11). Shaftesbury, after Plato (*Philebus*, 65a), argued for a unity of the three based on the formal properties of harmony and proportion exhibited in each of these norms (1732, III, p. 182). But Peirce is also likely to have been inspired by the systematic relation among Immanuel Kant’s three *Critiques*, his first philosophic mentor. Kant argued that the unity of theoretical and practical reason is through the idea of the purposiveness of nature, the subject of the third *Critique* (1781, A815–6; B843–4). This is perhaps why Peirce sees the study of esthetics in a non-traditional sense, as tied to the study of purpose, what ends are admirable and fine to pursue.

As this study of Peirce’s normative thought intends to show, Peirce strikes out his own path for the unity of truth, goodness and what ends are best to pursue. Peirce’s pragmatic maxim provides a simpler more elegant solution to the unity of theoretical and practical reasoning and connects it to purpose. “The most striking feature of the new theory,” Peirce notes, “was its recognition of an inseparable connection between rational cognition and rational purpose; and that consideration it was which determined the preference for the name pragmatism.” The pragmatic maxim showed how “the rational purport of a word or other expression, lies exclusively in its conceivable bearing upon the conduct of life" (1905, CP 5.412).

Peirce hoped to find a unity and coherence among truth, beauty and goodness in the development of his triad of normative sciences. In one of the drafts of his Harvard Lectures of 1903, he gives one of his most cogent accounts of the sense of these studies:

> Normative science ought to examine all questions relating to the possible consistent ends of phenomena. Not merely what the ends are and what are the conditions of conformity to those ends, or their mere quantity of goodness and badness, but also, the diversity in the different paths by which such ends may be pursued, and the different stadia in those paths; as well as the different ways in which the ends may be missed.
>
> (1903, R311, p. 9)

Peirce relished the study of ethics. He thought the study "entrancing" (1903, CP 5.36), and "the logical analysis of the conceptions connected with morals is one of the very best whetstones for the wits ever found" (1900, CN 2, p. 249). Although Peirce recognized that "my opinions on ethics and esthetics are not so well matured as my opinions on logic," (1903, R 311, p. 10), he wanted to make the study of the three normative sciences as scientific as possible, as he understood it:

> [I]t is above all the normative sciences, esthetics, ethics, and logic, that men are in dire need of having severely criticized, in their relation to the new world created by science. Unfortunately, this need is as unconscious as it is great. The evils are in some superficial way recognized; but it never occurs to anybody that the study of esthetics, ethics, and logic can be seriously important, because these sciences are conceived by all, but their deepest students, in the old way.
>
> (c. 1905, CP 5.513)

Peirce engaged in the study of the normative sciences at a point where science was undergoing significant transformation in methodology, with its growing emphasis on laboratory experimentalism. The late 19th century saw a marriage of science, industry and technology in practical life, especially in Peirce's own fields of chemistry and physics—and Peirce's pragmatic maxim presages it all. Peirce's pragmatism was essentially a herald of this coming confluence of theory and practice. But in his later years, he also saw that it had wrought the Gilded Age, Social Darwinism and a striking individualism and egoism that Peirce wrote strongly against. He worried that science itself may be corrupted by its very usefulness, and its noble end of truth-seeking usurped by instrumental and self-interested ends.

What is the way to study ethics and esthetics in light of "this new world created by science"? Unfortunately, although Peirce wrote substantially on logic and semiotic in published and unpublished work, his work on ethics and esthetics is in fragments. Perhaps the closest he got to putting his ethical thought together was in the fourth chapter of his projected *Minute Logic*, composed around 1901–1902 (c. 1902, R432-R-434), his Harvard Lectures in 1903, particularly the fifth lecture (1903, CP 5.120–150; 1903, HL, pp. 205–220; 1903, R 310–312), and some of the Lowell Lectures, given later in that year (1903, R448). He never finished the chapter on ethics or the book on logic. The Harvard Lecture provides one of the best guides to his account of the normative sciences. But, by the turn of the century, the troubles of his life multiplied and the time needed to make whole this pursuit of the normative sciences diminished.

The primary purpose here is to complete as far as possible what is incomplete in Peirce's study of normativity and the normative sciences and to get a good sense of his ethical thought. This is not merely for the sake of understanding Peirce, but for the sake of introducing an insightful and innovative account of ethics, and an interesting rethinking of the study of esthetics. This effort is analogous to what the Gestalt psychologists called *the principle of closure*, the phenomenon in which people tend to perceive incomplete figures as complete when there is sufficient lead. The goal is to take the leads Peirce provides throughout his work and develop them further in that direction, to fill in the gaps in his line of thought on the matter of normativity, and to present a coherent picture of his ethics and esthetics while situating it in the context of contemporary thought. A sketch of this picture is due to the reader.

Peirce adopts two seemingly contradictory positions on the matter of ethics. In his first of the Cambridge Lectures in 1898, "Philosophy and the Conduct of Life," Peirce presents an argument for a *conservative sentimentalism*. It is a position in line with the moral sentimentalists of the 18th century, particularly the common-sense philosophy of Thomas Reid. Among its theses is that in "vital matters" reason should defer to the moral sentiments and instincts (1898, CP 1.630). Moreover, ethical theory is in such a poor state that it is "useless" for the guidance of the conduct of life, if not downright "dangerous" (1898, CP 1.666; 1898, CP 1.667). Yet, on the other hand, Peirce devotes himself to the development of ethics as a normative science. He declares a few years later that he has "no doubt" that the study of ethics "is more or less favorable to right living" (1903, CP 1.600). How are these reconciled?

The key to the resolution of these differing views is the theory of evolution. Reid and the British sentimentalists such as Francis Hutcheson and David Hume thought that the moral sentiments were present in the constitution of human beings, and common-sense morality self-evident. But, thanks to Darwin's theory of evolution—something that came on the scene in Peirce's time like lightning at midnight—Peirce understood these moral sentiments and habits of conduct as something honed by evolution, as adaptations sufficient to ensure cooperation and stability in societies. Peirce thought now that the matter of ethics "lies in the evolutionary process in some way" (1902, CP 5.4).

But Peirce was never satisfied with Darwin's theory as a complete account of evolution, particularly cultural evolution, and it certainly did not explain the evolution of practices such as science. Cultural evolution seemed more Lamarckian, where the primary mechanism of adaptation was through learning, whereby the practices of life were improved and those improvements intentionally passed on (1893, CP 6.296–6.300). Whereas Darwinian evolution was mechanical and directed by chance, Lamarckian evolution was purposively directed (Liszka, 2014a).

In this way, Peirce thought that there were at least two paths through which evolution works itself out: the first through natural selection, and the luck of the draw; the second, purposive, through learning by inquiry. Inquiry can accelerate evolution. It will bring about truth and knowledge "most speedily" (1903, CP 1.615). Darwinian evolution is the result of natural experiments of living made through the dumb mechanism of the selection of random variations. Inquiry is deliberate reasoning engaged with those experiments of living. Peirce's complaint about the tradition in ethics is not about the significance of the study, but the lack of scientific attitude and methodology (1898, RLT, pp. 107–108). Peirce's common-sense ethic, as opposed to Reid's, is *critical* common sense, one that is guided by fallibilism, where even the so-called instincts are subject to change, and where there is a careful sorting of genuinely evolved habits of conduct from cultural biases and conventions (1905, CP 5.438–5.451).

With this rationale, Peirce sets about to develop his three normative sciences. The normative sciences as normative are concerned with what people *ought* to do. Logic is concerned with how people ought to reason; ethics with how they should act; and esthetics with what sorts of ends admirable to pursue (1903, CP 1.186, CP 1.191). But what is the nature of this normativity, this "ought?" Peirce begins with the assumption that moral agents have some degree of voluntariness, some self-control in their actions and that they are primarily goal-seeking. Peirce argues that the concept of normativity is tied to such end-seeking conduct: "the word 'ought' has no meaning except relatively to an end" (1898, CP 5.594). There is a connection between norm and purpose. What a person ought to do depends "upon what the purpose of his action is" (1901, CP 7.186). Without an end, whether in the form of a goal or ideal, there is no way to measure what is done, compared with what ought to be done. Conduct can be corrected relative to an end. Is this the right path to an end, is this the right way to attain it? Ends, like truth and goodness, function critically, that is, they serve to correct human conduct and the direction humanity ought to take. The voluntariness in moral agency allows for self-direction—aiming at some end—and self-correction through self-control, the ability to correct from one path to another in order to attain that end. This self-control "is precisely that that gives room for an ought-to-be of conduct, I mean Morality. . . ." (c. 1902, CP 4.540).

Peirce analyzes the characteristics of such purposive conduct through the framework of Alexander Bain's desire-belief model of human motivation. Peirce thought pragmatism "scarce more than a corollary" to Bain's notion of belief (1906, CP 5.12). Bain claimed that "belief is preparedness to act, for a given end, in a given way" (Bain, 1889, p. 508). "Under given conditions," Peirce says, a person "will have formed the habit of acting in a given way whenever he may desire a given kind of result" (c. 1906, CP 5.491). Peirce thinks purposive conduct is a triadic relation among some desire or motive for an end, a belief concerning how best to attain the end, and the intention and resolution to act on what one believes will attain that end. The purposiveness of the act becomes degenerative if one or more of the triadic elements is missing.

Bain's desire-belief model, in turn, serves as the armature for practical reasoning (c. 1902, CP 5.538). Practical reasoning is reasoning about the means by which ends are likely to be attained (c. 1906, CP 5.491). The core of practical reasoning is what Peirce calls a "practical belief," that is, what is likely to attain the end in question. But practical reasoning is also guided by an implicit norm which, in Peirce's language, is to do "what is most conducive to an end" (1898, CP 5.594). People ought to do what is likely to attain their ends. "Belief," Peirce claims, "consists mainly in being deliberately prepared to adopt the formula believed in as the guide to action." As such, "the proposition believed in can itself be nothing but a maxim of conduct" (1903, CP 5.27). "A practical belief is what a man proposes to go upon" (1901, CP 7.186).

The pragmatic maxim is at the core of Peirce's thinking on practical reasoning. As formulated in "How to Make Our Ideas Clear," it commands the thinker to "consider what effects, that might conceivably have practical bearings, we conceive the object of our conception to have. Then, our conception of these effects is the whole of our conception of the object" (1878, CP 5.402). The pragmatic maxim shows two things in regard to practical reasoning and practical beliefs in particular. First, the truth of a practical belief depends on the truth of its corresponding theoretical claim, and the meaning of theoretical claims is found in their corresponding practical beliefs. As Peirce pointed out in the formulation of his maxim, each concept (or belief or hypothesis) has "practical bearings," by which he means that it could be transposed into what Kant called a hypothetical imperative. For example, the scratch-hardness of diamonds means that it can cut glass rather than being cut by glass (1878, CP 5.403). If that is true, then it entails a corresponding hypothetical imperative: "if you desire to cut glass, use a diamond cutter." "Every proposition has its practical aspect. If it means anything it will, on some possible occasion, determine the conduct of the person who accepts it"

(1902, NEM 4, p. 291). Kant called these hypothetical but also "pragmatic" imperatives, "action good to some purpose" (1785, pp. 31–32n4). As Peirce characterizes it, a practical belief may be described as "a habit of purposive conduct" (c. 1902, CP 5.538).

But there is a problem with practical reasoning from an ethical point of view. The norm implicit in practical reasoning—that people ought to do what is likely to attain their ends is wanting ethically speaking. It is purely instrumental since it does not discriminate among good or bad ends or right or vicious ways and means to those ends.

By the turn of the century, Peirce came to recognize the dangers of this instrumentalism in the form of the excesses of the Gilded Age, the rise of Social Darwinism and the corruption of science away from the noble end of truth to that of utility. The merging of modern, scientific experimental method with capitalism, industry and technology had led to such a result. The pragmatic maxim had presaged the essence of modern experimental science—how theoretical beliefs and hypotheses could be transposed into practical ones—but it had not considered any ethical constraint on those ends. Peirce now realized that logic had to yield to ethics, and eventually to esthetics, as he understood it, to determine what ends would be worthy of pursuit. As he says in a letter to William James, "the true nature of pragmatism cannot be understood without them" (1902, CP 8.256). Peirce had to find a way to transform the practical reasoning inherent in the pragmatic maxim into one that had ethical constraints. Peirce did not complete this task entirely, but there is a way to gather Peirce's thought on this matter to give a coherent account of that attempt.

Practical reasoning, if it is to become ethical, must implicitly appeal to three norms: truth, righteousness and goodness. What ends are good to pursue? What are the right means to use in attaining them? Which among righteous means will likely attain the end? These three questions can be deeply broadened: To what ends ought humankind strive; what are the more likely means by which it will achieve them; and among those likely, which are right and good to do? "Ethics," Peirce says, is "right action" that is in "conformity" to ends that people are "prepared deliberately to adopt as *ultimate*" (1903, CP 5.130). The key for him was to determine an ultimate end, a *summum bonum*, which could order all other worthy ends into their proper place. The normative sciences are to divide up this labor. Esthetics is concerned with identifying those ends that can be counted as ultimate and inherently admirable; ethics is concerned with which, among the admirable ends, are good to pursue and the righteous constraints on the means to those ends; logic, broadly understood as truth-apt methodology, is concerned with what will likely achieve those ends (1906, CP 1.573; 1903, CP 1.191). "It is only after the moralist has shown us what is our ultimate aim," Peirce writes, "that the logician can tell how we ought to think in order to conform to that end" (1901, CP 8.158n3). This, at least in design, transforms practical reasoning from being purely instrumental to one that incorporates an ethical project—the pursuit of good ends by righteous means.

If this is the ethical project, then the attainment of these goals is a matter of inquiry. How is it known among the many claims to what is good and right, which are true? Peirce is a realist, and it can be assumed that he is a moral realist. The hallmark of moral realism is that there is such a thing as moral truth that can be determined objectively, independently of what people may happen to believe, or what cultures happen to adopt at any point in their history.

How is the truth of a moral claim to be measured? Peirce developed a rather novel theory, often called the convergence theory of truth. For Peirce, true claims would be those that were the result of inquiries rightly done, sufficiently long, so that further inquiries find little or no reason to doubt such claims. A true claim is one in which the beliefs about the claim among inquirers over time tend to converge toward the same opinion about the claim (1878, CP 5.407; 1902, CP 2.781). Peirce argues that the convergence theory would also apply to the determination of the truth of moral claims, that "conduct controlled by ethical reason tends toward fixing certain habits of conduct" (1905, CP 5.430), so that "good morals" are the kind of human behavior that "would come to be approved if studies of right behavior were carried sufficiently far" (c. 1911, R 673, p. 12).

Peirce characterizes convergence in three correlated senses. Each can be translated to criteria for measuring the truth of moral claims. One indication of true claims is inductive approximation, meaning that continued sampling does not appear to change the expected value of the ratio of the target variable in the population sampled (1878, CP 2.748). As applied to ethical reasoning, a true ethical norm would be one that cannot seem to be improved on, that it approximates the limits of its improvability. A second sense of convergence to the truth in Peirce is the idea that any inquirer with good methods should reach the same conclusion if the claim is true (1878, CP 5.407). One indication of the truth of an ethical norm might then be whether it was adopted by different cultures. In other words, there would be evidence that among all known cultures, there is statistically high number of them that have adopted a similar norm. The third indicator of truth for Peirce is a convergence of a belief among those who have inquired into the matter over time (1877, CP 5.407). True claims tend to promote consensus, false ones diverge opinion. Similarly, an indication of the truth of a moral claim or norm would be that more and more people adopt it as a standard or best practice over time, and continue to prefer it over the old ways. It is something that informs the conduct of a wide swath of the community. In general, "If . . . the future development of man's moral nature will only lead to a firmer satisfaction with the described ideal, the doctrine is true" (1906, CP 5.566), that is, *morally* true.

The fact of convergence would demonstrate what is *generalizable* in the way of belief, conduct and sentiment. It shows which beliefs, which norms of conduct, or which sentimental attitudes can have widespread adherence and consistently work with the constraints of lived experience. To be generalizable is to have a law-like character (1901, CP 7.187; Aydin, 2009, p. 439).

Peirce links generalizability with what he calls *reasonableness*. Convergence is a process that happens over time. The good is not discovered through "individual reactions in their segregation, but in something general or continuous." "The ultimate good," Peirce says, is realized in an "evolutionary process." It is "the coalescence, the becoming continuous, the becoming governed by laws, the becoming instinct with general ideas." It is all "phases" of "the growth of reasonableness" (1902, CP 5.4).

For individuals, reasonableness is an aspect of self-correction, the core of the purposive agency (Ayin, 2009, p. 431). It involves casting off false beliefs and adopting less erroneous ones in a progression toward ones which resist error. The truth cannot be known if people cannot detect error and ends cannot be attained if people refuse to change false paths. Truth cannot be known, as Peirce writes in "The Fixation of Beliefs," if people hold onto beliefs tenaciously despite evidence, or if they believe something simply because it serves their interests (1877, CP 5.378). Truth cannot be known if beliefs are imposed by authority, coercion or force (1877, CP 5.380). It cannot be known if people believe merely on the basis of what others believe (1877, CP 5. 383). To be reasonable means to go wherever truth leads, "to discover whatever there may be that is true (1901, CP 7.186).

The test of the truth of a moral claim, norm or rule of conduct is whether it is generalizable, law-like, meaning that it is something that achieves some measure of convergence. This may seem similar to the claims of Kant's categorical imperative: Act as if the maxim of one's action were to become a universal law. However, Peirce rejects the *analytic* methodology of Kant's categorical imperative. The truth of a moral claim is not satisfactorily met by means of a formal contradiction or *reductio ad absurdum* (1902, CP 5.4). Its truth cannot be established once and for all in a thought experiment. Instead, it must be a *synthetical* process of testing, rooted in experience, developmental and evolving out of the experiments of living together and the sort of constraints it places on norms and ideals (1902, CP 5.4). Convergence is achieved through this process of inquiry that wrestles with the experiences of living together, a living laboratory, accompanied by the pain of trial and error.

If moral truths are the result of inquiries, done in the context of experiments of living, and done rightly and sufficiently enduring so that further inquiries show little reason to doubt their truth, then determining the truth of a moral claim relies on proper inquiry. What Peirce realized early on was that proper inquiries not only need a good method but require inquirers to have certain moral sentiments, virtues conducive to inquiry and certain ethical norms guiding the practice of inquiry (1902, CP 7.87). In other words, inquiry itself harbors the initial norms needed to seek any moral truths.

Inquiries are successful when they attain their end. The end of all inquiry is the truth about the matter investigated. To be successful, inquirers must have all the features of reasonableness. They should cultivate certain sentiments characteristic of reasonableness. Above all, they must have a disinterested love in truth, truth as a cause that puts it above self-interest, so that inquirers identify their interests with the interests of a larger community of inquiry (1878, 2.654). Since inquiries often require generations to solve and depend on inquiries that have come before, inquirers must become intergenerationally altruistic—an "evolutionary love" as Peirce calls it—to do one's part for the sake of those to come, to fix what is broken now and improve on it while passing on what is best (1893, CP 6.289; 1902, CP 7.87). In the process of inquiry, inquirers must exercise certain virtues, honesty above all, fair-mindedness, the humility of the scholar and the courage to advocate for claims that break convention (1901, CP 8.136; 1902, CP 2.82; 1903, CP 1.49). These sentiments and virtues ensure that inquirers will cast off erroneous beliefs rather than hold on tenaciously to self-interested ones. It ensures that they will be devoted to the truth in the long run rather than what is of self-interest or popularly held in the short run.

Communities of inquiry also have implicit norms. As Peirce sees it, these fall out of the speech acts of making claims, making assertions about what is true or right to do. To make an assertion is to be committed to providing reasons or justifications to others, sufficient for them to believe as one does in the assertion (c. 1895, CP 2.335; 1905, CP 8.313). It is also as Robert Brandom (1994, p. 202) and Cheryl Misak (2000, pp. 73–74) have pointed out, a commitment to any inferences or entailments from those assertions. Thus, to claim that people ought to do something is an assertion like any other and, as such, people are committed to providing reasons for why something should be done, in a way that echoes the thought of T.M. Scanlon (2000).

Making assertions imply that others have a right to question it, to make counter-assertions. Thinkers such as Karl-Otto Apel (1980) and Jürgen Habermas (1990) have developed ethical theories based on Peirce's notion of the community of inquiry in this respect. Inquiries, in which inquirers are attempting to come to some consensus about what is true and right, must make assertions, but also must abide by norms that permit openness to inquiry, such as the equality of roles in give and take in debate and justification, lack of coercion or force to press a claim and the fact that certain inquirers cannot be excluded from ongoing inquiries simply on the basis of what they believe, or who they are. Following these norms gives some assurance that communities of inquiry will not be guided by the imposition of authority or the pressure of conventional beliefs that foil genuine inquiry. "The first rule of reason," Peirce says, is "do not block the way of inquiry" (c. 1905, CP 1.135). The norms of the practices and institutions of such communities must also express the key features of reasonableness.

Peirce provides an account of moral truth as a convergence of sentiment, habits of conduct and beliefs. He shows the sentiments, habits of conduct and norms essential for reasonable communities of inquiry and reasonable inquirers. But why should people engage in such inquiries? More fundamentally, why should people pursue moral truths—why should people be reasonable?

This is a matter for the last of the normative sciences—esthetics, a study which has "the deepest characteristics of normative science" (1906, CP 5.551). Peirce defines esthetics in what most would consider a nontraditional sense as the study of what makes ends ultimate and admirable. But Alexander Baumgarten, thought to be the originator of study, defines it as the ability "to judge perfections and imperfections sensibly" (1739, sect 452, p. 139). This is not too far afield from a contemporary of Peirce, George Santayana, who defined in *The Sense of Beauty*, published in 1896, as "the perception of value" (Santayana, 1896, p. 16). To the extent that Peirce's esthetics studies what makes ends admirable, then it is not too far off the mark from these thinkers.

To the question of why pursue ultimate ends such as truth and goodness, the tradition has offered two types of answers: duty or love. The first path is the way of the Stoics, Cicero, Aquinas and Immanuel Kant. Reason is the master and calls on some version of the natural law. It commands to do good and avoid evil, so says Aquinas (1265–1274, *Summa Theologica*, Q.94. Art 2). The second path is the way of sentiment. The true and the good are lovable and beautiful, *kalos*, as Plato and Shaftesbury argue. It is a "disinterested" love as Shaftesbury would have it. It is loved for itself not because it is bound up with some self-interest.

Peirce chooses, instead a way between these two and allies himself with Friedrich Schiller. Peirce's first exposure to esthetics was through the German poet and philosopher, and he read *The Aesthetic Education of Man* with delight as a young man (1902, CP 2.197). Peirce may have been inspired by Schiller's insight that "if truth is to gain the victory in the struggle with Force," then truth must "become herself a force." There must be "some impulse to champion" truth. It is the only "motive" in the "sensible world." (1795, p. 48). In response to Kant, although the "command of law," Schiller says, can "inspire us to duty," it is "the aesthetic attitude [that] can enable human beings to go beyond duty to nobility" (1795, p. 48).

There are certain other themes in Schiller that sit well with Peirce. The most important of these is Schiller's notion of *play impulse—Spieltrieb*.

The play impulse is manifested in beauty, which in that sphere of freedom, rethinks the way things are ordered and through some new shape, unites sense and form, reasoning and feeling in equilibrium. As such it gives an object a *living shape*, it is sensuous matter neither without form, nor form without feeling, but its balance (1795, p. 76). In this way, reason and sentiment are set in harmony. The living shape has a family resemblance with Peirce's notion of concrete reasonableness. The appeal of reasonableness must be through the living shape it takes, the design it has in the practices of communities and the conduct of individuals. If certain principles of justice are to be counted as reasonable, then their manifestations in the norms of practices and institutions of a community must take on an appealing form, a design such as proportion, balance, equality, solidarity and unity that is concrete, admirable and lovable, much in the way in which great art shapes matter with form. Injustice is ugly, unsatisfying, ignoble. It divides rather than unifies.

Peirce was also influenced by the classical Greek notion of *to kalon*, as indicated in his detailed study of Plato. Indeed, he prefers the term *to kalon* to "beauty" (c. 1902, CP 2.199; 1903, CP 1.586). Standard interpretations of Plato's notion suggest three themes that likely influenced Peirce. The first characterizes *to kalon* as the design of parts that constitute a whole, so organized that it fits its end or purpose Something is *kalos* if its design best suits its end or purpose (Barney, 2010, p. 365). What makes something good in part is the order of whole by means of the relation of its parts (Philebus, 64e-65a; Gorgias, 506e; Barney, 2010, pp. 364–365). Peirce does define esthetic goodness in terms of the organization of parts and wholes that produces a certain quality in their totality (1903, CP 5.132). Peirce stresses: "The question of the goodness of anything is whether that thing fulfills its end" (1903, CP 5.197). Form must follow function.

Second, the function must be beneficial or good (*Greater Hippias*, 296c; Grube, 1927, p. 272). Peirce sees this as an essential role for ethics (1903, HL, pp. 212–213; 1903, CP 1.191). Third, Plato associates *to kalon* with certain kinds of pleasures or feelings. What is *kalos* is what is pleasing, what is lovable in itself. In *The Symposium*, Plato sees *to kalon* as motivational as something erotic or lovable (Barney, 2010, p. 375).

In this way, there is an outline of what makes an end admirable. It must be something so designed to achieve its purpose, its purpose is good and, in doing so, becomes lovable and admirable.

Peirce also seems inspired by Kant's notion of the architectonic in this respect, the idea of systematic unity of reason (1781, A840; B686). The model of such systematic unity for Peirce is science. Peirce supposed that there would be an order to knowledge that eventually "becomes an absolutely perfect, rational, and symmetrical system" (1891, CP 6.33). The classification of the sciences reveals a systematic unity and order of the particular sciences. Its design best fulfills its function of acquiring knowledge. Its practice in communities of inquiry exemplifies a concrete reasonableness in terms of its ability to correct itself, the virtues and sentiments of its practitioners, all of which allow it to grow progressively in the accumulation of knowledge and admiration.

If esthetics has to do with the worthiness or value of ends, what are the candidates for such honors? Around 1900, Peirce takes a stab at making such a list. It is motivated by a review of Frank Thilly's *Introduction to Ethics* and a review of Karl Pearson's *The Grammar of Science* a year later. Peirce is unhappy with Thilly's classification because it is not comprehensive, and he is unhappy with Pearson's characterizations of the ends of science. Peirce sets about providing a more systematic list of candidate ends for the purpose of assessing their qualifications for the honor of *summum bonum* and making a case for his choice.

Peirce sees three grand theory types in the tradition. First, those based on the end of pleasure or satisfaction of desires. This represents the hedonistic, Epicurean and utilitarian traditions. There are those who aim at what is conducive to the continuation of the human race and stability of societies, represented by the contractualist traditions. Finally, there are those who identify the end as some general ideal, something with "the same kind of being that a law of nature has, making it lie in the rationalization of the universe" (1900, CP 1.590). These are represented by Stoic, natural law and Kantian traditions.

Each of these, in turn, can be generalizable, that is, something that can be pursued consistently with lived experience. The utilitarian principle expresses the generalizability of pleasure—the greatest pleasure for the greatest number (1900, R 1429, p. 14). The end of maximizing pleasure and minimizing pain for the most is certainly more generalizable than doing so for the fewest.

Since cooperation fosters stability of societies and the continuation of the race and conflict diminishes those ends, then an end that is generalizable in this respect is a maximization of cooperation and a minimization of conflict. The end of cultivating altruism in people fosters cooperation and minimizes conflict. To the extent that societies are needed for the continuation of the human race, then their peace and prosperity is certainly a more generalizable end than constant war, poverty and destitution (1900, R 1429, p. 14).

What then is generalizable in regard to generalizable ideals? Peirce proclaims that this is "not definable in advance." It is a process by which such an ideal would be realized "in the long run" (1900, R 1429, p. 14). Such a process must involve, then, the process of inquiry that would result in that determination. But for such inquiries to be successful, inquirers must be reasonable in that they adopt the sentiments and virtues needed for self-correction, and communities themselves must be constituted by norms that thwart the authoritarianism and irrationality that block the road of inquiry. In other words, what is generalizable in the pursuit of generalizable ideals is reasonableness itself.

This, "the reasonable itself," he declares in the review of Pearson's *Grammar of Science*, must be the *summum bonum* (1901, CP 8.140). This is the highest end that Peirce seeks. The highest good consists "in that process of evolution whereby the existent comes more and more to embody those generals which were just now said to be *destined*, which is what we strive to express in calling them *reasonable*" (1905, CP 5.433). One could not, Peirce believes, "have a more satisfying ideal of the admirable" (1903, CP 1.615). It would seem that Peirce is not rejecting the pleasurable, peaceful and prosperous life as a worthy end, only that it is not the highest. It would be hard to reject the end of a pleasurable life in a society marked by peace and prosperity. However, these ends, among others, must fit into a whole so that's its totality is marked by a certain esthetic goodness, *kalos*, admirable and noble.

Peirce goes on to develop more detailed classifications of ends in the Pearson review and its associated drafts. He ends up with 28 candidates (1901, CP 8.138; R.1434). These are likely the 28 he intends to review in the chapter on ethics for *The Minute Logic* and assess their worthiness for the *summum bonum* (1902, R 434 Draft B, p. 28; 1902, CP 1.581). He never completes the task.

Peirce had taken up one of the critical tasks of many philosophers and thinkers of the 18th century—the unity among truth, goodness and beauty. But he attempted to apply 19th-century concepts to this problem: the pragmatic maxim, experimental scientific methodology and the understanding of evolution. For Peirce, the answer to their coherence lies in a living, "concrete" reasonableness—a living shape to the practices of inquiry, the communities of inquiry and the inquirers themselves. It is a living shape that is conducive to self-correction, to cast off what is in error and to retain what is not.

Peirce's account of the normative sciences allies in various ways with strains of thought in contemporary ethical thinkers such as Thomas Nagel (1978), Karl-Otto Apel (1980), David Wiggins (1998), Jürgen Habermas (1990), Robert Brandom (1994), T.M. Scanlon (2000), Michael Bratman (1999), Cheryl Misak (2000), David Copp (2004) and Philip Kitcher (2011). His thought also adds importantly to current debates in metaethics concerning the nature of moral agency, normativity, moral truth, realism, internalism and externalism. But Peirce also opens up a reconsideration of the role of esthetics in ethical matters, understood more broadly as concerned with the valuation of ends, and the direction which is best for humankind.

1 Influences on Peirce's Ethical Thought

Peirce came rather late in his career to the study of ethics. As a practicing scientist with a broad and deep understanding of philosophy, Peirce was primarily concerned with logic and scientific methodology. He developed a theory of signs to explain how information, inference and inquiry worked together to produce reliable knowledge. Once he realized that logic, understood in one aspect as a normative science, was dependent on ethics, he began an intense study of the subject somewhere around 1883. Even then, it wasn't until the late 1890s that he attempted to clarify the relation between logic and ethics (1902, CP 2.198). By 1901, he certainly made a point of it (Kent, 1987, p. 110; 1901, CP 8.158).

As Peirce recalls the matter in 1903, he became convinced that logic was a normative science in the sense that it argued for how we ought to think. Since thinking is a species of conduct, then logic was dependent upon ethics, which studies what we ought to do generally (1903, CP 5.108; 1903, CP 5.111; Liszka, 2012, pp. 48ff). Logic was deliberate thought, that is, self-controlled thought and self-control was an ethical matter (Kent, 1987, p. 111; 1901, R 692, pp. 3–4). Self-controlled thinking was thinking guided by standards and directed to some end or purpose. The end of logical reasoning was the truth, and the test of the right standards of thinking was whether they lead to true claims in the long run (1902, CP 2.144; Liszka, 2012, pp. 52ff). But why should people seek truth, and why should they reason by certain logical standards? Since the subject of ethics was the matter of good ends and standards of conduct, then ethics could answer these very fundamental normative questions.

Getting a sense of where Peirce situates himself in the tradition of ethical theory should certainly help in understanding his own theory. However, Peirce is rather eclectic and draws on a number of different sources, some of which are contrary in theoretical outlook. On the one hand, his emphasis on the power and glory of logical reasoning would suggest that he sits in a line of those from Plato to Immanuel Kant, who saw reason as the way and means to what counts as good and right. On the other hand, he is clearly influenced by the 18th-century moral sentimentalists, Shaftesbury, Francis Hutcheson and Thomas Reid in particular. Peirce attempts to reconcile these two traditions by defining the right angle between the orthogonal vectors of cognitivism and non-cognitivism. Peirce also adds a novel perspective to the mix, applying the framework of 19th-century experimental science to the study of ethics, and trying to show how the discipline fits and functions in the system of mathematics and the empirical sciences. Peirce was also greatly influenced by evolutionary theory, and this allowed him to frame ethics and folk morality in a different way than the tradition.

Peirce began his work on ethics in 1883 with a study of "the great moralists" as he says (1903, CP 5.111). Other than Kant, Peirce does not mention them here by name. But, if they were great, they most certainly included Plato, Aristotle, the Stoics, Aquinas, Hume and the utilitarians of his own time. He certainly had a goodly scholarly acquaintance with these thinkers. Peirce also mentions some lesser ethical thinkers. His first classroom study of ethics as a Harvard student was Theodor Jouffroy (1903, CP 5.111). Joseph Brent notes that Peirce had also read Ralph Cudworth, Spinoza, Hobbes, Hume and James Mill during his Harvard days (Brent, 1998, p. 364). Peirce also mentions elsewhere his later study of the British and Scottish moralists of the 17th and 18th centuries: Thomas Hobbes and Ralph Cudworth, Shaftesbury, along with Edward Herbert and Richard Cumberland (n.d., R 683, pp. 20–21). He was especially familiar with the work of Francis Hutcheson and seems to favor him to Hume (1901, EP2, p. 71). As noted, he was clearly influenced by the common-sense philosopher, Thomas Reid (1905, CP 5.444).

As the son of a Harvard professor and esteemed mathematician as well as a socially and politically connected mother, Peirce was steeped in the rich, intellectual culture of Cambridge of the mid-19th century (Brent, 1998, pp. 28–29). It was a time of high intellectual activity, and likely forged some of his ethical temper. Transcendentalism was one of the better known philosophies of this time, and Emerson was headquartered nearby in Concord. Peirce claimed no truck with Emerson's philosophy, but acknowledges "that some form of the disease was implanted in my soul, unawares, and that now, after long incubation, it comes to the surface, modified by mathematical conceptions and by training in physical investigations" (1892, CP 6.102). He also seemed influenced by the rather exotic theology of the elder Henry James, which Peirce referred to approvingly (1878, 5.402n3). Richard Trammell, who studied this relation, suggests that they shared some similar themes. Among these is James's view of God as a creative, all-encompassing love and Peirce's notion of evolutionary love, a love that encompasses even what is hateful, what is opposed to it, and moves it to "loveliness" (1973, p. 202). They also shared similar views of the negativity of the individual self, and the importance of community (1973, p. 207).

But it might be reasonably supposed that his first serious study of ethics—the ethics of Jouffroy—left some lasting impressions that colored his own thinking and influenced certain themes in his moral outlook. For this reason, it might be a good place to start analyzing the influences on Peirce.

Peirce studied Jouffroy under the tutelage of President Walker at Harvard (1903, CP 5.111). It was the custom in the 19th century for the college president to teach moral philosophy—a course considered to be "the most important" in the college curriculum, and usually "required of all senior students" (Sloan, 1979). If it was studied in his senior year, then Peirce took the course in 1859, at the age of 20. Now forgotten, Jouffroy was quite well known in the mid-19th century. He was also apparently popular among the American transcendentalists and, so, possibly present in the intellectual environment of Boston in Peirce's formative years (Leighton, 1908, p. 40). From all accounts, his *Introduction to Ethics* was a very well-received textbook of the day, and probably the one that Peirce studied under Walker (1903, 5.111n1-n2).

Jouffroy was originally drawn to the Scottish common-sense school, a tradition which, as noted, Peirce also shared (Madden and Manns, 1987). Jouffroy thought that philosophies that contravene common sense do so because of a misuse of ordinary language. Once this misuse is exposed, the absurdity of the position becomes manifest. One good example is his critique of Thomas Hobbes, a favorite target of most 17th- and 18th-century ethicists. Hobbes, he complained, used the concepts of right and duty inconsistently. In the state of nature, each person has a right to all things. However, common sense would dictate that all rights entail duties. If each has a right to life, then each has a duty to refrain from taking life—otherwise, no one can, in practice, have such a right. Rights must be acknowledged through consensus, generating a corresponding duty. But the right to everything cannot generate a corresponding duty. If each has a right to everything, then no one will have a right to anything, since no one has a duty to observe such a right. If everyone acknowledges that each has a right to anything, then no person can uphold that duty, since to acknowledge it for one is to deny it to the other. On the other hand, if each person acknowledges each one's right to life, the duty to preserve the life of others is consistently possible (1840, 1, p. 313).

Although influenced by the common-sense school, Jouffroy was eclectic in his ethical thought. He believed that every philosophy contains an element of truth (Madden and Manns, 1987, p. 580). If all the great philosophers were in one place and "translated into the same philosophical language," compared and with errors removed, these views would provide "the whole philosophical truth" (1838, 1, pp. 335–350). Eclecticism was the view that "every opinion is necessarily true and necessarily false," so that the task is to select what is true in each. As such "it admits every system . . . for future use" (1838, 2, p. 100). Each age reflects a truth but becomes distorted when it is claimed to be the whole truth. The task of the philosopher is to restore the elements of truth in each philosophy.

Jouffroy's eclecticism is reflected in the *Introduction to Ethics*. It is a masterful blending of the various classical ethical theories of Plato, Aristotle, the Stoics, Kant and the utilitarians into one coherent story. However, his *Introduction to Ethics* is hardly a philosophical argument so much as a narrative and presents a very idealized picture of the order of things.

According to Jouffroy, there is but one duty for human beings, and that is to accomplish their destiny. Their destiny is found in the immanence of each person's nature, understood as part of a larger order of things. Given that this order is good, and that each species' nature is part of this order, then "good and evil are success or failure in the pursuit of those ends to which our nature aspires" (1840, p. 32). In this way, he interweaves the external and immanent teleologies of Plato, Aristotle and the Stoics.

Since every being has a particular end—which is the highest good for that being—and since that end is part of an eminently good order—each being is also fitted with faculties to accomplish that end. Because it is fitted to accomplish its end, each being has an impulse (by emotions and passions in human beings) toward that end and, at the same time, pleasured when such ends are being accomplished. Thus, happiness is the natural result of pursuing the end for which one is fitted, although such pleasure is not the end for which human beings struggle (1840, pp. 32, 37). In this regard, he echoes Aristotle's argument in the *Nicomachean Ethics*, namely that although pleasure is a good, the right sort of pleasure results from a life well-lived rather than being the end of life itself (*Nicomachean Ethics*, 1174b15–30).

The dark side of such impulses is the formation of self-interest, understood as a primary concern with one's own destiny (1840, p. 41). It was only when, with proper use of reason, that human beings could elevate themselves from the pursuit of self-interest to something greater than self, more universal, that true morality emerges (1840, p. 42).

> When reason has ascended to this conception, it has reached, for the first time, the idea of good. It had previously applied the name in a confused manner to the satisfaction of our nature. . . . Good—true good—good in itself—absolute good is the realization of the absolute end of the creation—is universal order.
>
> (1840, p. 43)

> The moment the idea of order is conceived, reason feels for it a sympathy so profound, true, immediate, that she prostrates herself before it, recognizes its consecrated and supreme right of control, adores it as a legitimate sovereign, honors it, and submits to it as the natural and eternal law.
>
> (1840, p. 43)

Here we have unfolded the Kantian stance of awe and respect before the law, with a heavy dose of natural law theory. It is only when our interest is a universal interest—"not our good alone—the good, the end of every creature," that we've achieved the moral stance (1840, p. 45). "All duty, right, obligation, and rules of morality, spring from this one source, the idea of good in itself—the idea of order. Destroy this idea, and no longer is there anything sacred in itself to the eye of reason" (1840, pp. 45–46).

One could see how this lofty language might influence impressionable young men at Harvard who, given their privilege in American society, might already be inclined to such noble ideas. And Peirce scholars will recognize some of Jouffroy's themes echoed in his grand outlook. Among these include the idea that there is an order to things, that the order is governed by reason. There is a highest good in this order, a good in-itself. And the highest good is bound up with reason, a good he names "concrete reasonableness" (1903, CP 1.615; 1902, CP 5.3). Peirce often uses the language of what is "destined." This highest good is "destined" so that, in the end, the use of reason rightly will prevail and disclose what is true and eschew what is false, in both the natural and moral realms (1896, CP 3.432; 1906, CP 4.547; 1878, CP 5.407; 1905, CP 5.430).

Truth can be known because the order of the human mind and the order of things are aligned (1893, CP 6.605). For individuals to come to know and align themselves with this order of things, they cannot be self-interested, but must work collectively in communities of inquiry, and do their part to discover what is good and true. This engenders a true ethic, a collective altruism (c. 1902, CP 7.87). "Why then the very first command that is laid upon you, your quite highest business and duty becomes to recognize a higher business than your business, not merely an avocation after your vocation has done its daily task, that of melting into continuity with the neighboring parts of the universal cosmos" (1898, R 436, p. 34). People must "execute" their "function in the operation of creation" by "rendering the world more reasonable" (1903, CP1.615; 1898, R 437, p. 26; 1905, CP 8.138n4).

But two important events happened after Peirce's graduation from Harvard in 1859 that undoubtedly influenced his thinking in all matters, including ethics. The first was a scientific revolution that occurred with the publication of Charles Darwin's *The Origin of the Species* later in 1859. The second was his admission to the *Lawrence Scientific School* at Harvard two years later in 1861, where he masters the methods of experimental, laboratory science. As Peirce reflects near the end of his life, "the modern recognition of evolution" along with "modern science . . . . has put us into quite another world; almost as much so as if it had transported our race to another planet" (c. 1905, CP 5.513). He found himself as a result "forced," as he says "by a great many different indications to the conclusion that an evolutionary philosophy of some kind must be accepted" (1893, CP 6.604). Peirce attempted to meld the theory of evolution and modern experimental science to his teleological picture of the reasonableness in the order of things. So that now "the *summum bonum*" does not "consist in action but makes it to consist in that process of evolution whereby the existent comes more and more to embody those generals which were just now said to be *destined*, which is what we strive to express in calling them *reasonable*" (1905, CP 5.433). But Peirce was wary of how Darwin's theory had been translated politically by the Social Darwinists of his day, so he proposed a counter to their egoistic interpretations in favor of a more Lamarckian form of social and cultural evolution, one that engendered intergenerational altruism, a kind of "evolutionary love" as he called it much later on (1893, CP 6.293–6.294).

All in all, based on his formative years, Peirce was led to a teleological picture of the order of things, but one that could be scientifically understood, rather than religiously grounded. In reference to the second law of thermodynamics, the order of things showed "a tendency toward ends" that "is so necessary a constituent of the universe that the mere action of chance upon innumerable atoms has an inevitable teleological result" (1885, CP 8.44). By analogy, individuals working collectively together to discover the truth would end their travail with an inevitable, "foreordained goal . . . like the operation of destiny" (1878, CP 5.407). Indeed, Peirce saw scientific practice as a model of an ethical community. It was a practice in search of the admirable end of truth, by means of right standards of reasoning, in which investigators adopt an intergenerational altruism, building on the work of others, but making contributions which they themselves "cannot hope to enjoy." "One contributes this, another that. Another company standing upon the shoulders of the first, strike a little higher, until at last the parapet is attained" (c. 1902, CP 7.87).

As Peirce opens up to the study of ethics in 1883, he looks to the "great ethics thinkers" now for their accounts of the good and the right, where he had previously mined them for their work on logic. It might be best to look at these influences chronologically, beginning with Plato.

Peirce clearly admires Plato and thinks that the study of the great Greek philosopher is one, among others, that cannot "fail to make men better" (1902, CP 2.201). Peirce apparently read every dialogue of Plato (1902, R 434). Plato plays a prominent role in drafts of Chapter 4 of his *Minute Logic* manuscript, written in 1902. The ostensible purpose of that chapter is to do a survey on the concepts of the good, starting with the Pre-Socratics, but he gets as far as Plato. He analyzes all of Plato's dialogues in order of their writing (1902, R 434). But he gets distracted, as he often does, and busies himself with the chronological ordering of the dialogues, supposedly to get at Plato's more mature formulations of the good.

It would not be surprising that he shares with classical Greek thinkers such as Plato and Aristotle the elevation of reason as a higher good than other candidates, if not the highest (1903, CP 1.602; 1903, CP 1.615).

In Chapter 4 of his *Minute Logic*, Peirce seems particularly interested in what Plato has to say about reason's chief rival for the crown—pleasure. He wrestles with Plato's differing formulations of pleasure in relation to the good, particularly in *The Phaedo, The Gorgias, The Republic* and *The Philebus* (1902, R 434, pp. 42, 84, 152 (2nd draft), 153–158). It is clear from his commentaries on these writings and elsewhere that Peirce is not a hedonist, and agrees with Plato that pleasure cannot be the ultimate good (1906, CP 5.561–5.562; Atkins, 2018, p. 175). But, at the same time, he seems to note the qualification that Plato makes about the "mixed life," in which pleasure and reason are in harmony (*Philebus*, 22a–d). Peirce may have found more satisfaction with Aristotle's solution in *The Nicomachean Ethics*, where pleasure is not sought as an end, but results from a life lived well (1174b15–30).

Plato's argument in *The Philebus* and elsewhere is that pleasure is without direction and so cannot be an ultimate good, since that is the function of such a good—to direct all other ends (*Euthydemus, 278e-282a*; Russell, 2005, pp. 17, 23). For Plato, that which gives direction is reason or wisdom. However, a life without pleasure may be possible for divine beings who can live the life of reason purely, but a second-best life is one possible for human beings, one that admixes pleasure and reason, but pleasure under the guidance of reason (*Philebus*, 22; Russell, 2005, p. 9). Peirce seems to dwell on this account of pleasure in *The Philebus* (1902, R434, pp. 153–155). Plato argues that this admixture must be ordered by "measure and proportion" (*Philebus*, 64d). So that Socrates says "so now we find that the good has taken refuge in the character of the beautiful, for the qualities of measure and proportion invariably, I imagine, constitute beauty (*to kalon*) and excellence" (*Philebus*, 64e). So, here is one classic account of the relation between the good and the beautiful that Peirce clearly notes (1902, R434, p. 156). Indeed, Peirce adopts the language of *to kalon* as a substitute for "beauty" in his work on esthetics (c. 1902, CP 2.199; 1903, CP 1.586). Peirce is clearly influenced by Plato's characterization of *to kalon* as good order, a design that fits its function and, in doing so, produces a pure pleasure (Grube, 1927).

Peirce, of course, was well-studied of Aristotle, particularly the works pertaining to logic. As he says, "to be well-read, or even fairly versed in philosophy (no easy accomplishment), it is quite indispensable to have studied Aristotle" (1893, CP 2.445n1). He "was by many lengths the greatest intellect that human history has to show . . .," and was the first pioneer in logic (1903, CP 6.96). Along with Kant, they were the "two greatest of metaphysical systematizers" (1902, CP 2.36). Peirce's development of his own logic and scientific methodology is clearly beholding to Aristotle.

It's less clear how Peirce stood with Aristotle's ethics. A review for *The Nation* in 1906 of a book on Aristotle's *Nicomachean Ethics* by Thomas Marshall shows that he had also read Aristotle's ethics closely, and was familiar with some of the secondary literature of the day. He does rather trivialize the theme of the work, even while admiring it:

> Aristotle's work, unlike modern treatises, is not chiefly occupied with the theory of morality. Its main purpose is practical: namely, to aid men to behave on all occasions with moderation and good sense. In that respect, it is certainly one of the most interesting and improving books that ever was written.
>
> (1906, CN, 3, p. 276)

In the review, he disputes Marshall's claim that Aristotle had a conventional view of right and wrong. Peirce points to the evidence of a more universal and natural foundation to ethics, as found in the fifth book (1906, CN, 3, p. 277). Peirce agrees with Aristotle that virtue is a matter of habituation but takes issue with Aristotle's claim that the power of the will, without the exercise of virtue, is capable of overcoming any temptation (1906, CN, 3, p. 278). There does not seem to be any other textual evidence of how Aristotle might have influenced his ethical thought.

Peirce was, of course, well-versed in the scholastics and adopted what he called a scholastic realism (1903, CP 5.49). But although he is indebted to their metaphysical and logical thinking, there is not much mention of their ethical thought. He is familiar, though, with Aquinas's natural law theory (c. 1901, CP 6.542).

Peirce seems particularly interested in the 17th- and 18th-century British and Scottish moralists. His influences here break roughly into three camps: the moral intuitionists, mostly among the Cambridge Platonists and their followers, such as Ralph Cudworth. Richard Cumberland defines a second group as a proto-utilitarian. There are then the moral sentimentalists, such as Shaftesbury, Francis Hutcheson, David Hume and Thomas Reid.

What is interesting about these thinkers is that they define three lines of thought that extend up to the present day. Cudworth starts a line of moral intuitionism and cognitivism that extends through Whewell (1846) to G.E. Moore (1903) and W. D. Ross (1930)—and which has something of a comeback recently among thinkers such as Robert Audi (2004) and Russ Shafer-Landau (2003). Richard Cumberland can be seen as a precursor to utilitarian and empirical thinking in ethics that extends through Jeremy Bentham, John Stuart Mill, Henry Sidgwick and among 20th-century utilitarians. Shaftesbury, Hutcheson and Hume are moral sentimentalists and noncognitivists, a line that extends through emotivists such as C.L. Stevenson (1944), A.J. Ayer (1936), and represented contemporarily by thinkers such as Simon Blackburn (1998), Allan Gibbard (1990) and Mark Schroeder (2013). What is most surprising and somewhat paradoxical is that Peirce, champion of reason, and cognitivist in most matters, is heavily influenced in his ethics by these moral sentimentalists.

It is clear that the center of attention and the foil for the development of all three camps of British-Scottish thinkers is Thomas Hobbes, whose egoism, hedonism and materialism these thinkers oppose. For this reason, Peirce argues that "the preliminary to any scientific investigation of its [ethics] problems seem to me to have begun with Hobbes" (n.d., R 683, p. 19). He is "too celebrated to need any remark. He seems to me an example of extreme perversity backed by great argumentative power" (n.d., R 683, p. 22).

As is well known, Hobbes imagined a miserable state of nature, primarily because human beings were a miserable lot. People without the force of law and authority tend to be limited in benevolence toward others. Human beings are motivated primarily by greed. Their judgments of good and bad are based primarily on their own subjective preferences. People's judgments are distorted by self-interest, the pleasures of the moment and various passions, above all the instinct of self-preservation. They are guided by certain implicit and intuitive rights of nature: First, to preserve their lives by any means which, when practiced by many, tend to become a right to do anything. Their practical reasoning, accordingly, is to use any means necessary to achieve one's ends. When collectively practiced this inevitably leads to state of war against all (Hobbes, 1641, Sect I).

Hobbes's bleak picture of the human condition was compounded by a seemingly mechanistic and materialistic account of nature. Even if some scholars disagree about this today, this seemed to be how Hobbes was read by interpreters such as Cudworth, Cumberland and Shaftesbury. Although they were to a man against Hobbes, they did not agree on the means of countering his claims. Peirce, too, throws in his lot with these thinkers against Hobbes:

> When Hobbes, for example, would persuade us that no man can act otherwise than for the sake of pleasure, it is clear that this belief would deeply modify our conceptions of men, and our plans of life; but when on asking what supports this momentous conclusion we learn that it is but the simple fact—if it can be dignified by that name—that every man desires to do what he does do, we are led at once to suspect that there is some sophistry in the process by which so novel a conclusion can be drawn from so familiar a premise.
>
> (c. 1873, CP 7.329)

Ralph Cudworth was part of the Cambridge Platonist movement. His work on ethics included *A Treatise Concerning Eternal and Immutable Morality* (1731) and *A Treatise on Freewill* (1848), both published posthumously. Interestingly, Cudworth has come into vogue with some contemporary philosophers in metaethics (Schroeder, 2014). Mark Schroeder uses Cudworth's souped-up argument from Plato's *Euthyphro* against voluntarism, namely, the position that obligations derive from commands, in order to dispute command theories in the Kantian mode, held by thinkers such as Christine Korsgaard (Schroeder, 2014, p. 19). It cannot be the case that some agent ought to do some action merely because God commands or authorizes it. That doesn't explain why God would command or authorize it. As Socrates argued, there must be some reason, some explanation why God commands what God commands other than the fact that God commands it (1731, pp. 17–22; Schroeder, 2014, pp. 20–21). This applies to Kant's notion of the moral law. But Peirce did not think much of Cudworth, claiming that his *Eternal and Immutable Morality* was "about the most unconvincing of books" (n.d., R 683, p. 22).

Cudworth is a moral innatist and intuitionist in Plato's mold. The human mind reflects the mind of God and involves the recollection of these ideas. Ideas of right and wrong, good and evil are, therefore, not a matter of convention, as Hobbes suggests, but are founded on what God thinks is good and right. In turn, what God wills as good and right is not arbitrary but based on reason, and moral principles are eternal and self-subsistent for this reason. The human will is not passive but active, and it is through an internal self-determination, rather than an external determination, that people are moved toward the good. Cudworth characterizes this internal self-determination in terms of the Stoic notion of *hegemonikon*, a faculty that integrates the higher capacities of human beings, such as reason, with the lower ones, such as animal appetites, and directs them toward good ends (1731, p. 178).

William Whewell follows in the line of British moral intuitionists, such as Cudworth and Richard Price. Although Peirce greatly admired Whewell's work on logic and scientific methodology and history, he did not seem to be too impressed by his work on ethics, calling it "wooden" (1903, CP 5.111). Whewell's theory is consistent with two principal claims of almost all of the intuitionists: (1) that there is some ability or faculty human beings have that allows us to grasp moral truths (Ross, 1930, p. 41) and (2) that these truths are self-evident, that is, their truth immediately apprehended (Ross, 1930, p. 29; Shafer-Landau, 2003, p. 247; Audi, 2001, p. 603). For Whewell, as for many of the intuitionists preceding him, conscience is the source of this ability or faculty by which human beings intuit right from wrong. Unlike some of the earlier intuitionists, particularly the Cambridge Platonists, he did not characterize conscience as a special kind of sense analogous to perception, but a rational process of some sort (1864, p. 11). What conscience intuited was so because moral truths, like the axioms of mathematics, were self-evident (1846, p. 58).

Based on his 1868 *Journal of Speculative Philosophy* series, Peirce objected to the Cartesian notion of intuition (1868, CP 5.213). To be consistent, Peirce would also object to these thinkers' notion of moral intuition. As to the question of conscience, although Peirce certainly recognizes the phenomenon of conscience as genuine, he does not see it as something innate, but acquired. Moreover, what conscience dictates is something that appears to change over time, depending on the changes in conventional morality. Conscience is "created by experience," but also "modified by further experience" (c. 1896, CP 1.56).

The 17th-century philosopher, Richard Cumberland, was also opposed to Hobbes's moral and political theory. But he was also opposed to the Cambridge Platonists' justification of moral laws by the argument of innateness, and he also avoided the justification of morality on the basis of revelation. Any laws of nature had to be discovered through experience.

In his book, *A Philosophical Inquiry Into the Laws of Nature* (1672), he questioned Hugo Grotius's justification of the so-called laws of nature on the basis of common consent. Instead, he proposed the notion of *the common good*, a view that the good of the whole is also the good of its parts. The pursuit of the collective good leads to the good of each, where good is understood as happiness (1672, Chapt. 3). In this regard, contrary to Hobbes's egoism, people can be assured that the happiness of each is attainable by working toward this common good, the ultimate end (1672, Chapt. 2). Morality, therefore, is end-driven, and eudaimonic in nature, the justification of morality being that it leads to happiness for the whole. This is summed in his Principle of Benevolence: an action is good only if it contributes to the collective happiness of people (1672, Chapt. 1).

Of the British and Scottish moral sentimentalists, Peirce seemed especially enamored of Shaftesbury, "if ever man hungered and thirsted after righteousness, he did" (n.d., R 683, p. 23). He is highlighted along with Plato and Kant as a philosopher whose study could not "fail to make men better" (1902, CO 2.201). He characterized him as a Stoicist of a certain stripe, especially influenced by Epictetus and Marcus Aurelius (1901, CN, 3, p. 27). Indeed, Stanley Grean notes that Shaftesbury's copy of the *Enchiridion* was heavily annotated (1967, p. 6). Shaftesbury's most important works were *An Inquiry Concerning Virtue or Merit* (1699), *A Letter Concerning Enthusiasm* (1708), *Sensus Communis* (1709) and *Characteristics of Men, Manners, Opinions, Times* (1711).

Shaftesbury was tutored by John Locke and like Locke and the Cambridge Platonists, he opposed Hobbes' egoism and mechanistic physics, but was also worried about Locke's empiricism and nominalism, which he thought could lead to a Hobbesian view of morality as simply socially constructed (1900, p. 403). His ethics seems to be a mix of Stoic and Platonic thought, along with Cumberland's doctrine of the public good, as well as other thoughts of the Cambridge Platonists (Grean, 1967, p. 7). As these influences suggest, Shaftesbury was a moral realist who argued that morality was not arbitrary, dependent on convention, but that there were things that were necessarily good, independent of culture and convention. Shaftesbury appears to be influenced by the Neoplatonic idea of the unity of truth, goodness and beauty (Grean, 1967, p. 247). What links all three is harmony and proportion: "What is beautiful is harmonious and proportionable; what is both beautiful and true is, of consequence, agreeable and good" (1711, p. 268). In this regard, he adheres to a classical sense of beauty, so that beauty lies in the proportion and arrangement of parts (Glauser and Savile, 2002, pp. 9, 27–28).

Moral form is also esthetic form: "Virtue has the same fixed standard" as beauty: "the same numbers, harmony and proportion will have place in morals and are discoverable in the characters and affections of mankind" (1711, pp. 157–158). In this way, moral beauty could be seen in the quality of good sentiments, the grace of action, the form of character and rational thought (1711, p. 62).

He distinguishes three degrees of beauty. The first level of beauty is found in the design or form of the thing, which he calls "dead forms." The second is in the designer. Beauty is the forming power in the thing, rather than the form itself: "the beautifying, not the beautified, is the really beautiful" (1711, p. 322). The third is found in the "Supreme Mind," which is the form that forms the form. If the second level of beauty is found in the human mind, the third is found in the reflection of the human mind in the divine (1711, p. 324).

Moral beauty also has three degrees (Glauser and Savile, 2002, p. 32). The first is the inner harmony of the body—its health in the form of mental balance, the disposition of character traits and the like. The second is a harmony between the inner organization and the outer organization of the type to which the thing belongs. The third is the beauty found in the rational mind, reasonableness in itself (1711, p. 172). Virtue is defined in terms of harmony as well, as in Stoic fashion, a harmony between inner and outer order.

Shaftesbury views the world itself as beautiful form, a rationally structured whole, a living, purposeful form that reflects the mind of God. Order is essentially the unity of design, a system of parts. In that regard it is teleological, aiming at a single end, just as the parts of an organism or a building are unified in a system of parts and whole (1711, p. 274). It is "the admiration and love of order, harmony and proportion, in whatever kind" that is "naturally improving to the temper, advantageous to social affection, and highly assistant to virtue, which is itself no other than the love of order and harmony in society" (1711, p. 191).

Shaftesbury developed a concept of *disinterested love* that also links the esthetic and the moral and is influential for Kant. Disinterest is not indifference toward the object, but an appreciation of the object in-itself, whether human or non-human, without consideration of how it could be used in the context of self-interest. It is sparked by the perceived beauty in something. It forms both the basis of the moral attitude toward others in sympathy, where one is concerned for the other rather than oneself, and for an appreciation of the beautiful object, where it is beheld in itself, with no intention of how it might be used (1711, pp. 318–320). This in effect links the good and beautiful.

In turn, Shaftesbury links disinterested love to *enthusiasm*: "all sound love and admiration is enthusiasm" (1711, p. 320). Enthusiasm for the true, good and beautiful elevated people to something higher, something greater than self (Grean, 1967, p. 20). Of all creatures, human beings alone are capable of grasping a relationship to the whole of being, and to acquire a sense of obligation to the good of the whole (Grean, 1967, pp. 33–34).

Shaftesbury, like Cumberland, also develops a notion of common good, a *sensus communis*, also influential for Kant (1711, pp. 48–53). Unlike Hobbes, and in agreement with the Cambridge Platonists, Shaftesbury argues that human beings are fitted to live in society. The common good is distinct from private good of self-interest. Private goods are what each person considers to be good and is a matter of self-interest. But the real good is harmony with the common good of one's group as a whole. Self-interest becomes bad when it conflicts with the common good (1711, p. 167). For an action to be good, it must be good for the system as a whole (1711, p. 169). For individuals to be counted as good, they must have an abiding affection for the common good, and act deliberately for its sake. The *sensus communis* is also the basis for moral taste, which must be cultivated. Everyone is born with capacity for moral taste, but they must be educated to acquire it properly—and it can be lost through the development of the wrong habits.

Peirce summarizes Shaftesbury's ethic as the "doctrine that we ought to be good because of the beauty of holiness" (n.d., R 638, p. 23). Some of the themes in Shaftesbury certainly reflect Peirce's thinking. As noted, Peirce too takes up the Neoplatonic quest of linking truth, goodness and beauty. Of course, Peirce does this in a way much different than Shaftesbury. Rather than arguing that they all share the properties of proportionality and harmony, Peirce claims they are hierarchically ordered so that they work together to determine what ends should be pursued and the standards by which they should be pursued. Shaftesbury expresses one of Peirce's favorite themes: the idea of a cosmos ordered by reason, an order that is "living and purposeful." Peirce's account of the disinterested inquirer, one who puts interest in the truth over self-interest, seems to have a family resemblance with Shaftesbury's concept of "disinterested love," the love of something for its own sake rather than how it might serve self-interest. Peirce's characterization of noble inquirers as people who have a "love of truth," and identify their interests with those of an unlimited community, also calls up Shaftesbury's notion of the *sensus communis* (1878, CP 2.654–2.655). Peirce often talks about admiration as one factor in identifying ultimate goods, and Shaftesbury uses this term quite frequently to express the proper attitude toward the order of things (1902, CP 1.191; 1903, CP 5.130; 1903, CP 5.36). Similar to Shaftesbury, Peirce uses a classical account of beauty as a certain relation of parts to whole, to define his notion of "esthetic goodness" (1903, CP 5.132). Shaftesbury had influenced Schiller, and Schiller had influenced Peirce as a young man (1902, CP 2.197).

If Peirce admired Shaftesbury, he also admired Francis Hutcheson, who Peirce thinks "the great light" during the early 18th century (1901, EP, 2, p. 71). Hutcheson shared many of Shaftesbury's views. Like Shaftesbury, he claimed that there was a moral sense that served as the center of judgments of right and wrong. This moral sense was God-given and based on a pleasure for the nobler things in life, such as altruism, social cooperation and harmony with others (Hutcheson, 1725, I.VIII, p. 83). It was not a cognitive judgment, but a judgment based on feeling—and not exactly an emotion—but more of a feeling associated with the way in which people might value something. It was felt after an encounter with the thing or event approved or disapproved (Hutcheson, 1728, I, p. 408). Reason functions to give a representation of what is apprehended in the moral sense, but it does not play a role in its approval (1728, I, p. 411). The test of the goodness of one's own actions or the actions of others is whether the thought of it pleases and makes that person attractive, in the sense of someone to admire (1728, p. 403).

For Hutcheson, reason and desire play two different roles in action, and characterizes what is called contemporarily an internalist account of moral motivation (Williams, 1993, p. 102). Desire for an end is associated with the will and the only source of motivation for that reason. As Aristotle suggests, happiness is the ultimate desire and so the overarching motivator for action (Hutcheson, 1728, I, pp. 405–406). Reason functions to determine the means to those ends and is not motivating. "What is Reason but that Sagacity we have in prosecuting any End?" (Hutcheson, 1725, I, 115). "Why does a Luxurious Man pursue Wealth?" he asks. Because of the truth that "wealth is useful to purchase pleasures" (Hutcheson, 1728, I, 404). As he emphasizes, "a Truth shewing an Action to be fit to attain an End does not justify it [the end] . . . for the worst Actions may be conduce to their Ends, and reasonable in that Sense. The justifying Reasons then must be about the Ends themselves." Here, he says, "we must recur to a Sense" (1728, I, 407–408). The approval of this end is the work of a moral sense (Frankena, 1955, pp. 362–363). People *approve* of happiness not because it is a self-evident reason, as the intuitionists would argue, but because of this moral sense.

In this context, Hutcheson points to two different types of norms, two different types of obligations in what is generally called practical reasoning, reasoning about means to ends. One concerns what is necessary to obtain the end, the second, that every spectator must approve his action. The latter includes the moral sense (Hutcheson, 1728, I, p. 408).

Hutcheson also takes a page from Shaftesbury by arguing approval of an end is similar to the sort of approval people have in perceiving a beautiful form, or harmonious composition, or good music (1728, p. 242)

Hutcheson, like just about everyone else at this time, was keen to attack Hobbes's account of the state of nature based on these ideas. Because Hobbes characterized human motivation as *only* self-interested, then he has difficulty explaining a number of readily observable types of fellow-feeling, including love, friendship, esteem, gratitude and the pleasure of society and good company (Hutcheson, 1730, VI, p. 147). If people preferred the peaceable sociality brought about by political union, from where does that preference come? A general positive feeling toward benevolence and happiness seems to be part and parcel of a moral sense.

David Hume, of course, belongs to this school of British moral sentimentalists. In "Hume on Miracles and Laws of Nature," Peirce mentions Hume's *Principles of Morals* and claims it "merely modified Hutcheson's doctrine" (1901, EP 2, p. 71). Perhaps because of this estimation of Hume's work, Peirce did not engage in any substantial discussion of Hume's ethics. In fact, Peirce did not seem to be taken much by David Hume, claiming him to be an extreme nominalist, Peirce being an avowed realist. He vehemently rejects the claim by some that he is an imitator of Hume (1893, CP 6.605). As far as Peirce is concerned, Hume's greatness is due to taking nominalism out to its logical conclusion, but which also reduces it to absurdity (1871, CP 8.35). However, he does think kindly about Hume's theory of association, especially the notions of contiguity and resemblance, which Peirce uses to good effect in his theory of signs (c. 1893, CP 7.391). Peirce uses Hume's argument against miracles as a foil to discuss scientific methodology and his account of the laws of nature (1901, CP 6.522; 1901, EP 2, p. 67ff).

Hume is also seen by many contemporary ethicists as developing a theory of ethical internalism based on his desire-belief model of human action and motivation (Williams, 1993, p. 102). But, as noted, Hutcheson seems to be its predecessor. For whatever reason history favored Hume in this respect, it is still an important source of dispute in metaethics (Davidson, 2006; Schroeder, 2007). Like Hutcheson, Hume argued that the source of moral motivation is found in desire and the passions, and that beliefs alone, including moral beliefs, could not serve as such a motivation (1739, p. 413). "Reason," as he famously says, "is and ought to be slave to the passions" (1739, p. 415). Essentially, people will act morally only if they are already disposed by desire or moral sentiments. Fortunately, Hume argues, there is a moral sense, with sympathy at its core, which allows for fellow-feeling, and which makes possible the various moral sentiments (1739, p. 470; p. 320ff). Contemporary internalists do not advocate for something like the moral sense, which leaves it rather arbitrary and subjective as to why people might desire to do the good (Schroeder, 2007; Brandom, 2000, pp. 30–31).

Thomas Reid is often counted among this group of moral sentimentalists, although some interpreters, such as Terence Cuneo, argue that he falls more in the cognitive-intuitionist camp of ethics than among the sentimentalists (2004). In any case, he was certainly a significant influence on Peirce. Peirce claims in 1905 that his *critical* common-sensism is based on Reid's common- sense theory and, moreover, it follows from his pragmatism (1905, CP 5.439).

Reid argued that, because reason and virtue are later developments of human capacity, and are imperfectly exercised by human beings, people should rely on their God-given instincts. As imperfect as they are, they are still less imperfect than the use of reason in moral matters, which is in a nascent stage. If reason were perfect, it would lead people to the proper means of living but, as exercised so far, it is far from perfect (1788, pp. 138–139). Instead, nature has instilled some common-sense behaviors, including natural affection for offspring and family, gratitude toward benefactors, sympathy for those in distress, friendship, romantic love and affection for the wise and good, among others, in order to guide humans in the conduct of their lives, and to ensure their survival (1788, pp. 145–161).

Reid also argued, like the other British moral sentimentalists, that people are endowed with a moral sense, often expressed as conscience, in which people perceive what is right and wrong. It is just as reliable as any of the perceptual senses (1788, p. 231). Despite the innateness of the moral sense, people still need education and training in morals, since it requires a process to bring to maturity, thanks specifically to the family and society in which people are raised (1788, p. 373). Without such a sense, no reasoning can persuade people to the good, or avoid evil (1788, p. 234). All moral reasoning rests on self-evident practical principles, not derived from reasoning, and it is the moral sense which perceives them as self-evident (1788, p. 235).

Among common-sense moral principles, Reid includes the claim that there are some things in human conduct that merit approbation and others that merit blame and punishment; what is not voluntary can be neither blamed nor praised; people ought to prefer a greater good and less evil to greater evil; people are not born for themselves and so are naturally social; and there is a common acceptance of the golden rule (1788, pp. 364–366).

Reid also dismisses the need for ethical theory as a guide or moral life. As he writes in a rather long passage,

> By the theory of morals is meant, a just account of the structure of our moral powers. . . . [I]t has little connection with the knowledge of our duty; and those who differ most in the theory of our moral powers, agree in the partial rules of morals which they dictate. . . . As a man may be a good judge of colours . . . without any knowledge of the anatomy of the eye, and of the theory of vision; so a man may

> have a very clear and comprehensive knowledge of what is right and what is wrong in human conduct, who never studies the structure of our moral powers.
>
> (1788, pp. 376–377)

"Men may be led into this gross mistake," he says, "which I wish to obviate, that in order to understand his duty, man must need be a philosopher and a metaphysician" (1788, p. 377). Theories of morals are quite varied, but there is wide agreement among the practical rules of morals, which are based on common sense. From this "we may judge, that the rules of morality stand upon another and a firmer foundation than the theory." People only need to heed their conscience to know what is right and wrong, but to judge the various theories of moral requires analysis. By analogy to the eye, "the learned and the unlearned see objects with equal distinctness," and, "the former have not title to dictate to the latter" (1788, p. 386). Reid concludes that

> [w]here we find any disagreement between the practical rules of morality, which have been received in all ages, and the principles of any of the theories advanced upon this subject, the practical rules ought to be the standard by which the theory is to be corrected; and that it is both unsafe and unphilosophical to warp the practical rules, in order to make them tally with a favourite theory.
>
> (1788, p. 387)

Reid also picks up some of the themes from Shaftesbury on the relation among truth, beauty and goodness. Taste is the capability of discerning and enjoying the beauty of nature and the fine arts. However, it depends on the constitution of people whether they perceive it or not. Because there can be a taste for the good, the true and the beautiful, the three are comparable in some respect, such that there can be moral beauties as well as natural ones, and beauties in intellectual objects as well (1785, p. 758). Beauty, where it really is, is an excellence derived from its own constitution, not any person's (1785, p. 753).

Peirce is much influenced by the British and Scottish moral sentimentalists. His version is a *conservative sentimentalism* (1898, CP 1.661), which he presents in one of his most controversial writings, "Philosophy and the Conduct of Life," delivered in Cambridge in 1898. Like Reid, Peirce argues that people should rely on their moral instincts and sentiments rather than ethical theory for guidance in the conduct of life. Moreover, ethical theory is both useless and dangerous in this respect (1898, CP 1.666–1.667). Many Peirce scholars find his doctrine perplexing (Atkins, 2018, pp. 6–7). But at least the source of it can provide some context to Peirce's seemingly radical claims here.

As Peirce outlines it in his first Cambridge lecture, the claims appear to controvert much of Peirce's pragmatic philosophy, his adoration of reason, reasoning and reasonableness, his cognitivism, the connection between theory and practice, his meliorism and advocacy of concrete reasonableness as the *sumum bonum* (Hookway, 2002, p. 14; De Waal, 2012, p. 87; Misak, 2004, p. 163). To understand Peirce's ethics fully, this conflict between his cognitivist and non-cognitivist leanings has to be worked out. Although Peirce admired the moral sentimentalists, he had a more complicated account of moral motivation than their internalist theory would hold. He sided with Alexander Bain on the matter of the relation between belief and desire, which allowed that beliefs could be motivational in a way that comes close to an externalist view (1906, CP 5.12). His theory of desire also shows that beliefs can influence desire as well, something contrary especially to Hume (1902, CP 1.205).

Moving to other influences, there is of course Immanuel Kant, who was a very formative influence on Peirce's thinking, along with Plato and Shaftesbury (1902, CP 2.201). He was the first philosopher he studied in any detail and became "a passionate devotee" (1898, CP 4.2). He was someone "I *more* than admire." But he had his disagreements, some of them fatal to Kant's thinking, especially the concept of the D*ing an sich* (c. 1905, CP 5.525) and his transcendentalist arguments (1902, CP 2.114). As Peirce writes, "the present writer was a pure Kantist until he was forced by successive steps into Pragmaticism" (1905, CP 5.452). It is clear that he had a thorough understanding of the three *Critiques*, certainly Kant's work on logic, and his *Anthropology*. Peirce derives his own categories from a critical analysis of Kant's and his three types of reasoning from problems with Kant's logic. Indeed, it is likely the case that Peirce's schema of the normative sciences—logic, ethics, esthetics—rests on the general architectonic of Kant's three *Critiques*, and the hierarchical dependency that Kant envisions between pure reason, practical reason, the esthetic and teleological judgment, may be reflected in Peirce's own ethical theory (Kant, 1790, p. 174).

It's surprising, then, that Peirce's ethics is not in Kant's mold, except perhaps with some affinity between Peirce's notion of self-control and Kant's notion of autonomy as self-governance, but that is also present in the work of Thomas Reid. Peirce is certainly not a deontologist, and because he rejects transcendental arguments, he would not accept Kant's transcendental justification of the categorical imperative. As Peirce says, he is "not one of those transcendental apothecaries . . . who call for a quantity of big admissions, as indispensable *Voraussetzungen* [presuppositions]," and claims that he is "not so indulgent . . . to suppose that they can seriously expect as much as half their demands to be allowed" (1902, CP 2.113). Transcendental arguments tend to make what is proved have no other reason for its justification than a necessary presupposition:

> Kant, as you know, proposes to allow that categorical imperative to stand unchallenged—an eternal pronouncement. His position is in

> extreme disfavor now, and not without reason. The whole question is whether or not this categorical imperative be beyond control. If this voice of conscience is unsupported by ulterior reasons, is it not simply an insistent irrational how, the hooting of an owl which we may disregard if we can? *Why should* we pay any more attention to it than we would to the barking of a cur? If we *cannot* disregard conscience, all homilies and moral maxims are perfectly idle. But if it can be disregarded, it is, in one sense, not beyond control. It leaves us free to control ourselves.
>
> (1903, CP 5.133)

As this passage suggests, Peirce thinks that the categorical imperative functions much like conscience, calling out what is one's duty to do or not to do. Peirce also rejects the use of formal inconsistency, the *reductio ad absurdum* that Kant employs in the categorical imperative. For Kant, as is well known, the test of the good of an action is whether it could be consistently pursued under universalization. Making a promise with the intention of breaking it, if universalized, would make promise-making senseless. But for Peirce, the test of the moral rightness of promise-keeping is its generalizability, a consistency indicated by its widespread embodiment in the habits of people and practices and persistence in the long run. It is, as Peirce says, a matter of a synthetic rather than analytic test (1902, CP 5.4).

Peirce was also certainly conversant with the signature ethic of his day—utilitarianism, although his reaction is somewhat mixed and inconsistent at times (1901, CP 8.138; CP 8.141). Sometimes he praises the ethical theory, as in this passage: "For I do not know what other system of philosophy has wrought so much good in the world as that same utilitarianism. Bentham may be a shallow logician: but such truths as he saw, he saw most nobly" (1903, CP 5.158). Utilitarianism is "one of the few theories of morals which have manifestly brought about any amelioration of society" (1900, CN 2, p. 250). He even calls it an "improved substitute for the Gospel" (1893, CP 6.297). On one occasion, he defends it against the charge that it is a simple hedonistic philosophy (1901, CP 8.136n3), yet on other occasions, he criticizes Bentham's version because it reduces happiness to pleasure and pleasure to immediate feelings. As noted, since Peirce does not see pleasure, particularly as it is characterized by Bentham as the highest good or ultimate striving of humankind, Peirce's ethic cannot be characterized as utilitarian. Peirce argues, "if the pursuit of pleasure is not a satisfactory ultimate motive for me, why should I enslave myself to procuring it for others?" (1901, CP 8.141). He is particularly dismissive of the "vulgar utilitarian":

> As for the vulgar utilitarian, his fault does not lie in his pressing too much the question of what would be the good of this or that. On the

> contrary his fault is that he never presses the question half far enough or rather he never really raises the question at all. He simply rests in his present desires as if desire were beyond all dialectic. He wants, perhaps, to go to heaven. But he forgets to ask what would be the good of his going to heaven. He would be happy there, he thinks. But that is a mere word. It is no real answer to the question.
>
> (1903, CP 5.158)

Peirce makes it clear his notion of evolutionary love is not to be confused with the greatest good for the greatest number, particularly if the good is characterized as pleasure. Like utilitarianism, it is a concern for the whole, for the community, but with a different purpose in mind. Evolutionary love, by means of sympathy and fellow-feeling, seeks to make better what is imperfect or lacking in others, and to cultivate what is best in others. It is not concerned to fulfill people's desires, whatever they may be, of as many people as possible (1893, CP 6.288).

There may have been other influences on Peirce's ethical thought but, if there is, he does not elaborate. This review of his most significant influences allows some summary of the themes in the history of ethical thought that most reflect Peirce's own thinking. First, Peirce agrees with the 17th and 18th century thinkers surveyed that, against Hobbes, self-interest is neither a common basis for ethics nor a worthy moral position. His abnegation of self-interest in favor of devotion to something greater than self is something writ large all over his philosophy and is exemplified by his devotion to science and the theoretical life, much in the way in which Aristotle touted the contemplative life as best (*Nicomachean Ethics*, 1177a 20–25). It is "in the contemplation of . . . those universal things with which philosophy deals, the factors of the universe" that "man [is] to find his highest occupation." Such a vocation, Peirce argues, "completes your personality by melting it into the neighboring parts of the universal cosmos." As he says blissfully, "in fulfilling this command, man prepares himself for transmutation into a new form of life, the joyful Nirvana in which the discontinuities of his will shall have all but disappeared" (1898, CP 1.673).

Second, consonant with the first supposition, Peirce follows Cumberland, Shaftesbury, Jouffroy and the utilitarians in holding to a collective, common good. In Cumberland's phrase—the good of the whole is the good of its parts. Peirce's ethics is clearly at odds with those ethical positions, such as Adam Smith's "invisible hand" theory, or the Social Darwinists of his day, who argued the converse, namely that each individual pursuing self-interest is good for the whole (1893, CP 6.290). This is probably most pronounced in Peirce's own account of *evolutionary love*, understood not as self-sacrifice, but a deep altruism toward helping to pass on what is best and improving on what is wanting (1893, CP 6.289). Although Peirce's notion of evolutionary love does not quite fit with Shaftesbury's notion of disinterested love, there is a family resemblance. Through disinterested love, people can step outside of their own self-interest and appreciate another person, intrinsically, much in the way in which one can appreciate a beautiful object, without malice, gain, or control. In this way, people are capable of adopting something larger than self. Evolutionary love, similarly, drives people to forego their self-interest and make things better for those who come after. It even seeks to change that which is hateful, so that it moves things toward loveliness (1893, CP 6.289).

Third, consonant with the notion of a collective good, Peirce argues, along with Jouffroy, that people find their highest calling in putting whatever talents and abilities they have to this higher, collective good:

> Here we are in this workaday world, little creatures, mere cells in a social organism itself poor and little thing enough, and we must look to see what little and definite task our circumstances have set before our little strength to do.
>
> (1898, CP 1.647)

As he says, science—indeed logic—"requires a conceived identification of one's interests with those of an unlimited community." "To be logical men should not be selfish" (1878, CP 2.654). In a famous passage, he argues that

> logicality inexorably requires that our interests shall *not* be limited. They must not stop at our own fate, but must embrace the whole community. This community, again, must not be limited, but must extend to all races of beings with whom we can come into immediate or mediate intellectual relation. . . . He who would not sacrifice his own soul to save the whole world, is, as it seems to me, illogical in all his inferences, collectively. Logic is rooted in the social principle.
>
> (1878, CP 2.653)

Fourth, Peirce tends to agree with the moral sentimentalists that nature has provided human beings with moral instincts and sentiments to guide their conduct of life. However, he characterizes instincts and sentiments in terms of his notion of habit, as evolved dispositions, subject to change, and some of which can be partially controlled (1902–1905, R 1343). His conservative sentimentalism seems to accord with Reid's view that the moral sentiments are a more reliable guide to the conduct of life than ethical theory, at least until ethics can prove itself worthy of trust, and not simply serve as an ideological tool for the ethical conventions of the day.

A fifth theme that seems to conflict with the fourth is one espoused by Jouffroy and has a Stoical ring, namely, to find accord with the order of things through reason and logic. There is an element of reasonableness in the world, Peirce says, "to which we can train our own reason to conform more and more" (1903, CP 5.160). Indeed, for Peirce, the ultimate end of human endeavor is what he calls *concrete reasonableness*, a celebration of the ability to discover what is true and good by self-correcting from error (1902, CP 5.3). Reasonableness itself is admirable for no ulterior reason other than it leads us along the right path, wherever that may lead (1903, CP 1.615). Peirce was convinced that there was some sort of teleology in the order of things, that even chance begets order (1893, CP 6.297). However, he could not see his way to proclaim that way to the good, true and right was only wholly through reason. Yes, right reason was essential, but also the right sentiments were needed, and the right sort of community in which both reason and sentiment could be exercised in furthering human conduct.

2 Morality, Ethics and Peirce's Conservative Sentimentalism

Like many philosophers, Peirce distinguishes between morality and ethics. Whereas morality is "a description of the facts of moral life," ethics is "the logical analysis of the conceptions connected with morals" (1900, R 1429, p. 1). Morality is what people have internalized about what is right or wrong, relative to their cultural milieu and upbringing (1898, CP 1.654). It runs mostly on sentiment, habits and instinct. Ethics, on the other hand, is the study of what is right or wrong (1903, CP 1.191). It uses logical reasoning and the keen (coenoscopic) observation of the experience of practical life to formulate its theories (1902, CP 1.241; 1901, CP 8.158; 1905, CP 1.126). There are "two different distinctions of right and wrong . . . generally recognized," one has to do with how people act in accordance with their conscience and personal ideals of conduct. "But there is another question,—the question of the science of morality." This asks, "what are the ideals of conduct most fitting to man and on what principles are they to be allowed to be so? This has been a deep study from the dawn of history" (1903, R453, p. 14).

Morality

"What is morality?" Peirce answers,

> We are brought up to have a horror of doing certain things and of not doing other things. The habit which we thus contract of associating certain emotions with certain acts . . . becomes a very powerful one, and the necessity which we thus feel ourselves to be under of acting in a certain way we term a moral necessity.
>
> (n.d., R 892, p. 1)

Morality is the accumulation through evolution over time of common-sense rules together with the moral conventions of the time and the folkways of the culture (1898, CP 1.654)—what Frank Jackson calls "mature folk morality" (1998, p. 133). Peirce writes in a review of an ethics book by Sidney Mezes, "the author [Mezes] belongs to that school of ethics which is probably nearest right—that is to say, to the school which makes tribal tradition a main factor of morality, and which is thus enabled to frame an evolutionary theory of it" (1901, CP 8.158). Peirce explains this in another passage:

> Morality consists in the folklore of right conduct. A man is brought up to think he ought to behave in certain ways. If he behaves otherwise, he is uncomfortable. His conscience pricks him. That system of morals is the traditional wisdom of ages of experience. If a man cuts loose from it, he will become the victim of his passions. It is not safe for him even to reason about it, except in a purely speculative way. Hence, morality is essentially conservative. Good morals and good manners are identical, except that tradition attaches less importance to the latter. The gentleman is imbued with conservatism. This conservatism is a habit, and it is the law of habit that it tends to spread and extend itself over more and more of the life.
>
> (c. 1896, CP 1.50)

Following the British moral sentimentalists, Peirce believes that conscience is the embodiment of these embedded folkways. As he says, "a stay-at-home conscience does the most to render earth habitable" (1901, CP 8.162). He traces this idea to the scholastic's notion of *conscentia moralis*, which he defines as "acts of pronouncing a moral judgement, springing from a moral habit, whether inborn or developed" (1902, R 434, p. 12). He also refers to Plato and Aristotle's concept of *synderesis*, which the Medieval thinkers also adopted. Peirce understands it "to mean an immediate appreciation of an end as good or otherwise, antecedently to having settled the conception of moral good" (1902, R 434, p. 14). Aristotle defined it in the *Nicomachean Ethics*, according to Peirce, as "the power of correctly weighing different considerations as to the desirability of a line of conduct, after those considerations have been urged" (1902, R 434, p. 19 (2nd draft)). Conscience is a faculty of self-governance and he likens it to the different branches of government, having a tripartite division of legislative, judicial and executive (1903, R 451, p. 7). The legislative conscience lays down the ideals of conduct, the judicial approves or disapproves of the action (1903, R 453, pp. 16–17) and the executive transitions intention into determination to act (1903, R 451, p. 7).

Peirce thinks that conscience is something that is ingrained in the individual, not innately, but developmentally:

> Conscience really belongs to the subconscious man, to that part of the soul which is hardly distinct in different individuals, a sort of community-consciousness, or public spirit, not absolutely one and the same in different citizens, and yet not by any means independent

> in them. Conscience has been created by experience just as any knowledge is; but it is modified by further experience only with secular slowness.
>
> (c. 1896, CP 1.56)

Having a conscience is not a deliberate choice but comes about developmentally under normal conditions. As Peirce writes somewhat sarcastically,

> The pursuit of a conscience, if one hasn't one already, or of a religion, which is the subjective basis of conscience, seems to me an aimless and hypochondriac pursuit. If a man finds himself under no sense of obligation, let him congratulate himself. For such a man to hanker after a bondage to conscience, is as if a man with a good digestion should cast about for a regimen of food. A conscience, too, is not a theorem or a piece of information which may be acquired by reading a book; it must be bred in a man from infancy or it will be a poor imitation of the genuine article. If a man has a conscience, it may be an article of faith with him, that he should reflect upon that conscience, and thus it may receive a further development. But it never will do him the least good to get up a make-believe scepticism and pretend to himself not to believe what he really does believe.
>
> (1885, CP 8.45)

Conscience is a reliable guide in moral decision-making. At the same time, because conscience is evolved and developmental, it is subject to change (c. 1896, CP 1.56). Peirce cautions that it is certainly subject to error: "But we are by no means to think that the utterances of this faculty are infallible" (1902, R 434, p. 15).

Conservative Sentimentalism

The tradition among ethical thinkers is that the study of ethics can serve as a guide to the conduct of life—why else study it? Both Peirce and James are cautious of this claim.

In "The Moral Philosopher and the Moral Life," a talk delivered to the Yale Philosophy Department in 1891, William James thought that even after some 2300 years of attempts, ethical thinkers had not come to any agreement about what is to count as the good (1891, p. 607). In any case, it was dangerous to rely on any thinker's "clean shaven" system as a guide for the rough-and-tumble of practical life. Instead of relying on philosophers to figure out what is good and right, it was better to rely on the collective results wrought from experiments of living. The good cannot be pre-conceived and then applied artificially to human practices. James states this theme directly: "the main purpose of this paper is to show that there is no such thing possible as an ethical philosophy dogmatically made up in advance. We all help to determine the content of ethical philosophy so far as we contribute to the race's moral life" (1891, p. 595). Indeed, James is worried that individual moralists might be in a position of authority to decide right and wrong, "to determine which good shall be butchered and which shall be suffered to survive" "The notion," he says, "really turns one pale." So afraid of this possibility that he exhorts "better chaos forever than an order based on any closet-philosopher's rule, even though he were the most enlightened possible member of his tribe" (1891, p. 610). The answers to which ideals are the best guides have to wait on the long experience of human experiment.

Peirce says much the same thing less eloquently in "Philosophy and the Conduct of Life," Peirce's opening lecture in the Cambridge series at Harvard, arranged by William James in 1898. It is in this lecture that he makes a case for a conservative *sentimentalism*, following many of the themes of the British and Scottish moral sentimentalists. He gave a preview of it five years earlier in his article, "Evolutionary Love." There he defines sentimentalism as "the doctrine that great respect should be paid to the natural judgments of the sensible heart" (1893, CP 6.292).

In this first lecture of the Cambridge series, Peirce makes some rather radical claims. First, that theory and practice should not mingle (1898, CP 1.618). Second, in vital matters, reason should defer to sentiment and instinct (1898, CP 1.630); in fact, reasoning is subordinate to sentiment in this regard (1898, R 436, p. 34). Third, not only is the science of ethics useless for the conduct of life (1898, CP 1.666), it is, fourth, downright dangerous (1898, CP 1.667). Fifth, given the first four claims, people should conduct their lives not on the basis of ethical theories, but on their sentiments and instincts (1898, CP 1.666). These doctrines constitute his conservative *sentimentalism*. By *conservatism*, Peirce means "to believe in thinking as you have been brought up to think" (1898, CP 1.666). By *sentimentalism*, Peirce means something akin to reliance on feeling, conscience, emotion and instinct.

Peirce certainly is inspired by Thomas Reid's similar positions on these matters, articulated a century earlier. Recall that, for Reid, reason shouldn't be trusted as a guide to life because it is a nascent ability and currently imperfectly employed by humankind (1788, pp. 138–139). The moral instincts and sentiments are more reliable guides for this reason (1788, pp. 145–161). Ethical theory has little connection with the moral conduct of our life, and is in a sorry state, bound up in disagreements (1788, pp. 376–377). When ethical theories conflict with moral sentiments and instincts, it is unsafe to warp the common-sense rules with those theories (1788, p. 387).

Many Peirce scholars find "Philosophy and the Conduct of Life" vexing (Misak, 2004, p. 164; Hookway, 2002, pp. 23, 224). What perplexes them is that these theses seem to be inconsistent with the body of Peirce's pragmatist doctrine. Even if Reid is the influence, it still raises the question why Peirce would side with the British moral sentimentalists on ethical matters, given the principal theses of his pragmatism.

The first thesis against the mix of theory and practice would seem to be contrary to the letter and spirit of the pragmatic maxim, and so the most perplexing of the claims in this lecture of 1898. Peirce's pragmatic maxim makes it clear that the import of a theoretical claim is found in its corresponding practical maxim, so there is an inherent transposition of theoretical into practical reasoning (1903, CP 5.18). It is also inconsistent with themes in "The Fixation of Belief," where Peirce argues that science can play an important social function in securing the fixation of belief, better than alternatives, particularly methods of authority—which his conservative sentimentalism seems to invoke. Peirce's claim that science has nothing to do with belief is also befuddling, given the claim in "Fixation" that science is the best means for "fixing" beliefs (1877, CP 5.387; Hookway, 2002, p. 14).

The second thesis that reason rests on sentiment appears contrary to Peirce's promotion of reasonableness as the *summum bonum*, and his advocacy of cognitivism in almost all matters and claims that feelings are cognitive phenomena (1903, CP 1.615; c.1890, CP 1.381). The British sentimentalists were noncognitivists in moral matters, yet Peirce was a dye-in-the-wool cognitivist in most everything (1868, CP 5.265). In one passage, he even seems to support the Humean thesis that reason is and ought to be "a slave to the passions" (1898, CP 1.673; Hume, 1739, p. 413).

If the third thesis is correct, that the science of ethics is useless in the conduct of life then as Cornelis De Waal points out, it would deny the validity of a science of ethics as useful for logic (2012, p. 87).

The claim that ethics is dangerous is contradicted by the history of ethics which, by all accounts, has introduced norms and ideas that seem to have assisted in the improvement of the human condition. Indeed, Peirce himself, on occasion, considered utilitarianism favorably, and utilitarianism certainly was an ethical theory that had been developed in fairly recent times (1903, CP 5.158).

As to the fifth thesis on conservative sentimentalism, this would seem to fly in the face of Peirce's evolutionism, synechism, meliorism and agapism, all of which suggest a change for the better (1893, CP 6.303). *Conservative* sentimentalism would seem to advocate keeping whatever is in place, which stands in contrast to Peirce's arguments against authoritarianism, dogmatism and methods of tenacity in the "Fixation of Belief."

Peirce's theses in "Philosophy and the Conduct of Life" seem to upend most of Peirce's thinking prior to this time in the ways just mentioned. There are three plausible interpretations to explain these apparent inconsistencies: Peirce changed his mind and is now disavowing the earlier theses of his pragmatism; this lecture is an aberration or meant to be ironic or sarcastic; there is some interpretation of the lectures that reconciles his views in the lecture with the principal themes of his pragmatism.

As to the first explanation, Peirce continues to proclaim pragmatism as the hallmark of his philosophy after 1898, although he clarifies his version of it under the name of *pragmaticism* (1907, CP 4.540). But there is also continued support for the pragmatic maxim well into his later years (1903, CP 5.14). So, it is unlikely that he intends to disavow the fundamental theses of pragmatism in the Cambridge lectures of 1898.

There is some evidence to back up the second interpretation that Peirce was being ironic or sarcastic. Some drafts of the lecture are indeed very sarcastic and bitter, particularly about Harvard, given that he had been rejected for a position there by President Charles Eliot (1898, CP 1.650). At this time, Peirce's life situation was desperate financially and professionally while others less talented had flourished. This would certainly foster resentment.

James had arranged for Peirce to give this series of lectures. These were part of the Cambridge Conference series, funded by local citizens of Cambridge, and were clearly meant to be popular lectures. Titles included "the ethics of altruism," "ethics of trade or commerce," "ethics of citizenship," "ethical issues in education," among other similar topics. Peirce, probably not aware of the context, wanted to present very technical, abstract and theoretical topics on logic and mathematics. When they were proposed to James, he tried to coach Peirce away from those topics and emphasized that Peirce should do something "on topics of a vitally important character." Peirce's reply to James shows an edgy acceptance of the suggestion, parroting James's phrase in quotations. In another letter, he proposes to rename his whole lecture with the phrase "vitally important topics," with the first lecture on that topic (Ketner and Putnam, 1992, pp. 26–28). Peirce is clearly upset that James does not consider his work on logic a "vitally important matter."

Peirce certainly tends to exaggerate in this lecture. Whereas he says there that the study of ethics is "useless" and "dangerous," in 1902 in drafts of *Minute Logic*, he says, as if referring to himself, "Some writers on ethics deny that it affords any aid toward a moral life. I cannot but think that this is an exaggeration. I do not see how the study of Plato, or Shaftesbury, or Kant can fail to make men better" (1902, CP 2.201).

That aside, one problem with this claim is that although Peirce might have been ironic or sarcastic about some of the claims in his first lecture, he does seem to take his conservative sentimentalism seriously afterward. Noted previously is the claim, in a review of a book by Sidney Mezes in 1901, that "the school which makes tribal tradition a main factor of morality, and which is thus enabled to frame an evolutionary theory of it" is "that school of ethics which is probably nearest right." "Conservatism in morals is most needful in practice, and, of course, is theoretically defensible" (1901, CP 8.158).

This would suggest that the third alternative is more plausible. Richard Atkins thinks that the explanation is that Peirce is providing an "oblique" criticism of James's *The Will to Believe*. It is well-known that Peirce, like other contemporaries, such as Alfred Lloyd could not accept James's account of the justification of religious faith (Lloyd, 1907; 1908, CP 6.485). But, if it is oblique, it is very oblique. As noted, James says much the same thing in "The Moral Philosopher and the Moral Life" as Peirce does in this lecture. Moreover, Atkins's interpretation doesn't explain very well the larger inconsistencies with Peirce's pragmatism and synechism. There must be a certain interpretation of his conservative sentimentalism that makes it consistent with his more fundamental theses of pragmatism.

Here are the highlights of the interpretation proposed here. First, the "conservative" in Peirce's conservative sentimentalism is consistent with his fallibilism. There is "good" and "bad" conservatism; the first is fallibilistic and the second is absolutist. Second, the way in which he interprets the "sentimentalism" among the British moral sentimentalists is consistent with his *critical* common-sensism, synechism and evolutionism. Third, Peirce's worry about the separation of theory and practice is founded on a genuine concern that practical interests can corrupt the objectivity of theoretical pursuits, particularly in the matter of ethics. This is tied to his rather perplexing claim that belief "has no place in science at all" (1898, CP 1.635). He does not deny that theoretical claims have practical application only that, if the goal is to pursue truth, practical interests should not interfere with theoretical pursuits.

Peirce's fallibilism is essentially the position that there is no reason for people to doubt their beliefs until there is a reason to doubt them (c. 1897, CP 1.13). Doubt must arise genuinely and is a prompt for further inquiry. Beliefs that are not doubted are, literally, indubitable. That does not mean they are infallible or cannot become dubitable. Peirce thought that what was counted as indubitable might change quickly, but his own preliminary study suggested that they tend to change slightly from generation to generation (1905, CP 5.444). Of course, history does not bear that out very well. Often, they do change quite rapidly. Additionally, there are some beliefs that are indubitable because they are acritical (1905, CP 5.440). However, although there is no absolute certainty about any belief, some beliefs are *practically* certain, meaning that they have persisted sufficiently over time such that they are unlikely to be doubted in the future. Peirce gives the example of moral beliefs that it is wrong to murder and steal (c. 1897, CP 1.151).

Fallibilism is Janus-faced for this reason, looking through the past at what has persisted over time but also to the future, open to the possibility that what was once believed may be doubted at some time. Its opponent is infallibilism, and religion and morals are the most frequent subscribers to that doctrine (c. 1897, CP 1.8). "The doctrine of fallibilism will also be denied by those who fear its consequences for science, for religion, and for morality" (c. 1897, CP 1.148). Bad conservatives tend to be infallibilists. "To return to our friends the Conservatives; these ladies and gentlemen will tell me this doctrine of fallibilism can never be admitted because the consequences from it would undermine Religion" (c. 1897, CP 1.151). Peirce claims that "sentiment lays no claim to infallibility," even if the actor feels his sentiments are such (1898, CP 1.661). Peirce insists in *The Minute Logic*, a few years after the Cambridge Lectures, that "we are by no means to think that the utterances of this faculty [our heart and conscience] are infallible" (1902, R 434, p. 15). On the contrary, "nobody needs to be told that nothing is more insincere or ignorant of itself than the human heart. It is a dull and mendacious witness that needs to be cross-examined closely, in order to extract from it the real truth" (1902, R 434, p. 27). Further in these passages, Peirce clarifies the roles of sentiment and reason. He uses the metaphor of the trial, where "the heart is witness but the head as jury," "the heart must be skillfully interrogated; and from her responses the head is to draw its own conclusions, whether the heart can be brought to acquiesce in them, or not" (1902, R 434, p. 29).

This can only mean that Peirce takes a fallibilist position toward any body of sentiment-based norms. Peirce is against those conservative moralists who think their moral rules are *infallible*. "But morality, doctrinaire conservatist that it is, destroys its own vitality by resisting change, and positively insisting, This is eternally right: That is eternally wrong" (1902, CP 2.197). As Richard Atkins notes, "Peirce's view . . . is not that our sentiments are infallible guides to conduct but that they are inductive generalizations that help guide our action well enough to avoid disaster. They are practically infallible in the sense that they are the best we have" (2018, p. 76). Peirce recognizes that for the fallibilist position to work properly, people do have to have indubitable beliefs, otherwise they become itinerant skeptics, paper doubters. Moreover, he could agree that the persistence of certain rules over time, such as prohibitions against murder, theft and incest, is a good indication that some norms are *practically* certain. As Peirce says, "practically, we know that questions do generally get settled in time, when they come to be scientifically investigated; and this is practically and pragmatically enough" (c. 1906, CP 5.494; 1878, CP 2.664). Peirce argues, for example, that the moral beliefs that it is wrong to murder and steal are "practically and substantially" established in this sense (c. 1897, CP 1.151).

Peirce explains that because of its Janus-like character, there is an affinity between the doctrine of fallibilism and the principle of continuity. The latter is "the idea of fallibilism objectified." Fallibilism is the view that all beliefs "swim" in a continuum of uncertainty and indeterminacy (c. 1897, CP 1.171). In turn, fallibilism "cannot be appreciated . . . until evolution has been considered" (c. 1897, CP 1.173), and "evolution means nothing but *growth* in the widest sense of that word" (c. 1897, CP 1.174).

One aspect of growth is "diversification," which is possible only because of some element of spontaneity; pure deterministic mechanism could never generate anything novel (c. 1897, CP 1.174). Another aspect of growth is the organization of that diversity, an "organized heterogeneity" or "rationalized variety," as Peirce calls it (1903, CP 6.101). Perhaps the best example that Peirce gives of what he means by growth is learning (1893, CP 6.301). Learning is the incorporation of new into existing information (1867, CP 2.419). If science is illustrative of learning, then the system of sciences exemplifies what Peirce means by growth. In science, one has a continuous diversification of studies, physics, geology, biology, chemistry, psychology and sociology, each of which also has its subbranches. Yet, despite the diversity, they can be organized architectonically, where principles of the more fundamental sciences serve as foundations for other sciences, but where individual sciences may provide outcomes that inform or modify existing principles, as well as other sciences. In general, as more knowledge is acquired, its organization grows more systematically over time. Growth is exemplified by this sort of architectonic of learning.

Thus, with these few insights, Peirce connects the ideas of fallibilism, synechism and evolution. Evolutionism infers that any moral norms that are practically certain are not brought down from on high, complete from the beginning, but have worked their way into the gut as instincts and sentiments over time, as they persist through experiment with a variety of ways of living. "The infallibilist," Peirce says, "thinks that everything always was substantially as it is now" (c. 1897, CP 1.175). But the fallibilist appreciates the role of evolution, self-correction and growth in moral development.

Although Peirce agrees with the British moralists that sentiments and instincts are the best guide for the conduct of life—at least for now—he does not agree that they have been set in people's psyche from the very get-go. Peirce insists that "instinct is capable of development and growth—though by a movement which is slow in the proportion in which it is vital." But, most importantly, and consistent with his cognitivism, he argues that the development of instincts and sentiments parallel reasoning. "This development," of the instincts and sentiments,

> takes place upon lines which are altogether parallel to those of reasoning. And just as reasoning springs from experience, so the developement of sentiment arises from the soul's Inward and Outward Experiences. Not only is it of the same nature as the developement of cognition; but it chiefly takes place through the instrumentality of cognition.
>
> (1898, CP 1.648)

Peirce notes that "reasoning has no monopoly of the process of generalization—Sentiment also generalizes itself" (1898, R435s.), and that nature also makes abductive and inductive inferences (1898, RLT, p. 161). De Waal concludes much the same thing about Peirce: "like reason, instinct is a product of the individual's interaction with the environment and as such it is a reflection of the reasonableness of the universe" (2012, p. 94).

At bottom, while people should rely on their common-sense beliefs as a guide to practical moral life, as fallibilists, people should be prepared to modify them as their knowledge and experience grow. Peirce argues, "Common sense corrects itself, improves its conclusions," so "we see social, political, religious common sense modifying itself insensibly in course of generations, ideas of rights of man acquiring new meaning, thaumaturgic elements of Christianity sinking, spiritual rising in religious consciousness" (c. 1905, CP 6.573). But, as he emphasizes, if "common sense improves; it does not, then, attain infallibility" (c. 1905, CP 6.574). Indeed, Peirce stresses that, at times, it is difficult to sort out what are moral instincts from what are simply cultural conventions and biases: "there is a danger in following what appear to be our natural instincts too closely; and partly because we cannot distinguish between true instincts and mere prejudices" (1911, NEM 3, p. 204). Atkins thinks that prejudices might be sorted out for Peirce based on the evidence of transcultural adoption. For example, Peirce seems to think that incest is an instinctual prohibition, but suicide not, since its acceptance varies among a sufficient number of cultures and circumstances (Atkins, 2018, p. 75). Instincts can also fail us in novel situations, of which life presents many times over (c. 1894, R 410, p. 3).

Peirce also distinguishes instincts from sentiments more carefully than the British moralists, and even engages in attempts at their typology (1902, R 1300; 1902–1905, R 1343). Richard Atkins summarizes this effort nicely:

> moral sentiments are feelings of approval or disapproval about certain proposed or accomplished courses of action. Instincts are inherited habits, though the line of demarcation between inherited habits and those resulting from infantile conditioning is vague and so the latter may also be regarded as instincts. Some of our moral sentiments have a basis in instincts, but not all of them do. It is not clear whether all of our moral sentiments have a basis in some habit, whether inherited or acquired. . . . We must distinguish between habits and instincts, on the one hand, and sentiments, on the other.
>
> (2018, p. 54)

Although Peirce adopts Reid's common-sense theory, he adopts it in a modified form he calls *critical* common-sense. He summarizes it with six characteristics. Whereas the Scottish school argued for certain indubitable beliefs, Peirce argues that there are indubitable beliefs, but only because they are acritical, and cannot be proven (1905, CP 5.440). For example, a common acritical presumption of inquirers is that there is an order to nature. Inquiry without that belief would not seem possible, yet one cannot prove such a proposition, and such propositions are inherently vague (1905, CP 5.446). Related to this, rather than using the notion of "self-evident" intuitions, as the common-sense philosophers do, Peirce purposefully uses the term *indubitable*, literally, not doubtful. He is wary of the claims of self-evidence, having witnessed the upending of long-standing Euclidean axioms with Riemannian and Lobachewskian geometry and Cantor's transfinite arithmetic. As he says directly, "I am a total disbeliever in axioms" (1903, CP 7.622). Moreover, many of the moral intuitionists relied on the Cartesian criteria of being clear and distinct, so that the mere understanding of the moral claim justifies its belief. Of course, Peirce eschews the Cartesian criteria in favor of the pragmatic maxim so that the clarity of a concept is found in the sorts of practical dispositions or habits it displays under observable, experiential or experimental conditions.

Second, indubitable beliefs are also vague and indeterminate (1905, CP 5.446). Third, what is counted as indubitable seems to change over time (1905, CP 5.444). Fourth, whereas the Scottish philosophers counted indubitable beliefs as instincts, critical common-sense understands instincts as Darwin explains them in his evolutionary theory. As such instincts can be modified, even over a short period (1905, CP 5.445). Fifth, critical common-sensism differs from the traditional common-sense philosophy since it promotes fallibilism, as noted. What counts as indubitable can become dubitable (1905, CP 5.451). Sixth, he calls it *critical*, because it is a modification of Kant's philosophy (1905, CP 5.452). Peirce concludes,

> Man, like any other animal, is gifted with the power of understanding sufficient for the conduct of life. . . . Pragmaticism . . . implies faith in common sense and in instinct, though only as they issue from the cupel-furnace of measured criticism.
>
> (1908, CP 6.480)

Taking all of this into consideration, if this interpretation of "Philosophy and the Conduct of Life" holds, Peirce's conservative sentimentalism is compatible with his fallibilism, synechism, evolutionism and critical common-sensism. This leads one to think that Peirce's sentimentalism should be called *critical* rather than *conservative* sentimentalism. But that's not what Peirce chose. Nonetheless, this critical sentimentalism may mollify some of Cornelis De Waal's criticisms of Peirce's theory. He has two main ones. Some sentiments should be rejected on ethical grounds. It would commit the worse sort of naturalistic fallacy to accept the moral validity of a sentiment simply because of its predominance

(2012, p. 92). Second, what is relied on when there are competing sentiments, or no sentiments in novel situations, or they are not sufficiently fine-grained to be useful in certain situations (2012, p. 93). In regard to the first objection, Peirce agrees with what is to be called the naturalistic fallacy: "to urge that anything is sound and good logically, morally, or esthetically, for no better reason than that men have a natural tendency to think so . . . is as pernicious a fallacy as ever was" (1903, HL, p. 210). Most people do rely on their moral instincts and sentiments when making decisions. But, given his fallibilism and other statements just discussed, it's clear that he thinks those very sentiments and instincts are fallible and subject to criticism. In regard to the second objection, Peirce does seem to acknowledge this as a problem (c. 1894, R 410, p. 4).

What about his thesis concerning the uselessness of ethical theory? Peirce, like James and Reid, believes that moral philosophy is at present in an "infantile condition," and its practitioners cannot come to any agreement. This is what makes it "useless" as a guide to the conduct of life. He complains that the problem is a lack of scientific attitude and methodology in the study of ethics. He complains that

> it has chiefly been pursued by men who have not been nurtured in dissecting-rooms and other laboratories, and who consequently have not been animated by the true scientific Eros, but who have on the contrary come from theological seminaries, and have consequently been inflamed with a desire to amend the lives of themselves and others . . . radically unfitting them for the task of scientific investigation.
>
> (1898, RLT, pp. 107–108)

But, unlike James, Peirce seems to hold out some hope that the study of ethics, done scientifically, could eventually redeem itself and become a fairly reliable guide for the conduct of life:

> We do not say that sentiment is never to be influenced by reason, nor that under no circumstances would we advocate radical reforms. We only say that the man who would allow his religious life to be wounded by any sudden acceptance of a philosophy of religion or who would precipitately change his code of morals, at the dictate of a philosophical ethics . . . is a man whom we should consider unwise.
>
> (1898, CP 1.633)

A few years later, he seems to be very confident about the possibilities of a science of ethics: "I myself have no doubt that the study [of theoretical ethics] is more or less favorable to right living" (1903, CP 1.600). He also bemoans the fact that theoretical or normative ethics is not employed enough by the practical sciences:

> The influence of philosophy upon the practical sciences is less direct. It is only here and there that it can be detected; and ethics is the division of philosophy which most concerns these sciences. Ethics is courteously invited to make a suggestion now and then in law, jurisprudence, and sociology. Its sedulous exclusion from diplomacy and economics is immense folly. We are unhappily debarred from calling this folly stupendous or egregious, because it is merely the ordinary blindness of those who profoundly believe that lies are the most wholesome of diet. . . . Right is a silly thing without wealth or vigor in this work-a-day world. One day man shall start up out of his slumber to see by broad daylight that that despised idea has all along been the one irresistible power. Then may begin an era when it is counted within the practical sciences, one and all—when, in a word, a man will not design a stove nor order a coat without stopping first and sifting out his real desire—and it is prophecy as simple as Barbara, that, when that comes to pass, those sciences will answer even their lower and nearest purposes far more perfectly than at present they do.
>
> (1902, CP 1.251)

If Peirce still holds out some hope for a science of ethics that could, at the conclusion of its investigations, serve as a guide for the conduct of life, then why does he dismiss the "mingling" between theory and practice? "Now two masters, *theory* and *practice*, you cannot both serve" (1898, CP 1.642). Peirce's position seems to be that although the results of theory could serve practice, doing theory with practical interests in mind would ruin theory. "That perfect balance of attention which is requisite for observing the system of things is utterly lost if human desires intervene, and all the more so the higher and holier those desires may be" (1898, CP 1.642). To do theoretical ethics, inquirers must eschew their conservatism, and that is what makes the study of ethics "dangerous." As he says a year earlier:

> But I will take leave to say to these highly conservative gentlemen that however competent they may be to direct the affairs of a church or other corporations, they had better not try to manage science in that way. Conservatism—in the sense of a dread of consequences—is altogether out of place in science—which has on the contrary always been forwarded by radicals and radicalism, in the sense of the eagerness to carry consequences to their extremes. Not the radicalism that is cocksure, however, but the radicalism that tries experiments. Indeed, it is precisely among men animated by the spirit of science that the doctrine of fallibilism will find supporters.
>
> (c. 1897, CP 1.148)

He repeats this point in his review of Mezes's book on ethics:

> Now, conservatism in morals is most needful in practice, and, of course, is theoretically defensible. But that defence itself is not conservative: on the contrary, it is rationalistic; and in pure theory, especially in a theory of aims, conservatism is irrational and out of place.
>
> (1901, CP 8.158)

This is why Peirce thinks the study of ethics "dangerous" (1898, CP 1.667). Ethics must be practiced in a manner that allows the possibility to detach itself from moral conventions to evaluate those norms at some level—as hard as that might be to do. Peirce is expressing the genuine tensions in the culture between those who live the morality of the culture, and those who study it. The risk in this is that the work of theoretical ethicists, paradoxically, will often be labeled immoral by doctrinaire moralists if it is contrary to the dominant norms of the culture (1898, CP 1.666). In one striking passage, he argues, like Nietzsche, that ethicists are in a certain sense immoral since they may raise questions or concerns about existing conventional morality: "Hence, ethics, which is reasoning out an explanation of morality is—I will not say immoral, [for] that would be going too far—composed of the very substance of immorality" (1898, CP 1.666; Nietzsche, 1886, sect 228).

In regard to the problem of mixing theory and practice, Peirce may be expressing a concern he is seeing by the 1890s at a point in the industrial revolution. He sees science being used more and more for its practical uses and is worried that the purposes of what he calls "pure" theoretical science may be in jeopardy. This, of course, is ironic since Peirce's prescient pragmatic maxim shows how theoretical propositions can be translated to practical maxims, thus anticipating the direct transposition of theoretical science into practical application.

In this regard, Peirce notes three different types of inquirers based on three different purposes for inquiry (Liszka, 2018). There are those who inquire purely for the sake of truth, the true scientists (c. 1896, CP 1.44). There are the applied scientists who inquire to apply theoretical knowledge to some practical end (c. 1896, CP 1.45). Finally, there are the practically minded folks who, given that they aim at certain ends, must adopt means that they believe will accomplish those ends, means and ends to which they are committed to accomplish. Peirce writes, "the practical man . . . must believe with all the force of his manhood that the object for which he strives is good and that the theory of his plan is correct." Whereas "the scientific man is above all things desirous of learning the truth and, in order to do so, ardently desires to have his present provisional beliefs (and all his beliefs are merely provisional) swept away, and will work hard to accomplish that object" (1898, CP 6.3). In other words, applied scientists and practical people of all sorts view science and theory instrumentally.

It is for the latter reason that Peirce argues that "pure science has nothing to do with *belief*" (1903, CP 7.606). Interestingly, he says this in the context of a review of research on telepathy, and in that review questions whether many of the researchers in psychical research are interested in the truth or interested in proving what they believe to be the case (Liszka and Babb, 2020, p. 227). This is why Peirce insists on *predesignation* in testing hypotheses as a reliable tool to prevent confirmation bias (1902, CP 2.775). Researchers must pre-designate what the outcomes of their hypotheses will predict rather than performing experiments and then sorting through the outcomes to find results that confirm the hypothesis. Peirce—along with his student Joseph Jastrow—were the first to develop a double-blind test in experiments and randomization, in order to avoid any subconscious bias or influence on the results of experiments by experimenters (Hacking, 1988, p. 430; Stigler, 1986, p. 248).

Certainly, Peirce's concerns are felt today. If the principal purpose for doing theory is to solve practical problems, then basic science is at risk. Yet, paradoxically, it is through the unfettered pursuit of theoretical science that practical applications are possible. At the same time, as in the case of climate science, if scientific results conflict with political goals or practical interests, then scientific research is questioned and placed in danger.

This problem is especially complicated for the scientific study of ethics since, as Peirce himself notes, of all the sciences, normative ethics is thought to have the most application to the practical sciences. De Waal sees this as a particularly difficult problem for Peirce. It would seem that there is a great deal of investment by investigators in what is studied in ethics. Since the ethics of inquiry requires a disinterest in the hypotheses or claims of the investigation, then "the ethics of inquiry seems to preclude ethical inquiry" (2012, p. 89). Indeed, it can be said that ethical theory is often developed in light of particular issues and concerns that arise in ethical life. Whereas advances in theoretical science may be generated out of problems or puzzles in scientifically observed phenomena, the field of study, the experimental lab for the ethical theorist, must be the practice of ethical life.

Thus, the study of ethics seems to be inherently practical in many respects, as opposed to theory in basic science. As practiced, morality has a tendency to be conservative and to resist change. Additionally, it often takes on an absolutist attitude that can obstruct genuine theoretical inquiry: "The tendency of philosophers has always been to make their assertions too absolute. Nothing stands more in the way of a comprehension of the universe and of the mind. But in morals, this tendency acquires triple strength" (1902, CP 2.197). Because of the life-investment in many practically held moral beliefs, people may be more tenacious in those beliefs, seeking support where they can, and ignoring evidence to the contrary. This, of course, is deadly for theoretical science, and creates what Peirce calls "sham" reasoning. In the field of theoretical science, Creationists, for example, have a pre-formed hypothesis which they will not yield—that life was created at once by a divine intelligence rather than evolved; thus, they seek evidence that will support it; and where evidence does not, they will employ clever (or not so clever) *ad hoc* hypotheses to assimilate the contrary evidence. The goal is to prove the hypothesis they want to believe; that violates the rule of pre-designation in induction and makes for bad science. It prevents any self-correction.

This is especially true for the study of ethics. "For ethical research begins only after we find ourselves already practically committed to moral positions." In this respect inquiry "can only reach a foregone conclusion" (n.d., R 893, p. 2). In practical or applied ethics, this sort of sham reasoning becomes another name for rationalization of what we already believe, as Peirce explains:

> When men begin to rationalize about their conduct, the first effect is to deliver them over to their passions and produce the most frightful demoralization, especially in sexual matters. . . . In short, it is no longer the reasoning which determines what the conclusion shall be, but it is the conclusion which determines what the reasoning shall be. This is sham reasoning. In short, as morality supposes self-control, men learn that they must not surrender themselves unreservedly to any method, without considering to what conclusions it will lead them. But this is utterly contrary to the single-mindedness that is requisite in science. In order that science may be successful, its votaries must hasten to surrender themselves at discretion to experimental inquiry, in advance of knowing what its decisions may be. There must be no reservations.
>
> (c. 1896, CP 1.57)

Peirce's concern is a genuine one. Consider, for example, the ethical arguments around the issue of slavery in Peirce's own time. There were several different defenses of slavery in antebellum America by slave owners, religious leaders, politicians, and those invested in the institution. As more and more controversy about slavery rose, those with interests in the practice produced a cannonade of rationalizations, some of which would stretch the common sense of Americans today. In order to make the suffering and oppression of slaves palatable, the "positive" effects of slavery were touted, making slave-owners even appear righteous. In his famous speech to the Senate of February 6, 1837, John Calhoun argued not as some did—that it was a necessary evil—but that it was a positive good (1837, p. 225; Bartlett, 1993, p. 227). Calhoun pointed to the long-enduring norm of the aristocrats using the common man to improve the community. Moreover, African slaves are better off than many laborers around the world, and certainly better off here in the U.S. than they were in Africa. But slavery also raised the status and improved the lives of poor white folk in South Carolina (see Bartlett, 1993, pp. 227–228). Many religious ministers and preachers from the South joined the chorus, justifying slavery on the basis of literal interpretations of the Bible. Frederick Dalcho, for example, argued that slaves were descendants of Ham, who was cursed by his father, Noah. As such this was "divinely inspired" by God who, of course, was the "epitome of justice and righteousness," clearly legitimating the practice of slavery (Dalcho, 1823).

If ethicists act like ideologues and end up simply being apologists for the dominant moral conventions, then ethical theory becomes suspect. Ethics must be practiced in a manner that allows the possibility for inquirers to detach themselves from moral conventions to evaluate those norms at some level—as hard as that might be to do. Peirce is expressing the genuine tensions in the culture between those who live the morality of the culture, and those who study it. In one passage Peirce sarcastically articulates this tension between morality and the study of ethics:

> Now what's the use of prying into the philosophical basis of morality? We all know what morality is: it is behaving as you were brought up to behave, that is, to think you ought to be punished for not behaving. But to believe in thinking as you have been brought up to think defines conservatism. It needs no reasoning to perceive that morality is conservatism. But conservatism again means, as you will surely agree, not trusting to one's reasoning powers. To be a moral man is to obey the traditional maxims of your community without hesitation or discussion.
>
> (1898, CP 1.666)

Initially, as ethical theorists introduce new ideas and criticize existing norms, there is a strong resistance among practitioners accustomed to them. Think for example of the rise in relatively recent times of arguments for women's rights, civil rights, anti-racism, animal ethics, so-called death-with dignity legislation, abortion, LGBTQ rights. Yet, often within a passing decade, the novel theories are accepted as if they had always been part of the tradition. It is hard to imagine slavery as an acceptable practice today, yet in Peirce's own time that issue was rife with controversy; and, although Peirce's own beliefs and position on slavery during the Civil War were distressingly conservative and on the wrong side of history, he undoubtedly could acknowledge the normative changes that happened to the American belief system on that issue over time.

Yet, if existing norms are the result of an evolutionary process, the result of changes or rejections to past prevailing ones and adoption of new ones, then any existing norms are liable to the same processes.

Certainly, history bears this out. It shows that changes are prompted by people's dissatisfaction with existing norms or troubled by the day's convention. Peirce himself notes this in 1893 in a rather long amendment to his 1878 article, "The Fixation of Belief":

> Now, in the course of ages, old questions pass out of mind: new questions become urgent. The sea advances or recedes. . . . In one way or another, commerce is diverted from its ancient roads. Such change brings novel experiences and new ideas. Men begin to rebel at doings of the authorities to which in former times they would have submitted. Questions never before raised come up for decision. . . . Disturbances occur; knots of men discuss the state of affairs; and a suspicion is kindled, which runs about like a train of gun powder, that the Dicta men have been reverencing, originated in caprice, in the pertinacity of some busybody, in the schemes of an ambitious man, or in other influences which are seen to edify a deliberative assembly. Men now begin to demand that, as the power which maintains the belief has become no longer capricious but public and methodical, so the propositions to be believed shall be determined in a public and methodical manner.
>
> (1893, CP 5.380 n1)

Peirce's conservative sentimentalism is both a descriptive and proscriptive theory of morality. It argues on the one hand that, as a matter of fact and for the most part, people rely on their upbringing, conscience, instincts and moral sentiments to guide their practical lives. Since these sentiments and instincts have been shaped by the forge of evolution and experience, there is reason to respect them. Yet they are fallible, and it can also be difficult at times to sort out those that have genuinely persisted for good reasons, and those that are merely cultural biases of the time. Even though ethical science is in no shape to serve as a more reliable guide, it's quite possible that it will be in the future as the science of ethics improves in its methods and results.

3 The Normative Science of Ethics

Although Peirce was dissatisfied with the current state of the study of ethics, he must have thought it redeemable given his serious attempt to develop a normative science of ethics around the turn of the century. His complaint about the tradition seems to center on the lack of scientific attitude and methodology in the study of ethics rather than significance of the discipline. As he worried, it has been taken up mostly "from theological seminaries," rather than those "nurtured" in the methodologies of modern laboratory science (1898, RLT, pp. 107–108). Even though in his 1898 Cambridge Lecture, "Philosophy and the Conduct of Life," he claimed the "uselessness" and "danger" of ethics as a guide to practical life, later statements show that he *does* believe that studying the great ethicists can be edifying (1902, CP 2.201). "I myself have no doubt that the study [of ethics] is more or less favorable to right living" (1903, CP 1.600). He also thought that ethics can make a real contribution to jurisprudence, law and sociology, among other disciplines and practices (1902, CP 1.251). Although the normative science is distinct from practical science, nonetheless "it tends to produce this" (1906, EP2, p. 376). In his Lowell Lectures of 1903, he thinks that the science of ethics "has been a deep study from the dawn of history," and that "there is no more encouraging chapter of history than that one recounts the gradual improvement of the science of ethics." He cautions that this is so even if the "fully satisfactory solution of the problem is still hidden from us" (1903, R 453, p. 14). If it is true that moral sentiments, instincts and habits of conduct evolve and correct over time then, surely, assistance from a science of ethics, rightly done, can act as an accelerant of this process (1903, CP 1.615). Just as science has accelerated the rate of knowledge, so a science of ethics could accelerate an understanding of what is right and good.

The Development of Peirce's Views About the Science of Ethics

The development of Peirce's ideas about the discipline of ethics can be pegged with his different classifications of the sciences, beginning in the early 1880s. The earliest ones consider ethics to be a practical study. As

Beverley Kent suggests, even as late as 1898, Peirce considers ethics "concerned with the life-demands of day-to-day existence" (1987, p. 109). The first time the study of ethics appears in a classification is in 1892, where it is considered a branch of practical psychology (1987, p. 94). Shortly thereafter, Peirce considers it a branch of sociology. In 1895, it is listed as an art, along with rhetoric and jurisprudence. However, Peirce was toying in 1895 with placing ethics under philosophy, "as an application of logic" (1987, p. 99).

Around 1896, he puts ethics under a division of a science entitled *pragmatics*, the third of three divisions, the first two being mathematics and the second "empirics or phenomenology." Philosophy is a branch of phenomenology or empirics, but so are the nomological sciences such as physics and psychology (1896, R 1345, p. 1; Kent, 1987, p. 101).

The notion of a science of pragmatics is an interesting development in Peirce, and worth discussing since it shows some sense of Peirce's notion of practical reasoning, which factors later on in his account of ethical reasoning generally. Pragmatics is roughly sketched, and he doesn't use the term again after 1896. Peirce provides three somewhat different definitions. The first is rather broad. It 'studies how we ought to act in the light of experience" (1896, R 1345, p. 4). A second is more specific, as "the study of how we ought to behave in the light of the truths of empirics" (1896, R 1345, p. 1). Empirics, as it is formulated here, is the study of phenomena generally, and includes logic, metaphysics and the nomological sciences of psychology and physics. A third definition characterizes it essentially as practical reasoning. Pragmatics "studies the processes by which the outer world is to be brought into accordance with our wishes" (1896, R 1345, p. 2). In other words, it is reasoning about the means to achieve desired ends.

Pragmatics is divided into ethics, "the universal ("general" is sometimes used) principles of conduct"; arts, "or the study of general problems not going back to first principles"; and "policy, or the study of special problems" (1896, R 1345, p. 5), or as "the study of the course proper to be pursued in special cases arising in history" (1896, R 1345, p. 15).

Ethics is subdivided into "hedonics," presumably the study of what pleasures ought to be pursued; "social ethics, or how one should consider others"; and "polity, the principles of social action" (1896, R 1345, p. 30).

The pragmatic arts focus on "how to attain given ends," including the ends of bodily well-being, such as food, health, clothing, shelter, light, warmth and so forth; general mental needs, special communication and mechanical ends, such as transportation (1896, R 1345, p. 16). It also has to do with making things, such as metallurgy, glass-making, etc. (1896, R 1345, p. 24). But it also has to do with casuistry, "how to make the best of given circumstances" (1896, R 1345, p. 24). The casuistical arts include political economy, commerce, insurance, agriculture (1896, R 1345, pp. 31–32).

Given that William James is yet to coin the term "pragmatism" in 1898, Peirce is likely using the term "pragmatics" in Kant's sense in *Anthropology from a Pragmatic Point of View*, which Peirce calls a work in "practical ethics" (1902, CP 5.1). In *Anthropology*, "pragmatic" knowledge is described as a knowledge of what human beings can or should make of themselves as freely acting beings. This is contrasted with a physiological knowledge, which aims primarily to figure out what "nature makes of man" (1798, p. 3). Thus, the pragmatic is focused on the attainment of ends and goals, doing and becoming, rather than something about the nature of human beings. This is consistent with his sense of "pragmatic" in the *Foundations of the Metaphysics of Morals*. There he characterizes pragmatic imperatives as essential prudential rules of how best to attain ends (1785, pp. 31–32n4). He defines it as a form of prudence that "instructs the world how it could provide for its interest better than, or at least as well as has been done in the past" (1785, p. 34n6). In *Anthropology* pragmatic knowledge for Kant "aims at improvement" (1798, p. 4). Moreover, all kinds of knowledge of nature only become pragmatic when it is incorporated into knowledge of human beings as "citizens of the world" (1798, p. 4). "Having a world" means the actual participation in the world, as opposed to the speculative or theoretically scientific account of the world. The pragmatic viewpoint, then, is future-looking and action oriented. However, the very notion of improvement implies concepts such as ideals and purposes; a pragmatic viewpoint necessarily presupposes a focus on purposes and goals. A human being has "a character which he himself creates because he is capable of perfecting himself according to purposes which he himself adopts" (1798, p. 238): "the human species can work itself up to its destiny only through continuous progress within an endless sequence of many generations" (1798, p. 240).

With this interpretation of Kant's use of the term in mind, Peirce's pragmatics can be thought of as a practical study of which ends to pursue and how to realize them, that is, practical reasoning in a general sense. Just as Kant defined pragmatic knowledge as knowledge about what human beings should make of themselves Peirce, as noted, defines it as bringing about things according to our wishes (1896, R 1345, p. 2).

In classifications the following year of 1897, there is a rather significant shift in the role and function of ethics, hinted at in some earlier classifications in 1896. Now it is treated as a positive theoretical science, along with logic and metaphysics, and it is concerned with "the philosophy of purpose," although he still considers it "partly an art" (c. 1897, R 1135; Kent, 1987, p. 104). But this inclusion of ethics in the theoretical sciences is rejected two years later in 1898, and Peirce considers discussions of purposes more a matter for the psychological sciences. As a result, he returns to thinking of ethics as an "applied science or art" (1898, R 437, pp. 18–22; Kent, 1987, p. 105).

It is around 1900–1901 that Peirce sees a more defined relation between logic and ethics, and his idea of ethics as a theoretical normative science begins to appear in his classifications of the sciences (Kent, 1987, p. 110). This coincides with Peirce's own account of the transformation of his thinking about ethics and its relation to logic shortly after the Cambridge Lectures of 1898 (1902, CP 8.255). As Peirce develops his thought, he realizes that the aim of logic and science is an important concern and that the subject of aims is a matter of ethics. It has to be supposed, as noted, that Peirce was worried about the fate of science in the Gilded Age (1894, RLT, p. 13; c. 1905, CP 6.564). His worry that science itself might be harmed by the corruption of its ends toward utility rather than truth seems to grow, and that is borne out in his Cambridge Lectures of 1898. In a piece he did for the *New York Evening Post* in 1900, "The Century's Great Men in Science," Peirce praises these thinkers for their "devotion to the pursuit of truth for truth's sake" (1900, VC, p. 267), and is hopeful that the earlier age in which "knowledge was power" had transformed into one in which knowledge was pursued for its own sake (1900, VC, p. 274).

Because of these concerns, it became clear to Peirce that logic and scientific methodology needed the guidance of ethics. The pragmatic maxim in itself could be interpreted instrumentally, therefore, amorally. It showed how theoretical beliefs or hypotheses could be translated into practical maxims, relative to an end, but it didn't specify anything about the moral aspects of those ends, or how they were to be attained. Pragmatism was in danger of becoming an instrumentalist ethic, just as science was being used by industrialists at the time for any practical ends. Certainly, by 1902, he now saw clearly that logic and science were dependent on ethics (1902, CP 8.255). He complains in the letter to James that his Cambridge lectures in 1898 had not really gotten "to the bottom of it," and he had not "seen the unity of the whole thing" (1902, CP 8.255). Not only was logic dependent on ethics, but ethics on esthetics as he understood it (1902, CP 8.255). But with the trivium of the normative sciences in place, Peirce now declared that "the true nature of pragmatism cannot be understood without them" (1902, CP 8.256). It was the normative sciences that were needed to transform pragmatism from mere instrumentalism to a proper ethical outlook by supplying the proper ends of human endeavor and righteous means by which they might be attained.

By 1902, the trivium of the normative sciences begins to appear in his classifications of the sciences. In drafts of Chapter 2 of *The Minute Logic*, Peirce introduces such a classification, but now the task is to make their division of labor clear. Earlier in 1901, in a draft of a report to the National Academy of Sciences, "The Logic of Drawing History from Ancient Documents," he introduces the term *pure* ethics. Its task is to answer the question of "the purpose of man" (1901, CP 7.185), "what can a man deliberately accept as his ultimate purpose" (1901, CP

7.201). Pure ethics shows up again in drafts of Chapters 2 and 4 of *The Minute Logic*. He claims that its subject is the *summum bonum* (1902, CP 1.575). It is clearly described as "the science of aims." It is a "theatre of discussion" for "the gradual development of a distinct recognition of a satisfactory aim" (1902, CP 4.243). It tries to answer the question "what is good?" (1902, CP 1.577).

Peirce ruminates about certain characteristics of pure ethics. He is uncertain whether it is a normative or pre-normative science. His reasoning is that, by his definition of normative as the relation of phenomena to its ends and, given that pure ethics is the study of ends only, then it does not "seek the conditions . . . of its attainment" (1902, R 432, p. 5).

Peirce briefly discusses the relation between pure ethics as a theoretical science and practical ethics (1902, CP 1.577). If Peirce's science of pragmatics were still in play around this time, one could easily conclude that the results of the theoretical science of pure ethics would have informed the practical science of pragmatics since the latter is concerned with specific sorts of ends, such as pleasure, health and so forth. However, there appears to be no textual evidence making that link. In these passages, he now thinks practical ethics concerns primarily the study of rights and duties. He has high praise for the work in this area in the last three centuries, but emphasizes that such a study is less theoretical, and requires much experience, a "learned acquaintance with the structure of the society in which one lives," as well as "heavy drafts upon wisdom." Nonetheless, it is built upon theoretical ethics, a "superstructure upon ethics proper" (1902, 1.577).

Now that he has settled on pure ethics as the study of ultimate ends, the remainder of this draft to Chapter 4 is dedicated to the following task:

> What I propose now to do is to pass in review every one of the general classes of objects which anybody could suppose to be an ultimate good, and to question consciousness, first, as to whether or not each of these in turn could content us as the sole ultimate good independent of any ulterior result, and if not, whether it can be considered to be in itself a good at all, irrespective of its effects.
>
> (1902, CP 1.581)

This, of course, would be an enormous undertaking and Peirce never completes it, although he does provide a list of the 28 ends he intended to survey (1901, R 1434. Draft C, p. 7f). He briefly discusses the first few but gets bogged down in an exegesis of Plato's dialogues, presumably trying to get an account of his views of the good developmentally.

On the basis of these passages, James Feibleman argues that pure ethics is a special branch of the normative science of ethics (1943, p. 100). However, Peirce does not mention pure ethics in any of his classifications of the sciences, and other than these mentions noted in 1901 and 1902, there appears to be no other reference to it in his writings. To add to the confusion about this, Vincent Potter thinks that Peirce's introduction of the normative sciences in drafts of Chapter 2 of *The Minute* Logic suggests that pure ethics "sounds very much like" the characterization of esthetics in Chapter 2 (1967, p. 35).

But Peirce makes a subtle distinction in Chapter 2 between the roles of ethics and esthetics. Both are concerned with ends but in two different respects. Ethics is concerned about which ends people *ought* to pursue, whereas esthetics is concerned with which ends hold an attraction (1902, CP 2.199). Presumably, the two would work together so that the ends people ought to pursue are those that people would find attractive to pursue. It is here that Peirce wants to adopt the classical Greek notion of *to kalon* in place of *beauty* to make his point. As commonly interpreted among Plato scholars, *to kalon* is a broader notion than beauty. It is characterized as a well-ordered form designed to fulfill a beneficial purpose (Philebus, 64e-65a; Gorgias, 506e; Barney, 2010, pp. 364–365; Grube, 1927, pp. 273–274; Hoerber, 1964).

Peirce's account of esthetics will be discussed here later in Chapter 8, but in the drafts of *The Minute Logic*, he gives the reader a vague sense of the division of labor between ethics and esthetics. Both have to do with the matter of final or ultimate ends. This may be part of the reason that Potter claims they have similar duties. However, they have different functions in regard to those ends. Esthetics is to determine which ends are *kalos*, ends that have a design such that it produces a quality that is admirable. As he clarifies later in the Harvard Lectures, ethics is to determine among those that are admirable in that sense, which ought to be pursued (1903, HL, pp. 118–119). In any case, the drafts of Chapter 2 of *The Minute Logic* clearly tasks ethics with the study of ends (1902, CP 2.198–2.199), and pure ethics is given that same task in Chapter 4 (1902, CP 1.575). At least in that respect, the role assigned to ethics seems consistent.

Peirce introduces the normative sciences publicly for the first time in the Harvard Lectures, delivered in March of 1903. These are delivered just a few months prior to the November Lowell Lectures, where the classification of the normative sciences is finalized. Peirce does not use the term pure ethics here. Peirce discusses the normative sciences in both the opening and the fifth lecture of the series. In the first lecture, he affirms again that logic is dependent on ethics to the extent that logic is a doctrine of how "we ought to think," so a species of what we ought to do, which is the subject of ethics. He also reaffirms the differing roles of ethics and esthetics as he laid these out in *The Minute Logic*. "We cannot get any clue to the secret of Ethics . . . until we have first made up our formula for what it is that we are prepared to admire" (1903, HL, p. 118). It doesn't matter which doctrine of ethics is embraced, Peirce says, it will still raise the question of whether the end it implicitly or explicitly proposes is fine and admirable. Whether it is happiness or pleasure in the utilitarian theory, or the preservation of the species in Darwinian theories, or the satisfaction of impulses or desires in hedonism, all of these raise the question of admirable character of the end (1903, HL, pp. 118–119). This relatively clear presentation of the division of labor between ethics and esthetics is somewhat muddled in the Fifth Lecture with a rather confusing and enigmatic account of esthetics.

Peirce begins the fifth lecture with emphasizing that the normative sciences are theoretical rather than practical, although the practical science of ethics "may be probably expected to receive aid" from the normative sciences (1903, HL, p. 209). The normative science of ethics is also not a special science. Those are *idioscopic*, the empirical sciences of physics and psychology being examples (1903, HL, p. 209).

As in *The Minute Logic*, Peirce claims once more with emphasis that "*ethics is the study of what ends of action we are deliberately prepared to adopt*," which seems to be the task of what he previously called pure ethics. But he then qualifies this to say that it is the study of "*right action* which is in conformity to ends which we are prepared deliberately to adopt" (emphasis added) (1903, HL, p. 212). This adds another role to ethics. Ethics not only determines which among admirable ends people ought to adopt but also determines "right action," that is, action that is in conformity to those ends. This suggests that ethics is concerned with both the proper ends of actions and the righteous means toward those ends. It's quite possible that people can adopt a good end but attain it in a vicious way. At this point, Peirce seems to realize that concern with the ends is not sufficient, that the means by which those ends are to be attained also fall under the purview of ethics. It would seem he wants to avoid a Machiavellian claim that the end justifies the means.

Peirce also clarifies somewhat what he means by a *deliberate* adoption of an end. To be deliberately adopted is to be *reasonably* adopted (1903, HL, p. 213). For one thing, it can't be adopted for "ulterior reasons." It can be supposed he means that it cannot be adopted out of self-interest or particular biases. It must be adopted regardless of anyone's particular interests so that it has to "recommend itself in itself" as he says. Simply said, it should not be adopted because it happens to be personally beneficial. One way to characterize this is to say that to be reasonably adopted, it must be *generalizable*, so that anyone, not considering their self-interests, would adopt it. Peirce does associate the reasonable with the generalizable (1901, CP 7.186; 1905, CP 5.433).

After a rather enigmatic discussion of esthetics, Peirce returns to the issue of ethics and the adoption of ends. Assuming that esthetics has provided candidates for admirable ends, by what means or method does ethics go about figuring out which ends to deliberately adopt? He mentions the categorical imperative as one possibility: "the instant that an esthetic ideal is proposed as an ultimate end of action, at that instant a categorical imperative pronounces for or against it" (1903, HL, p. 214). But he rejects its formalism (1903, HL, p. 214). The hallmark of the categorical imperative is consistency of action under universalization. Would its generalization lead to some *reductio ad absurdum*? Making promises without the intention to keep them, if universalized, would lead to an absurdity. People could not make promises, since no one would keep them and no one could break promises since no one would believe a promise (Kant, 1785, p. 40).

Even though Peirce rejects the formalism of the categorical imperative, he thinks there is a process that is analogous to the consistency test of the categorical imperative. He suggests that the ends which esthetics nominates must also pass a test of possibility: "the problem of ethics is to ascertain what end is possible." The test is a test of consistency: "An aim," Peirce says, "which *cannot* be adopted and consistently pursued is a bad aim." However, it would not be a formal test of consistency as Kant proposes. Peirce thinks poorly of the *reductio ad absurdum*, even as a mathematical means of proof, and condemns both Hegel and Josiah Royce for its excessive and less than rigorous application (1900, CP 8.110). Rather, it should be a test based on the fact that it is "capable of being pursued in an indefinitely prolonged course of action" (1903, HL, p. 314). That is to say, it would become generalizable over the long run. That would be the sense of its consistency (Parker, 2003, pp. 33–34). Peirce's test of possibility, as he says elsewhere, is a test of "synthetic" or empirical consistency (1902, CP 5.4). One assumes that its test is like all laboratory tests but here in the laboratory of life. Is it an end that will be adopted in the long run and manifested in the habits of people's conduct and the norms of practices and institutions. The adoption of an end that persists over time in the practices and institutions of moral life would count as a good aim. As Peirce writes a few years later, "if . . . the future development of man's moral nature will only lead to a firmer satisfaction with the described ideal, the doctrine is true" (1906, CP 5.566). The possibility of an aim is based on its consistency with lived experience, how it plays out in the world. If the aim of democracy is liberty, as Aristotle argues (*Rhetoric*, 1366a2), then slavery and disenfranchisement of women are inconsistent with that end. In the course of history, one or the other would go—democracy or the true realization of equal liberty. It is in this sense that Peirce argues that "it is incumbent upon us to inquire what an ultimate aim, capable of being pursued in an indefinitely prolonged course of action, can be" (1903, HL, p. 214).

Peirce concludes this part of the lecture by saying that "the deduction of this is somewhat intricate on account of the number of points which have to be taken into account; and of course, I cannot go into details" (1903, HL, pp. 214–215). That's an understatement. Indeed, much of what Peirce says in the fifth of the Harvard Lectures was puzzling and obscure to the audience based on the reaction of the philosophers present, such as William James and George Santayana. In a letter to Christine Ladd-Franklin, Peirce reveals that James thought it not a good idea to print the lectures since "he could not understand them himself" (Brent, 1998, p. 291). However he may have seemed obscure to his audience, he was certainly right that the account of his position is "intricate." That is the task of the remainder of this book—to provide the underpinnings of the general sketch given here.

By the end of 1903, Peirce settled on a classification of the sciences that remained virtually unchanged into his later years (Kent, 1987, pp. 118, 121). It was distributed as a supplement to his Lowell Lectures around that time. It declared the three normative sciences to be logic, ethics and esthetics and discussed their hierarchical relation (1903, CP 1.191).

According to that classification, there are three main divisions of science: theoretical (sciences of discovery), science of review and practical (1903, CP 1.181). Peirce distinguishes the theoretical and practical sciences more strictly. Now corresponding to the theoretical, normative science of ethics, there is also practical ethics, and he claims that "the practical side of ethics is its most obviously important side," and concerns "the conduct of life" (1902, CP 2.198; 1903, CP 5.125). The term "pragmatics" is no longer used and there is no detailed elaboration of practical ethics, so it's not clear whether the two are synonymous.

He thought that practical ethics could benefit from the findings of the normative science of ethics but insists that they are not integral. He argues that theoretical and practical ethics are of two different sorts of inquiries (1903, CP 5.125). The subjects of practical ethics include rights and duties. Such a study, as Peirce says, rests upon experience of practical life, and the sort of wisdom and knowledge "which comes by reflection upon the total experience of a life-time, as well as upon a learned acquaintance with the structure of the society in which one lives" (c. 1902, CP 1.577). As noted earlier, he thought Kant's pragmatic anthropology was an example of practical ethics (1902, CP 5.1). He also thought Aristotle's *Nicomachean Ethics* was a good example of practical ethics (1906, CN 3, p. 276).

Richard Atkins thinks that Peirce thinks practical ethics is primarily casuistic in methodology (2018, p. 202). Cornelis De Waal thinks Peirce is more wary about casuistry (2012, p. 97). The textual evidence for Atkins's claim is thin but, if Aristotle is the model of practical ethics for Peirce then, certainly, casuists such as Albert Jonsen and Stephen Toulmin (1988) and Martha Nussbaum (1990) claim Aristotle as one of the original champions of the methodology. But there are other interpretations of Aristotle, and Peirce defends an interpretation that Aristotle is seeking an objective and universal basis for ethics, rather than a merely conventional one (1906, CN3, p. 277). Atkins notes a mention by Peirce of casuistry in a draft of the first of the Cambridge Lectures on "Philosophy and the Conduct of Life." There, as in his sketch of pragmatics, he defines it similarly as "discussions of what ought to be done in various difficult situations." He also emphasizes in this text, as he does elsewhere, that most theoretical treatises on ethics are certainly not casuistic in this sense (1898, R 345, p. 31; 1902, CP 1.577). Peirce mentions a book by Amelie Opie, *Illustrations of Lying* (1825), as a good example of casuistry (1898, R 345, p. 31; Atkins, 2018, p. 202). Recall, however, that in the sketch of pragmatics, practical ethics is a branch which concerns "general" principles of conduct, and casuistry is mostly associated with the practical arts of commerce and agriculture (1896, R 1345, p. 5). Most casuists are either cautious or dismissive of the idea of "general" ethical principles. In 1902, Peirce considers casuistry as mainly an analysis of conscience and belongs among the special psychical sciences for that reason (1902, R 433, pp. 7–8). This makes it questionable whether Peirce advocated a casuistic methodology for practical ethics.

With the distinction between the theoretical and practical sciences, the former are divided into two sub-branches: sciences of discovery and sciences of review, the latter concerned with the integration and dissemination of the sciences of discovery (1903, CP 1.181). There are three principal classes of the sciences of discovery: mathematics, philosophy and the empirical sciences, with the latter, subdivided into physics and psychics, or what we would call today a division between the natural and the behavioral, social and cultural sciences (1903, CP 1.183).

Philosophy is subdivided into Phenomenology, the study and classification of things as they appear to us; Normative Sciences, the study of things as they ought to be; and Metaphysics, or the study of what is. The normative sciences are subdivided into logic or semiotic, ethics and esthetics (1903, CP 1.186). There is a certain hierarchy among the normative sciences now established. Logic is guided by the leading principles of ethics, and ethics is guided by the leading principles of esthetics (1903, CP 1.191). "Thinking is a kind of action, and reasoning is a kind of deliberate action; and to call an argument illogical, or a proposition false, is a special kind of moral judgment" (c. 1904, CP 8.191). Since ethics is a study of right and wrong conduct generally, and logic is a study of right and wrong reasoning, it "must appeal to ethics for its principles." Ethics, in turn, "must appeal to Esthetics for aid in determining the *summum bonum* (1903, CP 1.191). The normative sciences as a whole are dependent on phenomenology and mathematics for their guiding principles (1903, CP 1.191). Mathematics is a propaedeutic to philosophy, and mathematics and philosophy jointly serve as a propaedeutic to the empirical sciences, serving as their methodological guide (1903, CP 1.180).

In this classification of 1903, Peirce defines ethics as "the science of right and wrong" (1903, CP 1.191). Vincent Potter thinks this is the principal definition of ethics, for Peirce, a study of what makes right, right and wrong, wrong (Potter, 1967, p. 32; 1902, CP 1.577). Peirce also characterizes logic analogously as "the theory of *right* reasoning, of what reasoning ought to be, not of what it is" (1902, CP 2.7). Ethics is also described in this classification as the theory of "self-controlled, deliberate conduct," as is logic, but in terms of the conduct of thinking (1903, CP 1.191). As Peirce clarifies later on, deliberate conduct implies controlled conduct, and control is making the conduct "conform to a purpose or ideal" (1906, EP 2, p. 376). In an interesting definition of logic that suits its role in the practical reasoning of normative sciences, Peirce proclaims that it "analyzes the problem of how, with given means, a required end is to be pursued" (1902, CP 4.240). Esthetics is defined here as "the science of ideals," what is "objectively admirable" (1903, CP 1.191).

These definitions associated with the final classification of the normative sciences suggest a clearer division of labor among esthetics, ethics and logic. Esthetics is the study of admirable ideals, what makes ends worthy of pursuit. Ethics is the study of which ends ought to be deliberately adopted, that is, those that are good for no ulterior reason or interest, but simply good in themselves. It also has the job of determining right conduct in pursuit of those ends. Logical—or scientific reasoning broadly—would be *in this context of normativity* concerned with reasoning from means to ends, that is, what is likely to attain the ends-in-view. Ethics would have a second role in determining which, among those means, are right to do. For example, in regard to logic, Peirce argues that the end of reasoning is truth, a "phase of the *summum bonum*." Truth is an inherently admirable ideal. Since truth leads wherever it leads, the truth cannot be attained if it is distorted by ulterior interests. People who see a personal or cultural benefit to a claim thought true could corrupt inquiry by confirmation bias, or some other sort of cherry-picking of evidence. What one wants to believe is true and what *is* true may not meet. The means by which truth of any claim is best attained is by logical and scientific reasoning, through sound inferences of deduction and induction (1902, CP 1.575). Proof by sound reasoning is morally good; making claims deceptively through persuasive but sophistical and fallacious reasoning is immoral. In this way, the ends and means of logic are ethically sound.

The organization of Aristotle's *Nicomachean Ethics* might serve to illustrate this ordering of the relation among esthetics, ethics and logical reasoning. It involves an account of the highest ends to pursue, what sort of conduct in regard to those ends ought to be adopted, and the sort of reasoning by which those ends are to be attained. In Book I, Aristotle discusses the principal criteria for what is to count as the highest good, and a discussion of which among the candidates for that office best fits this criteria (*Nicomachean. Ethics*, 1094a). Of course, Aristotle nominates flourishing (*eudaimonia*) as the highest human good and shows why its rivals—pleasure, wealth and fame do not meet the criteria of a highest good.

Once this is accomplished, he provides an account of flourishing (*Nicomachean Ethics*, 1094a-1098b). Aristotle goes on to claim that the way to flourish is through the virtuous life (*Nicomachean Ethics, 1098a*). Much of the remainder of Aristotle's work, thus, concerns an account of the various virtues. Aristotle divides the virtues into moral and intellectual, and the latter, such as *phronesis*, along with other faculties such as intuitive perception (*esthesis*) (*Nicomachean Ethics*, 1142a15–20), deliberation (*bouleuesthai*) (*Nicomachean Ethics*, 1142b30) good judgment (*krinein*) (*Nicomachean Ethics* 1143a15), *savoir-faire* (*deinoteta*) (*Nicomachean Ethics*, 1144a25) and understanding (*synesis*) (*Nicomachean Ethics*, 1143a15–20), make up the type of reasoning crucial for making the right judgment about what to do in particular situations (*Nicomachean Ethics*, 1103a14). Of course, most ethics scholars would count everything that is done in *The Nicomachean Ethics* as the subject of ethics, the study of ends, righteous or virtuous conduct and the sort of reasoning to make good ethical decisions.

Peirce differs with Aristotle on what counts as the highest end, even if he agrees with some of the properties of such an end. Where Aristotle argues that flourishing (happiness) as the highest good "is something which appears to be agreed upon" (*Nicomachean Ethics*, 1097b22–23), Peirce sees a need to study the reasons for its attraction. Peirce sees a need for a science of esthetics to answer this question.

In 1906, in some drafts related to "The Basis of Pragmaticism in the Normative Sciences," intended for publication in *The Monist*, Peirce gives a last attempt to provide a division of labor between ethics and esthetics. It is also a rather rough sketch. Ethics is defined here as the "theory of the control of conduct," by which he means conformity to a purpose or ideal (1906, EP2, p. 377). However, rather than calling this science ethics, he prefers the term *antethics*, which is another name for what he calls *practics*. Ethics, in its traditional sense, is broader than practics because it also comprehends the study of the ideals themselves, "the nature of the *summum bonum*" (1906, EP2, p. 377). This distinction between practics and ethics is consistent with his division of labor within ethics as outlined in the Harvard Lectures, namely, ethics in the broader sense as the study of what ends ought to be deliberately adopted—what he calls "pure ethics" in *The Minute Logic*—and the task of ethics concerning the standards of conduct that will conform to those ends—what he now calls *practics* (1903, HL, p. 212). Practics is also characterized in "The Basis of Pragmaticism" as distinguishing the "useful" from the "pernicious," that is, from actions that have good versus bad effects (1906, EP 2, p. 379).

Peirce complains however that those traditional studies of the ultimate end have been more or less "a sort of composite photography of the conscience of the members of the community." It is nothing more than a rationalization of the morality of the day, rather than a true "heuretic" science (1906, CP 1.573). If ethics studies what is to count as the *summum bonum*, and practics the study of what conduct would conform to that highest good, then Peirce's sense of ethics would seem to be fairly consistent with the task of ethics as presented in Aristotle's *Nicomachean Ethics:* what is the ultimate end that ought to be pursued, and what sort of conduct is most conducive to that end.

In the end, Peirce thinks that "the question where precisely the lines of separation between them [the normative sciences] are to be drawn is quite secondary." It might be best to agree with him here and consider that the three normative sciences "form one distinctly marked whole" (1906, EP, 2, p. 378). That whole can be characterized as the study of good ends and righteous means, the standards of conduct that are conducive to those ends, and the means most likely to attain them. This rather straightforward division of labor, modeled in the organization of the *Nicomachean Ethics*, seems to be the clearest and most direct account of the various roles of the normative sciences.

Normativity and the General Character of a Normative Science

Peirce came to the conclusion that logic is a *normative* science and that it needed the guidance of the normative sciences of ethics and esthetics in order to understand it in its entirety. If ethics is a normative science, what does Peirce mean by *normative?* Peirce attributes the original use of the term "normative" to Friedrich Schleiermacher or his "school," or to Überweg, "or who else about that time" (1902, CP 1.575; n.d., R 602, p. 11). So, it's not sure who that might be. Yet, at least according to Frederick Beiser, Schleiermacher claimed that ethics should *not* be understood as a normative science. Schleiermacher saw ethics as a study in ontology, rather than a study of norms. Schleiermacher argued strongly against Kant's universalist ethics and sided with Herder's more historical and culturally relativistic sense of ethics (Beiser, 2005, p. 68). Friedrich Überweg characterized logic as "the science of normative or ideal laws of human cognition" (Überweg, 1857).

The psychologist, Wilhelm Wundt also used the term in a way that seems closer to Peirce's sense. In a review of Frank Thilly's *Introduction to Ethics* for *The Nation* in 1900, Peirce demonstrates a real familiarity with Wundt's ethics even though he doesn't seem to think highly of it (1900, CN 2, pp. 247–248; 1905, CP 8.204). Wundt's account of normativity may have caught Peirce's eye. Wundt argued that all psychological processes have a normative dimension. Almost any human action is normative in the sense that it is goal-directed so that any action can be compared to what is appropriate in attaining some end. In the case of logic, for example, to infer is to draw the *right* conclusion from the premises (Wundt, 1908, 3, pp. 273–274; Mischel, 1970, p. 8). Thus, it is an inherently normative act. As noted, Peirce agrees with Wundt that calling an inference illogical or a proposition false is a normative judgment (c. 1904,

CP 8.191). As Theodore Mischel interprets Wundt, the "mental sciences," so-called, explain human conduct in terms of the goals that people seek, and all purposive activities have a normative aspect (1970, p. 9).

Peirce seems to agree with Wundt that normative conduct is tied to purposive or end-seeking, goal-directed conduct. As Peirce says obviously, normativity deals with what *ought* to be (1902, CP 1.281; 1902, 2.156). But "the word "ought" has no meaning except relatively to an end" (1898, CP 5.594). Logic, for example, is concerned with "self-controlled, deliberate thought" (1903, CP 1.191), and "to say any thinking is deliberate is to imply that it is controlled with a view of making it conform to a purpose or ideal" (1906, CP 1.573).

Normativity is nothing mysterious in Peirce's view. Nearly all actions or practices are normative in the sense that they are measured against their purpose. What sort of actions and how they are done relative to an end serves as the measure of the agent's performance. To say that people made the right conclusion is to consider the inference from the premises. To say that people acted properly at the table is to consider how they went about eating their food. As Thomas Short argues, alternatives such as success or failure, better or worse, good or bad begin to apply whenever there is a purpose, since it can be reasonably determined whether some action has met, exceeded, or fallen short of that end (2007, p. 154). Normativity is a matter of how people go about attaining their ends. It is by means of this chain of reasoning that Peirce claims that the "Normative Science treats of the laws of the relation of phenomena to ends" (1903, CP 5.123), logic to the end of truth, ethics to good ends and standards of right conduct, and esthetics to the end of the highest, admirable and noble ends (1903, CP 5.121).

Peirce discusses some other general features of normative sciences. The normative sciences in Peirce's thinking are both *formal* and *positive* sciences. Formal sciences study the necessary conditions for its subject (c. 1897, CP 2.227). The three normative sciences "may be regarded as being the sciences of the conditions of truth and falsity, of wise and foolish conduct, of attractive and repulsive ideas" (1906, CP 5.551). They are positive sciences since they make factual, true claims about experience on the basis of experience (1903, CP 1.184; c. 1896, CP 1.55; 1903, CP 5.39). Certainly, most logicians would agree that logic is a formal science, and perhaps many would agree that it is a normative science, but most would be puzzled by calling it a positive science. Metaethics does address formal questions about ethics in Peirce's sense, since it is concerned, in part, with the possibility of morality. But ethicists would probably also be puzzled by calling it a positive science in Peirce's sense.

Since Peirce has a lot more to say about logic than the other normative sciences, his analysis of logic might be helpful in understanding this claim. Peirce reasons that, if the goal of logical reasoning is to distinguish the true from the false, then its use in experience must prove up on those claims: "when logic tells us that we can reason about the real world . . . with security, it tells us a positive fact about the universe" (n.d., CP 7.524). "Its central department, called Critic, is the study of nature of the trust that ought to be placed in different kinds of reasoning" (n.d., R 602, p. 5). If logic claimed a type of inference to be valid, or an inductive methodology as truth-apt, yet their use in experience leads to many false conclusions or hypotheses, that would defeat the purpose of having a logic. Logic is a positive science in the sense that the validity of its claims about truth-production "rests on experience" (Hacking, 1991, p. 209). The claim is that, if people conducted their inquiries logically, then it is more likely that such inquirers will light on true propositions than false ones. The "logical warrant" for induction, for example, is that if "this method [is] persistently applied to the problem," it "must in the long run produce a convergence . . . to the truth" (1902, CP 2.775). The test of that claim is whether that happens cumulatively over time in the course of human history. Peirce concludes exactly that (c. 1885, CP 8.43). As Peirce's convergence theory of truth argues, truth would be the end result of inquiry sufficiently pursued over time (1907, CP 5.494). This includes inquiry into induction and deduction itself, and their changes occur because of failures in experience (Short, 2012, p. 312).

This perhaps gives some insight into why Peirce called ethics a positive science, since good conduct, like good reasoning, would find its ultimate test in experience, specifically in practical life, experiments of living. What ought to be accepted as good, Peirce says, "is a question of fact, and the solution of the problem must be based upon experience," the experience of "every-day life" (1901, R 1442, p. 4; cited in Robin, 1964, p. 276; 1901 CN 3, p. 51). In other words, Peirce is claiming that there are moral truths, whether in terms of what counts as good ends, or what are the standards of conduct by which they should be pursued. Peirce is a realist, and it would follow that he is a moral realist as well. If it were the case that ethical reasoning did not result over time in a generally approved or admired good, that would infer something the matter with the ethical standards, or with the concept of the good. The test of a good ethic is whether its characterization of what is good to pursue and how to pursue it accords with, is consistent with lived experience in the long run (1898, CP 5.594; 1903, HL, p. 314).

4 A Grammar of Ethics

Although Peirce provides some general characterization of ethics as a normative science, he does not give a sufficiently explicit account of its organization as a discipline. Based on some of the standard divisions of the sciences in Peirce's mature classifications, Beverly Kent suggests that ethics should be subdivided into physiology, classification and methodeutic (1987, p. 135). The physiology would be tasked with selecting among the aims disclosed by esthetics. "It would determine "the conditions of conformity to the ethical ideal" (1987, p. 166). It is something that "would be thought fine by anyone given sufficient time to contemplate it." It would "limit the general aim to what is attainable," circumscribed by abilities and opportunities (1987, p. 165). Classification would be "the conditions of right action." It would determine "the conditions of conformity to the ethical ideal" (1987, p. 166). Methodeutic, in turn, "studies the principles that render the ethical ideal existent" (1987, p. 166).

This is an interesting suggestion, but since Peirce claims all the normative sciences have a "family likeness," it is more likely that, had Peirce developed his ethics more fully, its organization would parallel that of his logic or semiotic, a normative science that is, indeed, well developed (1902, CP 2.156). Peirce divided his semiotic into three branches: formal grammar, critical logic and formal rhetoric. Semeiotic grammar, as Peirce understands it, is concerned primarily with the necessary conditions for something to count as a sign, how meaning accrues in signs, as well as their typology and classification. There is a focus on logical features of language, particularly terms and propositions—and this is what speculative grammars were about traditionally. An analysis of terms and propositions prepares for the next phase in logic, namely, how propositions may, in turn, be combined in inferences in arguments, the validity of which is the topic of the second branch of semeiotic—critical logic. For Peirce, this focuses primarily on the analysis and interrelation among abduction, deduction and induction in scientific reasoning. Since scientific reasoning is in the context of an actual practice of inquiry, this leads to Formal Rhetoric, finally, as a study of the proper conditions for a community of inquiry sufficiently effective to achieve its goal of attaining truth.

If the parallel to logic is a good assumption then, ethics as a normative science, should also have somewhat similar divisions. This would suggest three branches of the normative science of ethics, something like a grammar of ethics, a study of ethical reasoning or critical ethics, and finally, an ethical rhetoric, concerned with the conditions of a community of inquiry best suited toward the discovery of moral truths.

If there is a family resemblance between the organization of the study of semiotic and the study of the normative science of ethics, a grammar of ethics, by analogy, could be thought of as explaining the conditions under which conduct can be counted as ethical and characterizing the nature of its fundamental elements.

The Formal Features of Purposive Conduct

For Peirce, as for most thinkers, the possibility of ethical conduct rests on the possibility of some degree of voluntary action, some degree of agency (1903, CP 1.592). A claim that people "ought" to do something implies that they can do otherwise. If they cannot do otherwise then, in agreement with the Principle of Alternative Possibilities (Frankfurt, 1969), Peirce says that to blame or praise the behavior is "not less ridiculous than it would be to pronounce the growth of your hair to be morally good or bad" (1903, CP 5.109). Voluntary action is manifested in what Peirce calls *self-control* (1903, CP 1.191). Essentially, self-control defines agency for Peirce (Colapietro, 1989, p. 110ff). Indeed, he uses the term "conduct" technically to "mean action under an intention of self-control" (1909, CP 8.315; 1906, 8.322).

For Peirce, much of human conduct is purposive and goal-directed (Aydin, 2009, p. 430). Purposive conduct is voluntary, directed to some end. Therefore, "an end—the essential object of normative science—is germane to a voluntary act in a primary way in which it is germane to nothing else" (1903, CP 5.130). To act purposively is to direct oneself to some end rather than another, and to do some action rather than another believed to attain that end. Purposive conduct therefore assumes self-control. "All direction toward an end or good supposes self-control" (1905, R 283, p. 84). Self-control, in this sense, is similar to Kant's notion of autonomy in that it involves self-governance. However, rather than thinking of self-governance in terms of giving oneself a law to live by, Peirce characterizes it in terms of the deliberate adoption of motivated or desired ends and the means to those ends. Most importantly, it involves the ability to self-correct, either in terms of which ends to pursue or how to pursue them if those means fail or ends disappoint (Aydin, 2009, p. 431). Deliberate conduct implies controlled conduct, and control is making the conduct "conform to a purpose or ideal" (1906, EP 2, p. 376).

If, as discussed, normativity for Peirce is measured by an action relative to its end, whether that end be a certain outcome or an ideal of conduct, then all normative conduct, including ethical matters, have to do primarily with purposive action. What is meant by saying that people ought to do something is related to some end (1898, CP 5.594). Since purposive conduct is conduct under self-control, then "morality supposes self-control" (1903, CP 1.191; 1903, CP 1.606). Self-control, as Peirce says, "gives room for an ought-to-be of conduct, I mean Morality" (1906, CP 4.540). If "moral conduct is self-controlled conduct" (1904, CP 8.240), then "Ethics is the theory of self-controlled or deliberate, conduct" (1903, CP 1.191).

Self-control, as the ability to correct conduct toward an end, is the defining feature that distinguishes purposive from merely mechanical action. Peirce uses the language of Aristotle to distinguish the two. Mechanical action is efficient causation; purposive conduct is final causation (1902, CP 1.211). Mechanical action is dumb in the sense that it continues to produce the same result in the same way until it stops producing it for whatever reason. It is a completely determinate action (1902, CP 1.212). There is no growth or adaptation. Purposive conduct, on the other hand, acts like a final cause. "Final causation does not determine in what particular way it [the end] is to be brought about, but only that the result shall have a certain general character (1902, CP 1.211). Purposive conduct is intelligent. It allows for change, growth and adaptation. Peirce uses the term *reasonableness*, sometimes *rationality* to describe such processes. "The essence of rationality lies in the fact that the rational being will act so, as to attain certain ends. Prevent his doing so in one way, and he will act in some utterly different way which will produce the same result. Rationality is being governed by final causes" (1902, CP 2.66).

Although Peirce distinguishes between mechanical and purposive or goal-directed conduct, there are distinctions among different types of goal-directed behavior that are important to note. The distinction between *teleological* and *teleonomic* behavior might be helpful here in sorting out the difference between goal-directedness generally and goal-directed conduct under *self*-control, that is, under agency (Mayr, 1974). Teleological and teleonomic behaviors are goal-directed, but in the latter, the directedness and correction are by means of the evolved logic of the organism, an evolved program of behavior, rather than a deliberating agency.

For example, the behavior of even the lowly *E. coli* bacteria swimming in the gut is teleonomic in this sense. By means of its sensoria it can detect gradients of its food source—glucose—such that when a chemical threshold is reached, it will enact a chain of chemical messages that moves its flagellum counterclockwise, and toward the food source. Conversely, when its outer sensoria detect gradients of toxins to a certain threshold, that will cause a chain of chemical messages that rotates its flagellum so that it moves away from the source. In the absence of any chemical stimuli, chemical messages are sent to the flagellum that causes it to rotate in a manner that results in movement in random directions, that is, it changes the state of the *E. coli* to a search mode (Berg, 2004). Thus, the *E. coli* can correct its behavior in light of environmental circumstances and has a degree of voluntariness. The *E. coli* of course is not *self-directed* but has evolved a behavioral program to adapt to its environment in these ways. Peirce would say that it has acquired a set of instinctual *habits* in this respect (c. 1898, CP 7.495). It has a sort of organism logic, but not a deliberate one. Peirce notes this as well. "A decapitated frog almost reasons. The habit that is in his cerebellum serves as a major premiss. The excitation of a drop of acid is his minor premiss. And his conclusion is the act of wiping it away. . . . What he lacks is the power of preparatory meditation" (c. 1893, CP 6.286). Human superiority to animals is that they have a greater number of grades of self-control (1898, CP 5.533).

Although human beings are capable of the higher grades of self-control, their conduct is teleonomic in a number of ways. For example, Daniel Kahneman makes a distinction between *slow thinking* versus *fast thinking*. *System 1*, as he calls it, "operates automatically and quickly, with little or no effort and no sense of voluntary control." *System 2*, "slow thinking,"

> Allocates attention to the effortful mental activities that demand it, including complex computations. The operations of system 2 are often associated with the subjective experience of agency, choice, and concentration.
>
> (2011, pp. 20–21)

Peirce says something similar:

> All inferences are really performed under the influence of the law of association. But all psychical actions divide into two great classes, those which are performed under the uncontrolled governance of association and those in which by the "agency" of consciousness,—whatever that may mean,—the actions come under self-criticism and self-control. The latter class of actions may be pronounced good or bad; the former could not be otherwise than they were.
>
> (c. 1893, CP 7.444)

Purposive conduct exhibits full agency in the sense that it is primarily self-controlled conduct, such that people are self-directed to motivated ends, deliberate about means and intentionally act on what is deliberated. To the degree that actions are purposive, then agents can be held responsible for such actions, blamed or praised and held accountable. For this reason, Peirce's ethical theory focuses on the formal features of purposive, intentional, goal-directed behavior, behavior that has full agency.

Just as semeiotic grammar analyzes and categorizes the elements of a sign relation—sign, object and interpretant—then a grammar of ethics would likely take the same strategy. This would involve, first, identifying the basic elements involved in purposive conduct and, second, identifying the glue that binds them together. In semeiotic grammar, the elements are sign, object and interpretant, and the glue that binds them is their triadic relation. For something to count as a sign, it must be about something, convey something about the thing it is about, and convey that to something else (Liszka, 1996, pp. 18–19). Purposive actions are also triadic according to Peirce. In fact, Peirce often uses purposive behavior to explain the triadic character of signs and, incidentally, gives us a sense of his understanding of purposive conduct:

> Every sufficiently complete symbol is a final cause and influences real events, in precisely the same sense in which my desire to have the window open, that is, the symbol in my mind of the agreeability of it, influences the physical facts of my rising from my chair, going to the window and opening it.
>
> (1904, NEM: 4, p. 254; see Liszka, 1996, p. 32ff)

In this example, it might be more precise to say—assuming the scenario described occurs at Peirce's home on a hot Pennsylvania summer—that Peirce *desires* the *end* of having a cooler room (not just opening the window), *believes* that opening the window will likely cool the room, and *intended* to open the window for that reason. This basic armature of purposive action can be used to both *explain* and *evaluate* the action.

The explanation of the action is bound up with the elements of purposive action, the motives or desires for some end, the belief about the means to that end, and what the agent intended to do. It is because Peirce wanted to cool the room and believed that opening the window would do so, that he opened the window.

The evaluation of the action is a normative matter, concerning how the action is related to its end. Breaking the window rather than opening it would be a poor choice of means to ventilate the room. Although both actions would ventilate the room, prudence would dictate opening the window simply out of good economy. There would be good justification to say it was wrong of Peirce to break the window. On the other hand, if the end was to escape from a burning, smoke-filled room, breaking the window might be a good thing to do, particularly if the window was stuck, or there was so much smoke that a person couldn't see the latch. The proper justification of an action depends on its end.

This action of opening the window, as Peirce characterizes it, is a triadic relation among the end (cooling the room), the means (the belief that opening the window will cool the room), and the intention (to act on what is believed will likely attain the end). Mark Schroeder also characterizes such actions as triadic but with somewhat different elements: "a three-place relation between [*sic*] the thing that is the reason, the agent for whom it is a reason, and the action-type that it is a reason to perform" (2013, p. 17).

One test of this claim of the triadicity of purposive action is whether the person's conduct can be *explained* dyadically, as relations between pairs of the action elements. Just as for a sign to have meaning, it must involve the sign-object-interpretant relation, so for an action to be purposive, it must involve the motive-belief-intention relation. For example, if the action is explained dyadically by saying that the opened window caused the room to cool, this doesn't explain why the agent opened the window. Peirce may have opened the window to say hello to his wife in the yard, and incidentally that cooled the room. If the action is explained dyadically by saying that the agent caused the window to open by pulling the latch, that also doesn't explain why Peirce opened the window, although it explains how he did so. He may have been fiddling with the window and accidentally opened it rather than intentionally. If it is explained simply as a dyadic relation between the agent's motive not to be hot and the goal of cooling the room, it still doesn't explain why Peirce chose to open the window. Peirce had to believe that opening the window was a means to that end.

Peirce uses the example of giving a brooch to one's wife as making the same point. Explaining giving as dyadic would represent it simply as a mechanical process of handing something to someone who then takes it (1902, CP 2.86). Giving the brooch to a wife involves a triadic relation among the end (a desire to please, show appreciation, or reward one's wife); the means (the belief that giving a brooch or some gift will attain that end), and the intention of giving the brooch to the wife when the occasion arises, following through intentionally on that belief. As Peirce says "threeness . . . consists in A and B being really paired by virtue of a third object, C." He uses the example of getting his dog to fetch a book. Peirce desires the book, believes that if he commands the dog to get the book by uttering those commands, the dog will likely get the book for him; he commands the dog, and the dog fetches the book. The dog's act is also intentional, but for different ends—to obey or please the master (1902, CP 2.86).

Degenerative Cases of Purposive Conduct

A second test of the triadicity of purposive action is if its evaluation would change if one or more of the elements of purposive conduct were absent or attenuated. It would seem, in general, the less purposive the conduct, the less responsibility for the action and, therefore, the less praise or blame and accountability. For example, suppose the latch on Peirce's window was stuck and in using a hammer to knock the latch free, he accidentally broke the window. His behavior would be evaluated differently than if he took the hammer and intentionally broke the window.

He did not intend to break the window, he intended to free the latch, and it can be supposed that he had no desire for the outcome. This would also hold for cases where actions are coerced, forced or where people act under duress.

The attenuation of the triadic relation should be able to *explain* these sorts of behaviors that fall short of being purposive. Such attenuations also affect the normative *evaluation* of that conduct. They are an important consideration for assigning responsibility and culpability for actions in criminal and civil justice and almost all moral matters. These might be called *degenerative* cases of conduct after Peirce's term of art. Peirce borrowed the term from mathematics. Some geometric forms can be understood as degenerate forms of others, when one or more of latter's constitutive elements is zero or absent (c. 1890, CP 1.365). For example, all circles have a radius, but a point can be considered a degenerate circle, if the radius of the circle is zero. Correspondingly, there is a degeneracy in purposiveness if one or more of the triadic elements is attenuated or absent.

In order for conduct to be purposive, there must be some degree of self-control in its triadic elements. There has to be some level of self-control over desires or other motives for ends, there has to be some choice in the ends to be pursued, and alternative means to those ends. In matters of criminal and civil law, an underlying consideration of all responsibility and culpability for an action is the degree of voluntariness in the act (American Law Institute, 1962, p. 31). As Peirce writes, "actions beyond the reach of self-control are not subjects of blame" (c. 1904, CP 8.191).

Consider, for example, obsessive-compulsive behaviors. These lack self-control in regard to doing a certain action and the action lacks purpose. "A compulsion," Peirce says, is "brute." Brute actions are dyadic ones (1908, CP 6.454). A compulsion is the case where people are compelled to do some action repetitively, such as checking on a locked door or cleaning their hands. The door is locked but it still needs to be checked. The repetition of checking has no purpose if the door is locked. Another example is the tics caused by Tourette's syndrome, such as shrugging shoulders, facial grimacing, or vocalizations. Although it can be controlled and masked to some extent, as one person explains it, "my tics are a strange and erratic phenomenon. It often starts with a thought or suggestion in my head telling me to do something and it won't go away until I act on it; like a mosquito bite that needs to be scratched" (Grant, 2019). It is something that has to be done but it has no purpose.

It is more controversial as to the degree of self-control in drug and alcohol addiction, eating disorders and the like. Part of the controversy centers on the fact that drug and alcohol addictions are self-induced, but once in play, the agent has lost self-control of the cravings or desires. Much of scientific research shows addiction to be a subconscious process, whereby the drugs flood the *nucleus accumbens*, the so-called "pleasure center" of the brain, with dopamine and the hippocampus registers this overwhelming pleasure, setting up a conditioned response to stimuli associated with the drug. Dopamine interacts with another neurotransmitter, glutamate, which involves reward-related learning. This stimulates the same reward circuits responsible for primitive behaviors related to eating and sex. Compulsions for the drugs occur when the brain begins to adapt to the dopamine release, producing less of it in response to the drug. Even though the pleasure from the drug subsides, the deep memory persists, creating a craving or compulsion to have the drug (National Institute on Drug Abuse, 2014). However, the fact that alcoholics can control the cravings and drug addicts can stay sober, as difficult as that is, shows that the loss of control is not absolute. From a criminal justice consideration, even if alcoholics cannot control the cravings, they can control conduct such as driving an automobile while intoxicated (American Law Institute, 1962, p. 46).

Criminal and civil law looks at three factors when evaluating the criminality or liability of an action. First, of course, it has to be established that the action or outcome that the defendant is accused of is against the law or, in the case of civil law, that the harm done was wrongful. If so, the defendant can be held *accountable*. For example, murder is illegal, and the defendant is accused of killing someone. The second is *causation*, which is usually established by showing factually that the agent did a certain set of actions and those actions caused the outcome in question (American Law Institute, 1962, p. 34). This is usually called the *cause in fact* (Black, 1980, p. 221). If it can be shown that the defendant fired the weapon that killed the victim, then that establishes the cause in fact. In this way, the defendant can be held *responsible* for the death of the victim. But this is a purely dyadic consideration and is not sufficient for evaluating the degree of *culpability*. A third factor to establish culpability is *mens rea*. According to the American Law Institute's *Model Penal Code*, it comprehends the three elements of purposive actions as Peirce outlines it. It includes the determination of whether the defendant desired the outcome. It also considers the degree of belief in the likelihood that the actions which defendant took would result in the outcomes that happened, and intended to act on that belief knowing that it would likely result in that outcome (American Law Institute, 1962, p. 33).

The first consideration in *mens rea* is whether the defendant acted "purposely," that is, had a "conscious" aim in mind. Second, it has to be determined whether the defendant acted "knowingly," that is, the defendant believed that the action was practically certain to end in the result. On the other hand, the defendant may have not aimed at or desired the outcome but acted "recklessly." The defendant intended to do the action despite believing that there was a good likelihood that the action would cause the outcome. In other words, the defendant failed to carry out prudent precautions against risk. Also, defendants may not have had any desire or motive for the outcome but acted "negligently." They should have been aware of the risks that the action entailed, but failed to discover these (American Law Institute, 1962, p. 33). As Peirce says, someone who follows rules of prudence or caution cannot be held as responsible. "It is certainly just that a man, even though he had no evil intention, should be held responsible for the immediate effects of his actions: but only for such as might have been guarded against by a reasonable rule of prudence" (c. 1890, CP 1.366).

Culpability is of the highest degree when agents act "purposively" and "knowingly," that is, when the action is fully purposive, in Peirce's language. A defendant who kills another with "malice aforethought," and intended the action that knowingly would cause that victim's death, could certainly be charged with first-degree murder.

Acting recklessly or negligently entails less culpability because the triadic elements of purposive conduct are attenuated. They relate mostly in the context of accidents. A driver may intend to turn left at the intersection as a means of getting home but, because the driver did not see the car coming, causes an accident. It is true that the driver's action of turning left caused the accident, but the driver did not believe that turning left would do so. It can be supposed that had the driver known that turning left would cause an accident, the driver would not have turned left. Furthermore, the drive, it is presumed, did not desire or aim for the collision, but had the goal of getting home. The driver can be blamed for not looking twice for traffic and following normal rules of driving prudence but, because the driver did not desire the outcome, then the culpability of the agent is greatly diminished.

Peirce gives an example of accidental action in a tale from *The Arabian Nights*. While traveling, a merchant stops to feed his hunger, eating some dates. He throws away a date stone, which hits Jinnee's eye nearby, killing him. The father of the Jinnee then seeks revenge and plans to kill the merchant, as the story continues. This action, as Peirce says,

> was purely mechanical, and there was no genuine triplicity. The throwing and the striking were independent of one another. But had he aimed at the Jinnee's eye, there would have been more than merely throwing away the stone. There would have been genuine triplicity, the stone being not merely thrown, but thrown *at* the eye. Here, *intention*, the mind's action, would have come in.
>
> (1902, CP 2.86)

As Peirce explains elsewhere,

> here there were two independent facts, first that the merchant threw away the date-stone, and second that the date-stone struck and killed the jinnee's son. Had it been aimed at him, the case would have been

> different: for then there would have been a relation of aiming which would have connected together the aimer, the thing aimed, and the object aimed at, in one fact. What monstrous injustice and inhumanity on the part of that jinnee to hold that poor merchant responsible for such an accident! I remember how I wept at it, as I lay in my father's arms and he first told me the story.
>
> (c. 1890, CP 1.366)

Together, the determination of whether the defendant caused the outcome, whether the action or outcomes was against some law, and the degree of culpability in the action, are the key factors in criminal justice cases.

There are also other degenerative cases of purposive action germane to criminal and civil justice as well as ethics generally. Among these are actions that involve force, coercion and actions done under duress. Conduct produced by force is a purely dyadic, brute action. Someone who is raped has no desire for it and does not intend it.

Acting under duress is another case. The mugger holds a gun to the head of the victim, commanding him to turn over his wallet. In one interpretation, if the victim complies, this could be counted as a purposive act. The victim does not desire to die, believes that unless he gives the thief his wallet, he will be shot and likely die and, consequently, gives the wallet to the thief intentionally. However, if it is looked at transactionally, the interpretation can be quite different. There is an element of brute dyadic force here in the sense that the mugger is forcing a choice of ends on the victim who would, otherwise, choose not to be in the situation in which a choice between money or life must be made. The element of force reduces the self-control the agent has in choosing ends as well as the means to those ends.

Being forced to do or refrain from doing some act is the least voluntary of actions. Those who use force on others may do so purposively as means to an end they desire. The mugger desires money; mugging is the means to that end. However, from the viewpoint of the subject of force, it is a purely dyadic action. The subject of force does not intend the action enforced and does not believe that the enforced action will attain any desired or motivated end the agent has. Using force, however, is not inherently wrong. Self-defense may require using force on another, even deadly force. But, here, as in the case of mugging, the choice of kill or be killed is one that is controlled by the aggressor's actions.

An Analysis of the Elements of Purposive Action

Peirce's account of purposive or intentional action jibes with both the classical account of purposive action in Aristotle's *Nicomachean Ethics* and Michael Bratman's more recent one (1999). In both Aristotle and Bratman's analyses, there should be a clear distinction made in purposive action among the functions of desire or motives for an end, deliberation about the means to the end, and the intention to act on the result of the deliberation, a belief about what is likely to attain the end. Purposive behavior for Peirce is, as noted, based on a version of what is traditionally called the desire-belief model of behavior. People have some sort of pro-attitude toward an end—an impetus, desire or reason—believe that certain actions will likely attain that end, and form an intention or resolution to act on that belief under the right circumstances and opportunities. It's time to turn to an analysis of each of these three elements of purposive action in Peirce.

Peirce's Theory of Desire

Peirce has an interesting theory of desire. Desires are indeterminate—the objects of desire are obscure. They are indeterminate along three dimensions (1902, CP 1.205). First, desires are general in the sense that what people desire is "always some *kind* of thing or event" (emphasis added) (1902, CP 1.205; 1894, CP 1.341). For example, people want happiness, but typically what is meant by happiness is ill-defined, as Peirce said of the vulgar utilitarian (1903, CP 5.158).

Peirce argues that "desires become more specific in the pursuit of them" (1902, CP 1.205), that is, desires become more determinate as they get represented in the beliefs about how to attain them, the plan to attain them. For Peirce, something is general in the sense that its properties cannot be specified below a certain scale. Triangle is a general term but as such it cannot be said to be either scalene or equilateral. If people desire lighting, it is not clear what type is meant by that (1902, CP 1.205). If people desire apple pie, it's not clear which sort of apples they want in the pie, which sort of crust, whether it should be mixed with other fruit or nuts, and so forth—all they know is that they want something like the sort of general pleasure associated with an apple pie.

A second source of indeterminacy in desires is their vagueness, meaning that the desire has a certain latitude depending on circumstances. If people want economical heating with accessible fuel, people in more rural areas might find it more economical to use a wood furnace than a gas source; whereas in denser populations with sources of natural gas nearby, a gas furnace might fit the bill (1902, CP 1.206).

The third source of indeterminacy is what Peirce calls its longitude. "By this I mean that while a certain ideal state of things might most perfectly satisfy a desire, yet a situation somewhat differing from that will be far better than nothing" (1902, CP 1.207). For example, a brighter lamp might be better for reading, but the cost would hurt the pocketbook, thus some compromise between these two ends—an economical lamp and a bright lamp—is made (1902, CP 1.207). One might call the longitude the local optimum, relative to alternative choices.

Using a different model than the geographical one for this concept of desire, one might think of the determination of desire as a process mapped by a conical helix. The diameter of the base is its generality, its height its vagueness and the volume its longitude. The apex would represent the most determinate version of the desire. Starting at the base, the desire has the greatest generality, vagueness and lowest optimality (most longitude). As one pursues means to attain the desire, one climbs up the helix toward the apex, the diameter of the base shrinks, making the desire more specific, it gains in altitude as it moves closer to the apex, and the overall volume shrinks, bringing its pursuit to a more optimal result.

In both models, Peirce's account suggests that there is an interaction between desire for some end and deliberation about the means to attain end. Desire for an end may initially drive deliberation about how to get it, but deliberation may also drive desire. The desire for an end is initially something that is indeterminate and, so, functions as a delimiting rather than a causal force on deliberation. The desire delimits beliefs about how something might be attained, but it is also clear that the planning in the deliberation makes the desire become more determinate and may change or alter the desire.

Since desires become more determinate as the deliberation of the means for its attainment unfolds, Peirce would seem to disagree with David Hume's claim that desires have no representational content. If they did, then beliefs concerning that content could influence the desire. As Hume argues,

> A passion is an original existence . . . and contains not any representative quality, which renders it a copy of any other existence or modification. When I am angry, I am actually possest with the passion, and in that emotion have no more a reference to any other object, than when I am thirsty, or sick, or more than five foot high. 'Tis impossible, therefore, that this passion can be oppos'd by, or be contradictory to truth and reason; since this contradiction consists in the disagreement of ideas, considered'd as copies, with those objects which they represent.
>
> (1739, p. 415)

This claim is somewhat ambiguous since Hume seems to admit that desires have representational content when he states that beliefs can play the role of intense impressions that can influence the passions (1739, p. 119; Radcliffe, 1999, p. 105).

Peirce's theory of desires would seem to suggest that desires do have representational content. In Peirce's example of opening the window to cool the room, he says carefully that "my desire to have the window open, that is, *the symbol in my mind of the agreeability of it*, influences the physical facts of my rising from my chair, going to the window and opening it" (emphasis added) (1904, NEM 4, p. 254). This suggests that at least higher-order desires do have representational content. Desires as intentional states are directed to something, and that something is represented in the beliefs about it. As desires become more determinate so does the object of desire.

For example, according to a Harris poll (November 13, 2013), about 68% of Americans believe in heaven (down from 75%, 10 years previous). Within the Christian religion alone, there have been thousands of representations of heaven over the centuries. These have varied from hedonistic paradises, posh residences and streets paved with gold, to places that are absent of pain and suffering, opportunities to reunite with loved ones, abodes of peace and tranquility, sensoria of love and eternal bliss. The Unitarian pastor, John Haynes Holmes, summed it up nicely: "a place where every desire of the human heart for happiness was realized" (Holmes, 1915, pp. 285–286). But if people believed that heaven was a place of eternal boredom, or mindless existence, that belief would certainly influence the desire for heaven.

If people desire to go to heaven, then, unless they are just engaged in wishful thinking, they must have a belief not only that it exists, but that it has certain characteristics that make it desirable. If the only thing that makes heaven desirable for some people is that they will be reunited with their loved ones, but they learn from an authoritative source in their religion that that's not what heaven is like, they may change or modify their desire for heaven.

Deliberation and Belief in Peirce

Deliberation about the means to an end is typically formulated as a process of considering alternatives to that end with a belief that doing a set of actions is the most likely way to attain the desired end. In this way. This very standard formulation echoes the basic tenet of the pragmatic maxim (1878, CP 5.402). Just as the meaning of a concept is clarified by the practical bearings of that concept, so the meaning of a desire is clarified by deliberating about the practical means to its attainment. Deliberation delimits what is to be done to attain an end.

As Aristotle characterizes it, deliberation is about things people can do. Deliberation is concerned primarily with means, not ends. However, thinkers such as Henry Richardson argue that there can be deliberation about ends (1994, p. 49). Peirce would seem to agree since this is the primary purpose of his science of esthetics. In any case, Aristotle argued that the intention to act is preceded by deliberation and, for that reason, it is contrasted with spontaneous action. Deliberation, as Aristotle says, occurs when the matter of how to attain an end is not determined and somewhat unclear, so that it might be possible that the end is brought about by at least more than one means. Deliberation is a form of inquiry, although it is not like mathematical inquiry, but is of a practical sort. Deliberation is distinguished from intention, though they have the same objects. But intention judges what is deliberated to be worthy of action (*Nicomachean Ethics*, 1112a18–1112b12).

The end result of deliberation is what Peirce calls a *practical belief*: "A practical belief is what a man proposes to go upon. A decision is more or less pressing. What ought it to be? That must depend upon what the purpose of his action is" (1901, CP 7.185). A practical belief acts more or less like a hypothesis, but a practical hypothesis about what should be done. As David Velleman notes, the difference between desiring and believing is that desiring is an attitude concerned with "things that aren't the case but are to be brought about," whereas beliefs are about "things that are the case" (or at least believed to be the case) (1996, p. 707). A practical belief engenders "a habit of deliberate behavior." Deliberate behavior is behavior directed to some end, that is, "to one's present purpose" (c. 1902, CP 5.538). In this sense, practical beliefs serve as *reasons*, hence, motivations for acting. This brings up Peirce's theory of belief.

Peirce acknowledges that his theory of belief is based primarily on Alexander Bain's theory, developed mid-19th century. The innovation in Bain's theory is that he ties it to action, rather than something based solely on cognition or emotion (Bain, 1869, I, p. 394). As Peirce interprets Bain, a belief is "that upon which a man is prepared to act" (1906, CP 5.12); but that, further, the likelihood of acting on that belief is proportional to the intensity of belief (1898, 1.635). Indeed, Peirce thinks that "pragmatism is scarce more than a corollary" to Bain's account (1906, CP 5.12). Although Peirce's pragmatic maxim was originally intended to clarify the meanings of concepts by expressing them in terms of their experimental consequences, it also shows that any hypothesis formulated in terms of its practical consequences can be transposed to a practical maxim. To define the scratch-hardness of diamonds in terms of whether it will scratch glass also sets up a practical maxim. If it is true that diamonds scratch glass then, if one desires to cut glass, use a diamond to do so (Liszka, 2009). Peirce states the transposition of the theoretical to the practical more technically: "Pragmatism is the principle that every theoretical judgment expressible in a sentence in the indicative mood is a confused form of thought whose only meaning, if it has any, lies in its tendency to enforce a corresponding practical maxim expressible as a conditional sentence having its apodosis in the imperative mood" (1903, CP 5.18). In other words, a theoretical claim can be transposed to a hypothetical imperative. As Peirce says, "every theoretical belief is, at least indirectly, a practical belief," and will "have some possible bearing upon practice" (c. 1902, CP 5.539). "The most striking feature of the new theory," Peirce notes, "was its recognition of an inseparable connection between rational cognition and rational purpose; and that consideration it was which determined the preference for the name *pragmatism*" (1905, CP 5.412).

Bain claimed more precisely that "belief is preparedness to act, for a given end, in a given way" (Bain, 1889, p. 508). Unpacking this, Bain points to the three interrelated elements of purposive action similar to Peirce: directedness to an end, belief about how to attain that end, and the intention (preparedness) to act on that belief. It is the readiness, the intention to act on the belief, that constitutes the belief in what the belief is about (Fisch, 1954, p. 84).

For Peirce, a belief serves to *both* "guide" desire and "shape" action (1877, CP 5.371). Actually, given Peirce's theory of desire and belief, it might be better to say that beliefs *shape* desire and *guide* action. Belief is tied to habits of action. The stronger the belief, the more indurated the habit associated with it (1877, CP 5.371). For this reason, beliefs are conditional in the sense that, under the right conditions, as the occasion arises, people tend to act on their beliefs (1877, CP 5.372). In agreement with Bain, Peirce argues the opposite of belief is not disbelief, but doubt—a state of mind that is intolerable for most and needs resolution (1877, CP 5.372). As a result, people tend to seek means of settling doubts and tend to stick to what they have no reason to doubt (1877, CP 5.372).

Bain shows how beliefs, particularly what Peirce called practical beliefs, motivate action. Bain notes that, even if desires such as relief of pain and attainment of pleasure are motives, belief is instrumental in acting on those two goals. There is nothing in the pain of thirst that motivates a person to lift a cup of liquid water to the mouth or run to a brook. It is the belief that doing these actions will result in the relief of thirst that motivates one to act (1865, p. 525). It is, as he says, the presentation to the mind of the belief in the solution to relieving the pain that brings the person to act, not just the pain alone (1865, p. 525). Thomas Nagel says something similar. Thirst alone does not motivate someone to put money in a vending machine to get a drink; belief in the effectiveness of quenching a thirst by extracting a drink from the machine does (1978, p. 33). Nagel points to the difference between motivated and unmotivated desires in this respect (1978, p. 29). The latter, like thirst or hunger, simply appear without much cognitive mediation. Motivated desires, on the other hand, are informed by beliefs. When, as Peirce argues, the belief in the means translates the desire for an end as a set of actions that could conceivably attain what is desired, it also represents that desire more determinately and becomes motivational since what is desired is now at hand. An end that is believed to be possible is more motivating than one that is believed to be impossible. This practical belief, the result of deliberation, serves as the basis for the intention to act. One does not act on the desire, poorly formed, but on the practical belief that is the result of the deliberation about the means to achieve the thing desired.

There is sufficient current psychological theory to back up Bain's analysis. According to expectancy-value theory, for example, motivation to do something is not only based on the desire or the value of the goal but the belief that that behavior will likely lead to the goal (Atkinson, 1957; Wigfield and Eccles, 1992). As attribution theory suggests, people are more motivated to achieve a goal if they perceive a beneficial goal as more likely to be achieved (Eccles et al., 1983). Allan Wigfield and Jacquelynn Eccles (2000) used Albert Bandura's notion of self-efficacy in an interesting study. Bandura makes a distinction between the objective assessment that doing something will likely accomplish an end, and the belief by actors that they are competent to do those things (1977, p. 247). Their study concluded that people tend to value less, activities for which they show less competence. Thus, desires can be affected by means-ends beliefs, and the relation between belief and desire is more complex than Hume characterizes it.

Peirce's Account of Intention, Resolution and Determination

As Aristotle argues, acting intentionally is contrasted with acting spontaneously on the spur of the moment. Intention is preceded by deliberation. It is not to be confused with desire. Intention to do something can also oppose what is desired—a source of contention with Hume and thinkers that follow him. Aristotle does not think people are and—at least hopes they are not—as Hume is to argue, "slaves to the passions." Intention is not to be confused with wish, since one can wish for an impossible end such as immortality, as Aristotle says. A wish is about an end, whereas intention is of the means relative to an end (*Nicomachean Ethics*, 1111b 5–30).

Michael Bratman argues that the difference between desire and intention is that, although desires can *influence* behavior, intentions are *conduct-controlling* pro-attitudes toward an action. It involves "a special commitment" to action that desires do not exhibit. It is something that seems to resist reconsideration and has an inertia (1999, p. 16). As. T.M. Scanlon describes it,

> a person who intends to do A will not only feel favorably disposed, on balance, to that course of action, but will also tend to be on the lookout for ways of carrying out this intention (finding means, looking for ways of fitting it in with other plans, and so on), and will think of this intention as a prima facie objection when incompatible courses of action are proposed.
>
> (2000, p. 21)

Bratman believes that intentions are states of mind distinct from desires and beliefs as to the means to attain those desires (1999, p. 20).

Peirce seems to agree that what he calls self-control is primarily centered on what Bratman calls the intentional aspect of action. Around the turn of the century, Peirce foregoes his earlier archaic language of "volition" and "will" to describe this process of self-control in favor of the vocabulary of intention and its cognates (c. 1894, CP 1.330–1.334). He analyzes the process of self-control into three distinct phases: intention, resolution and determination, although "*they are not every one present in every case*" (1903, CP 1.601).

"The power of self-control," for Peirce "is certainly not a power over what one is doing at the very instant the operation of self-control is commenced" (1906, CP 8.320). It begins with an intention to make "conduct conform to a whole or to a part of" the ideals of conduct that the person "most thoroughly believes." Such intentions can be "strengthened" as "rules of conduct" are more rigidly "adopted" (n.d., R 1132, p. 15a).

This leads to "the formation of a resolve" (1906, CP 8.320), when an "occasion is going to arise" (n.d. R 1132, p. 15a). Like Bratman's notion of intention to act, which involves planning, Peirce says, a resolution "is of the nature of a plan; or, as one might almost say, a *diagram*." It is an "act of stamping with approval, "endorsing" as one's own, an imaginary line of conduct so that it shall give a general shape to our actual future conduct" (c. 1902, CP 5.538). Because it is "more or less general . . . it does not necessarily influence . . . conduct."

It is at this point that people go through a further process whereby the plan "is converted into a *determination*, by which I mean a really efficient agency, such that if one knows what its special character is one can forecast the man's conduct on the anticipated occasion" (n.d., R 1132, p. 16).

In general, "This operation of self-control is a process in which logical sequence is converted into mechanical sequence or something of the sort. How this happens, we are in my opinion as yet entirely ignorant" (1906, CP 8.320).

Peirce mentions one last thing in this respect that has relevance for his account of purposive conduct. "I have specially emphasized the fact that conduct is determined by what precedes it in time, while the recognition of the pleasure it brings follows after the action." He adds that "a *feeling*, as a mere appearance, can have no real power in itself to produce any effect whatever, however indirectly" (1903, CP 1.601).

The Desire-Belief Model of Human Conduct

As noted, Peirce's analysis of purposive behavior is a version of what is generally called the desire-belief model of human action—of which there are several variants (Anscombe, 1963; Goldman, 1970; Williams, 1993, p. 102; Davidson, 2006, p. 23). The classic Humean version is usually represented as having the following theses:

(1) ends are picked out by desires, not reasoned beliefs
(Hume, 1739, p. 413; see Korsgaard, 1999, p. 312)

(2) desire is the only motivation of action; reasoned beliefs are not—"reason is and ought to be a slave of the passions

(Hume, 1739, p. 413, 1739, p. 415; see Smith, 1987)

(3) desire has no representational quality

(Hume, 1739, p. 415); and

(4) beliefs cannot oppose a desire in directing the will, only passions can oppose passions.

(Hume, 1739, pp. 413, 415, 458)

Hume is what Bernard Williams calls an *internalist*. All variants of this position agree that reasons for doing something are inherently connected to an inner motivational set of the agent usually associated with desires of some sort (Williams, 1993, p. 102). Consequently, beliefs about what is right and wrong cannot *alone* be motivational (Korsgaard, 1999, p. 43). As Thomas Nagel explains it: "since all motivated action must result from the operation of some motivating factor within the agent, and since belief cannot by itself produce action, it follows that a desire of the agent must always be operative" (1978, p. 27). Robert Brandom characterizes it as the position that "talk of reasons for action and norms governing action" are really about "underlying preferences and desires, which are understood both as intrinsically motivating and as the only sorts of things that can be intrinsically motivating. Thus, any complete expression of a reason for action must include a specification of what it is that the agent wants, in virtue of which the reasons functions (motivationally) as a reason for that agent." (2000, p. 38). If true, this has significate impact for ethical theory. If moral beliefs or ideals cannot motivate action, then standards of conduct or ethical principles would not be motivational, nor could they counter desires. In regard to Peirce's theory in particular, if Hume is right, self-control, the core of ethical conduct, would seem questionable. The question is whether Peirce's version of the desire-belief model avoids this problem.

Hume's theory has some questionable consequences. For one, it would infer that people would only do the right thing if they already desired to do the right thing. There can be no appeal to an objective, agent-neutral norm, such as people should care for their children (Schroeder, 2013, p. 103). Motivation always has to be tied to the internal motivational set of the individual. This makes the decision to act morally purely subjective and arbitrary. But moral claims seem to have an authority that is agent-neutral and extends beyond the individual agent's desires.

If Hume is right, then internalism entails a subjectivist ethics. It would seem to deny the claim that people sometimes do what they don't desire to do precisely because they believe it is the right thing to do. That is, Hume's model does not capture the ordinary experiences of conscience and duty (Korsgaard, 1999, p. 43). The sense of duty usually kicks in precisely when people don't desire to do something, but do it nonetheless, precisely because they believe it is the right thing to do. They may understand perfectly well that following through on the duty could have *undesirable* consequences, but do it nonetheless. But how can people be motivated to do something that they don't desire to do, if desire is the sole motivating force (Morillo,1990). Some Humeans claim that the sense of duty requires a desire to do one's duty but, again, doing one's duty is often undesirable (Prichard, 1968). On the other hand, there must be some desire to do one's duty. Nagel's point that beliefs—specifically reasons for beliefs—can generate desires suggests a solution to the question of duty: belief in one's duty could generate a desire to do one's duty and oppose the desire not to do one's duty.

Internalism would also seem to lead to a subjectivism about the ends of action as well since they are picked out by desires. Since it is the desire for the end that justifies the end selected, then anything anyone desires would seem legitimate to pursue. People would have a good reason to bring about immoral, irrational, or eccentric ends merely because they desire it (Schroeder, 2013, p. 84).

The alternative to internalism is externalism, advocated by thinkers such as Christine Korsgaard and Thomas Nagel. They argue that reasons for action, such as moral beliefs, can be motivational (Korsgaard, 1999, p. 331; Nagel, 1978, p. 32; Velleman, 1996, p. 697). Nagel's position is somewhat more subtle than Korsgaard's. He argues that desires must be present in any motivation, but that not all desires are motivating; in some cases, the desire is the result of a reasoned belief. As noted, he makes a distinction between *unmotivated* and *motivated* desires, the former arise without the intervention of beliefs, while the latter are the result of beliefs (1978, p. 29). It might be argued that unmotivated desires, such as the desire that arises from hunger act more like drives, while motivated desires generate more of a feeling of commitment or obligation. This distinction would explain how it is possible to have a causal arrow from reasoned belief to desire. Believing that something is right or wrong would generate a desire, in the form of a feeling of commitment or obligation to either do or not do what is right or wrong. T.M. Scanlon agrees with Nagel that there are motivated desires, that is, desires that are formed on the basis of reasons, but he also argues that unmotivated desires are also not motivating. Instead, these desires, such as the desire for food or sex involve "having a tendency to see something as a reason." Scanlon characterizes these sorts of desires as simply directed-attention: "A person has a desire in the directed-attention sense that P if the thought of P keeps occurring to him or her in a favorable light, that is to say, if the person's attention is directed insistently toward considerations the present themselves as counting in favor of P" (2000, p. 39).

Peirce's theory of desire combined with his theory of belief suggests a rather interesting variant of the desire-belief model of moral motivation.

For one thing, like Michael Bratman, Peirce suggests that there is a third element in the desire-belief model, namely, intention to act on what is believed will attain an end. As Bratman notes and Robert Brandom concurs, both internalists and externalists tend to reduce intention to some combination of desire and belief (Bratman, 1999, p. 18; Davidson, 2006; Brandom, 2000, p. 82). Bratman argues, as Peirce seems to, that the intention (including resolution and determination) to act on what is deliberated is a third independent aspect of purposive behavior that is not reducible to the other two (the desire for an end and a belief that a set of actions will likely attain it). The intention to act on what is deliberated is an indispensable aspect of the triadic character of purposive action. If desire alone motivates action, then it is a purely dyadic relation; if belief alone motivates, it is also dyadic. Purposive behavior must involve all three aspects in a triadic relation.

The inclusion of intention allows for a different strategy of how desires may be opposed. Although Peirce notes that "it is a natural hypothesis that a man cannot *will* to do that which he has no sort of desire to do," he shows why and how it is the case that something other than desire can oppose desire (c. 1894, CP 1.331). In Peirce's language, a belief is something upon which people are "*prepared* to act" (emphasis added) (1907, CP 5.12). Intention includes the *resolution* to act on that belief. If, in pursuing an end, a deliberation shows that the only means to achieve the end is thievery, yet the agent *believes* that stealing is wrong, it is quite possible that that agent would oppose the desire for the end on the basis of the moral belief. A deliberation on the means to achieve the desired end may in fact lead to a resolution not to act on those means, just as easily as it might lead to a choice to act on some such deliberation. He agrees with the externalists that "a desire may perfectly well be discontented with volition, i.e., with what the man *will* do" (c. 1894, CP 1.331). It is quite possible that "the element of the will"—which Peirce specifies as resolution and determination—"is always exercised upon an individual object upon an individual occasion, becomes so predominant as to overrule the generalizing character of desire" (1902, CP 1.205). In this struggle between desire, belief and intention, it is clear that Peirce "cannot grant" that the will or intention to act is "nothing but the strongest desire" and argues against both Hobbes and John Stuart Mill on this point (c. 1890, CP 1.380). The strongest motive may be the strongest *reason*, but acting on a reason, that is, on a belief, is inherently voluntary (1868, CP 5.340n.1).

Thus, although he agrees with the externalists, that something other than desire can oppose desire, it is primarily through the intercession of the intention to act rather than the belief itself. If the belief itself were the motivation, this could not explain why people often fail to follow on their moral beliefs. In other words, externalists cannot account for the common phenomena of "weakness of will," the fact that people often fail to act on their beliefs of right and wrong (see Davidson, 2006, p. 72f).

Peirce appears to disagree with the internalists on their account that desires cannot be opposed by something other than desires. At the same time, based on his triadic theory of purposive action, he would seem to agree with them that desire is present in all purposive action and that the desire can be motivating. How is this to be reconciled?

It is precisely on the basis of the triadic interrelation that this can be explained. Based on his theory of desire, Peirce could argue that all purposive action is motivated by a desire for the end but, because desires are indeterminate—that obscure object of desire—then they are weakly motivational. It is through deliberation, ending in a practical belief about how best to achieve that desire, that the desire becomes more robustly represented and more strongly motivational. It is this belief in the means that forms the basis of the intention and resolution to act, the motivation to act, rather than the desire itself. Peirce's theories of desire and belief show an important interrelation between desire and deliberation. Because desires are indeterminate, they may motivate weakly. To repeat a quote from Peirce: "our beliefs guide our desires *and* shape our actions" [emphasis added] (1877, CP 5.371). In other words, even if the desire is initially motivational, it is weakly so in the way in which some vague desire for something might be, and the desire can lessen once the means for the attainment of that desire becomes more manifest. It is its refinement of the desire through deliberation that is more strongly motivational, and it is the practical belief that is the result of the deliberation that serves as the basis for the intention to act on that belief. Motivation runs throughout all the elements as they work triadically together in any purposive action.

In this regard, it is not clear why the two exceptions that Hume cites as to how reasoned beliefs influence the passions are not evidence that practical beliefs, as Peirce calls them, do influence the passions. The two exceptions he mentions are cases where it becomes known that the object does not exist, and cases where the means to attain what is desired is known to be insufficient (Hume, 1739, p. 416). If, for example, a recent Harris poll is correct and about 16% of Americans do not believe in the existence of heaven, it also has to be assumed that they also no longer desire it, unless they are just engaging in wishful thinking. As Hume notes,

> the moment we perceive the falsehood of any supposition, or when it chuses means insufficient for the design'd end, 'tis impossible, that reason and passion can ever oppose each other, or dispute for the government of the will and actions. The moment we perceive the falsehood of any supposition, or the insufficiency of any means our passions yield to our reason without any position.
>
> (1739, pp. 416–417)

As to the second exception, it might be handy to return to Bain's example. If a person stuck in the middle of the desert has the belief that no water is accessible within a life-saving radius, although it would not damper the desire to quench his thirst, it could be de-motivating since the situation is believed to be hopeless. In this way, too, belief can influence desires.

5 Ethical Reasoning

Critical logic is the second division of the normative science of semiotic after the grammar. It is concerned with the right method of reasoning, the types of arguments that will lead to true claims (1902, CP 2.97; 1903, CP 1.191). Assuming a parallel in the organization of the normative sciences, the grammar of ethics should be followed by the matter of ethical reasoning. If the grammar of ethics is concerned with the fundamental features of purposive, goal-directed conduct, then ethical reasoning would be about reasoning concerned with good ends, and what *ought* to be done in the pursuit of those ends sufficient to assure that such conduct will result in some good.

Practical Reasoning

Peirce explains purposive conduct as a variant of the desire-belief model of behavior. It is a triadic relation among desire for an end, belief about the means to attain it and the intention to follow through on those means. The belief about the means refines the desired end, and gives credence to its attainment, sufficient to build resolution to act on what is deliberated. This more-or-less captures the sense of *practical reasoning*. Practical reasoning falls out of the desire-belief model of human action and flows from the grammar of purposive conduct.

Peirce provides this example of practical reasoning in the context of the analysis of his desire-belief-intention account of purposive conduct:

> Now to say that a man believes anthracite to be a convenient fuel is to say no more nor less than that if he needs fuel, and no other seems particularly preferable, then, if he acts deliberately, bearing in mind his experiences, considering what he is doing, and exercising self-control, he will often use anthracite. A practical belief may, therefore, be described as a habit of deliberate behavior.
>
> (c. 1902, CP 5.538)

Presumably, the desired end here is to heat one's home, and the man believes that anthracite is the most convenient fuel to attain that end among alternatives. The deliberation ends with what Peirce calls a practical belief in reference to Bain's dictum concerning the nature of belief as "preparedness to act, for a given end, in a given way" (Bain, 1889, p. 508). If a person believes that anthracite coal is the best means of attaining the end of heating the house, then as the right opportunity arises, he will resolve to use anthracite coal.

However, where the matter of practical beliefs gets specifically spelled out is in the pragmatic maxim. As discussed, the pragmatic maxim is formulated to show that there is an inherent connection between theoretical, scientific, experimental reasoning and practical reasoning. As Peirce expressed the maxim, each concept (or belief, hypothesis etc.) has "practical bearings," by which he means that it could be transposed into a practical belief. For example, if the scratch-hardness of a diamond means that it can cut glass rather than being cut by glass, then, if that is true, it infers a corresponding practical belief: using a diamond cutter is the best way to cut glass. This makes it clear that the truth of the practical belief—the core feature of practical reasoning—is based on the truth of the empirical hypothesis that diamonds are in fact scratch-hard (and scratch harder than glass). As Peirce says, "For truth is neither more nor less than that character of a proposition which consists in this, that belief in the proposition would, with sufficient experience and reflection, lead us to such conduct as would tend to satisfy the desires we should then have. To say that truth means more than this is to say that it has no meaning at all" (1877, CP 5.375n2).

However, Peirce emphasizes that this is a *pragmatic maxim*. Note the two words. A maxim, as Kant defines it is a rule of action (1785, p. 38). To repeat an earlier quote, he shows how the *maxim* follows:

> Pragmatism is the principle that every theoretical judgment expressible in a sentence in the indicative mood is a confused form of thought whose only meaning, if it has any, lies in its tendency to enforce a corresponding practical maxim expressible as a conditional sentence having its apodosis in the imperative mood.
>
> (1903, CP 5.18)

This is a rather formal way of expressing Kant's notion of a hypothetical imperative: "a conditional sentence having its apodosis in the imperative mood." In the diamond example, the truth of the claim that diamonds cut glass, justifies the following hypothetical imperative: If one wants to cut glass, use a diamond cutter.

The maxim is also a *pragmatic* one, in the Kantian sense of that term. It is well known that Peirce never used the term "pragmatic" to title his maxim when it was first published in 1878 in "How to Make Our Ideas Clear." Peirce did use the term later to describe the maxim in various writings and presentations, most notably in the Harvard Lectures

(1903, HL, p. 109). There's some controversy around the first use of the term, particularly whether Peirce used it in describing the maxim in the "Metaphysical Club" in the early 1870s (Brent, 1998, pp. 82–88). After checking with William James, who was the first to use the term publicly in 1878, Peirce finally settled on these matters in a public statement attached to the entry for pragmatism for the *Century Dictionary*, in which he claims he used it in conversations in the Metaphysical Club in the early 1870s (Brent, 1998, p. 88).

No offense to William James, but a serious Kantian scholar such as Peirce would know the term and its import. He says as much in "What Pragmatism Is" in 1905, published in *The Monist*. There, Peirce says he rejected the suggestion from "some friends" to call it "practicalism." "But for one who had learned philosophy out of Kant . . . and who still thought in Kantian terms most readily, *praktisch* and *pragmatisch* were as far apart as the two poles, the former belonging in a region of thought where no mind of the experimentalist type can ever make sure of solid ground under is feet, the latter expressing relation to some definite human purpose." For Kant, *praktisch* has to do with the core of practical reason, understood as an aspect of the more ethereal realm of moral law. It is the connection between rational cognition and rational purpose that "determined the preference for the name *pragmatism*" (1905, CP 5.412).

Kant's sense of the "pragmatic" in *Anthropology* has already been discussed. There he calls pragmatic knowledge, knowledge of what human beings can or should make of themselves (1798, p. 3), and aims at improvement (1798, p. 4). This is consistent with his characterization of it in *The Foundations of the Metaphysics of Morals*. "Pragmatic" imperatives are forms of hypothetical imperatives, essentially prudential rules of how best to attain ends (1785, pp. 31–32n4). He defines it as a form of prudence that "instructs the world how it could provide for its interest better than, or at least as well as has been done in the past" (1785, p. 34n6). This is also consistent with Peirce's fledgling science of "pragmatics," which "studies the processes by which the outer world is to be brought into accordance with our wishes" (1896, R 1345, p. 2) and includes "how to attain given ends" (1896, R 1345, p. 16). Had Peirce developed his pragmatics and connected it with his pragmatic maxim and the normative science of ethics, it would have made for a more systematic connection between theoretical and practical ethics than what is proffered currently. As Peirce says, "My want of skill in practical affairs does not prevent me from perceiving the advantage of being well imbued with pragmatism in the conduct of life" (1903, HL, p. 109).

In any case, Peirce provides an outline of standard forms of practical reason. There are several variants of practical reasoning (Audi, 2006, pp. 62–82). However, practical reasoning generally consists of some pro-attitude, such as a desire, want, or need, toward some end. The second premise usually involves a *practical hypothesis*, or what Peirce calls a practical belief, a set of actions that, if executed, are believed by the agent to be likely means to that end. The belief in the practical hypothesis, at least under Peirce's and Bratman's account, further serves as the basis for an intention, resolve, or commitment to do what the practical hypothesis recommends.

Just as the desire-belief model can both explain and evaluate conduct, so can practical reasoning to which it is tied. It can determine what ought to be done or what should have been done, but it can also explain and predict conduct—although rather unreliably. Some people believe that drinking ten glasses of water a day is good for your health, and this would *explain* why they engage in that conduct on a daily basis—assuming they desire to be healthy. But the best evidence in medical research claims that hyper-hydration can be harmful to health. Therefore, they *ought not* to drink so much water daily if they desire to remain healthy. Whether the second premise in practical reasoning is a true belief or does not alter the explanation of why people drink so much water, but it does affect its normative *evaluation* (Williams, 1993, p. 102). As Mark Schroeder notes, "subjective normative reasons depend on what the agent believes, independently of how things actually are. Explanatory reasons are not normative at all; they are only reasons why something is the case" (2013, p. 14).

The fundamental norm underlying practical reasoning can be expressed generally in the following way: *one ought to do what is likely to attain one's end*. As Peirce expresses it: "That ought to be done which is conducive to a certain end" (1898, CP 5.594). This prudential norm, as Bernard Williams calls it, is supposed in all hypothetical imperatives (1993, p. 114). Hilary Putnam thinks this defines the notion of "rationality" or "reasonableness." He uses the latter term in the context of a puzzle concerning Peirce, but it's not clear if he's referring to Peirce's use of the term (1987, p. 84). The puzzle, which figures in a number of issues to be discussed, has Peirce supposing a situation in which a gambler must choose between selecting a card from a deck of cards that has 24 out of 25 red cards and another with 24 out of 25 black cards. A red card yields everlasting felicity, the black woe forever. Most, if not all people would formulate the following hypothetical imperative: if you want everlasting felicity, choose from the deck with 24 red cards. The reason is that it is more likely to attain that end than the alternative. That in turn is justified empirically on the basis of probability theory. In that case, the hypothetical imperative has its warrant in the truth of the empirical claim.

Putnam puzzles over the deeper issue of *why* people ought to do what is likely to attain one's end, that is, why people should be reasonable. Obviously, if the answer is that it will likely attain one's end, that is a merely circular response. He doesn't like Peirce's answer which, as he interprets it, goes something like the following. To do what is likely to attain an end, whether in fact it results in attaining that end or not, is to be part of an ongoing process of inquiry in which one is one in a sample of such results. One is in a train of others that, through an inductive process, will determine in the long run which practical reasonings work best. Putnam thinks this is an altruistic interpretation of a process that is basically motivated by self-interest. People act on what they believe will attain their ends because they want the end, not because they think they are part of this process of inquiry (1987, p. 83). In the end, Putnam thinks that the reason to be reasonable is a case where "my spade is turned"—to use a phrase of Wittgenstein. There is no further reason for the fundamental norm of practical reasoning, other than the norm (1987, p. 85).

Some philosophers, such as T. M. Scanlon, distinguish between being rational and reasonable (2000, pp. 32–33). The economic sense of rationality is, of course, most often characterized as the maximization one's own utility, relative to a finite set of actions (Gauthier, 1986, p. 22). To *actually* maximize one's utility would assume, as T.M. Scanlon notes, *ideal* rationality, in which actors are fully informed of all possibilities, and have impeccable reasoning—an ideal agent (2000, p. 32). This is perhaps why thinkers, such as Herbert Simon, argue that most rational people engage in *satisficing*, a form of bounded rationality whereby people choose an optimal alternative relative to an end, rather than one that maximizes it (1956, p. 129). John Rawls defines rationality more generally as agents who seek to advance their interests:

> a rational person is thought to have a coherent set of preferences between the options open to him. He ranks these options according to how well they further his purposes; he follows the plan which will satisfy more of his desires rather than less, and which has the greater chance of being successfully executed.
>
> (1971, p. 143)

As Scanlon explains it, rationality is the case where, should people judge that there are compelling grounds for forming an intention to act, they then search for ways to fulfill that intention, *ceteris paribus*, given any opportunities to so act (2000, p. 24). Irrationality are cases where people act contrarily to their considered intentions to act (2000, p. 25). Reasonableness, on the other hand, for Scanlon involves not just the recognition of one's own interests but recognizes the interests of others. People have certain aims and intend to attain them in certain ways. Since such pursuits are almost always in the context of some collectivity of people with varying interests, and will undoubtedly affect those interests, then to be reasonable is to aim at ends and attain them in ways that others could not reasonably reject (2000, pp. 5, 33).

Peirce sometimes uses the terms rationality and reasonableness interchangeably, but the core feature of reasonableness for him is something different and more general than just rationality in the economic sense of maximizing interest. As it applies to practical reasoning it is primarily a matter of self-correction, relative to an end (1902, CP 2.66). Peirce defines it in the following way:

> The essence of rationality lies in the fact that the rational being *will* act so at to attain certain ends. Prevent his doing so in one way, and he will act in some utterly different way which will produce the same result. Rationality is being governed by final causes.
>
> (1902, CP 2.66)

Reasonableness is essentially correcting one's errors relative to a goal. If purposive conduct aims at some end, then self-correction toward that end is critical since it is more likely that people will attain their ends if they abandon erroneous beliefs in favor of less erroneous ones. Reasonableness in Peirce's sense is not quite the same as Scanlon's sense. It would seem the latter would have to suppose the former. To reject or not reject a claim in Scanlon's sense would suppose people capable of identifying erroneous beliefs and their willingness to correct them.

Reasonableness is intelligent action. Mechanical action, as Peirce says, is dumb in that it employs the same means toward the same result without change. Self-correction is intelligent conduct in that it allows for change of belief based on evidence, leading to a better way to an end, or better ends. Self-correction is the essence of learning and makes possible growth, improvement and progress (1893, CP 6.301). To act reasonably is to act on what best evidence shows to be *true* practical beliefs. To act on practical beliefs one knows is false but politically expedient, or to believe what one wants to believe, or to prevent efforts to determine which are true, or to cast aside evidence that is contrary to what one believes, is to act unreasonably in Peirce's sense. Reasonableness is not only a feature of practical reasoners but a feature of practices such as science, which has demonstrated its success in truth-getting, and has also demonstrated progress in this respect (1898, CP 5.575; 1898, CP5.591; c. 1905, CP 2.769). More broadly, one can also consider natural processes, such as evolution, as a process of self-correction in this regard (1898, CP5.591).

Any end is more likely to be attained if goal-seeking agents act reasonably. That requires that people follow *true* practical beliefs. Self-correction entails commitment to what leads to truth. For example, if people want an effective vaccine against a communicable disease like COVID 19 then they also have to be committed to better methods and norms of inquiry and testing.

This is where the ethical dimension of reasonableness comes into play for Peirce. Truth-getting is an enterprise of inquiry and inquiry, done right, is a collective effort that requires not only effective methodologies, but certain moral sentiments, virtues and norms (1902, CP 7.87). Truth-getting as a collective effort requires all the norms and virtues of cooperation. It cannot be done on one's own. Even if, as Putnam argues, the gambler in Peirce's heaven-or-hell scenario is self-interested, the gambler is part of an inquiry whether the gambler thinks so or not. If unlucky, people will learn from the gambler's mistakes but, if lucky, they will learn as well. In making a choice, the gambler also relies on what has come before. And that is Peirce's point.

Practical Reasoning Made Ethical

The problem with practical reasoning is that even if people are committed to the truth of practical beliefs and the sort of ethical, communal and methodological commitments that entails, without some account of good ends, practical reasoning could still remain instrumental. As Jean Hampton notes, hypothetical imperatives are constitutive of instrumental rationality (1998, pp. 165–166). To abide by the fundamental prudential norm of practical reasoning—that one ought to do what is likely to attain one's end—is likely to attain people's ends, no matter what those ends might be, good or ill. The Nazi bureaucracy had studied what would be most effective in attaining the end of ethnic genocide. Also, practical reasoning does not seem to address any moral constraints on the means to those ends. Science has used all of its wherewithal to develop weapons of mass destruction that could effectively create untold human misery, even end the existence of humankind. Still, since abiding by the fundamental norm of practical reasoning will perforce likely attain *any end*, it is a norm, if followed, would likely attain *any good end*. Thus, it is a norm that is quasi-necessary to attain *good ends*, but not sufficient. It is quasi-necessary because of its statistical nature, in the sense that there is a chance that even doing something unlikely to attain an end, may still result in its attainment. It is not sufficient since it could recommend immoral actions as easily as moral ones.

One can understand Kant's motivation, then, for something like a *categorical* imperative, since it justifies an action independently of the consideration of ends or consequences and, as a result, would avoid the instrumentality of practical reasoning in moral matters. However, if Phillipa Foot is right, all categorical imperatives are hidden hypothetical ones, related to purpose. Just as abiding by the rules of etiquette are categorical in the sense that abiding by them has no other purpose than to abide by them, still they require followers of etiquette to have a desire, or some reason to engage in appropriate etiquette. The same is with morality. Categorical imperatives do not answer the question of why be moral, but they do tell people what they must do to have their actions counted as moral. People could still reject the categorical imperatives of morality if they have no interest in being moral. They could be called moral monsters, but they are still acting within the confines of practical reasoning (1978, pp. 160–161). Although Kant performs an admirable demonstration of how categorical imperatives follow from the concept of an absolutely goodwill, some would argue that it's not clear why people should adopt the stance of a goodwill, freed as it is from all subjective interest in the consequences of action, particularly since it could result in wrongful consequences (1785, p. 55).

Is there a way to make practical reasoning ethical without resorting to categorical imperatives? The problem with practical reasoning is that it treats truth as a means to an end. It constrains reasonable conduct in Peirce's sense to only the consideration of means to ends, whatever those ends may be. Since true practical beliefs are what are likely to attain ends, then truth is in service to those ends. To make practical reasoning ethical, people would need to consider the goodness of ends—not only the goodness of ends but also the righteousness of the means to those ends. But truth in regard to good ends and righteous means is a search for moral truths. As Peirce says, "since pragmaticism makes the purport to consist in a conditional proposition concerning conduct, a sufficiently deliberate consideration of that purport will reflect that the conditional conduct ought to be regulated by an ethical principle." Anticipating the role of esthetics in this matter, Peirce adds that "by further self-criticism may be made to accord with an esthetical ideal" (c. 1905, CP 5.535). "The question of the science of morality," Peirce writes, asks "what are the ideals of conduct most fitting to man and on what principles are they to be allowed to be so? This has been a deep study from the dawn of history" (1903, R453, p. 14). As Kelly Parker argues, "Peirce saw the importance" of the question concerning ". . . what desires we ought to entertain, how we ought acquire them, and the role that our various principles and beliefs ought to play in motivating our actions" (2003, p. 39).

To be ethical, practical reasoning must be constrained by three norms. The first is the just mentioned prudential norm of all hypothetical imperatives or practical beliefs. The second would concern good ends and the third, righteous means to those ends. In that respect, it must function something like the sort of practical reasoning that Aristotle called *phronesis*, or practical wisdom: "[*phronesis*] is the disposition with true reason and ability for *actions* concerning human goods" (*Nicomachean Ethics*, 1140b 20–21). People who have *phronesis* "can aim well at the things which are attainable by action and are best for man" (*Nicomachean Ethics*, 1141b12). Phronesic reasoning is the ability to aim at the right thing and attain it in the right way.

It is the job of the normative sciences of ethics and esthetics to figure out this matter of good ends and righteous means. Peirce explains this in a draft to the Harvard Lectures:

> Normative science ought to examine all questions relating to the possible consistent ends of phenomena. Not merely what the ends are and what are the conditions of conformity to those ends, or their mere quantity of goodness and badness, but also, the diversity in the

> different paths by which such ends may be pursued, and the different stadia in those paths; as well as the different ways in which the ends may be missed. I will not pretend that this description is all that might be desired. On the contrary, here is one of the innumerable points at which my doctrine is not sufficiently worked out.
>
> (1903, R 311, p. 9)

To reiterate what Peirce says in those lectures of 1903:

> *Ethics is the study of what ends of action we are deliberately prepared to adopt.* That is *right action* which is in conformity to ends which we are prepared deliberately to adopt. That is all there *can be* in the notion of righteousness, as it seems to me . . . ends as he is prepared deliberately to adopt as *ultimate*.
>
> (1903, CP 5.130)

Peirce emphasizes that it is important to identify the right ends to pursue:

> we cannot get any clue to the secret of Ethics . . . until we have first made up our formula for what it is that we are prepared to admire. I do not care what doctrine of ethics be embraced, it will always be so. Suppose, for example, our maxim of ethics to be . . . that all our action ought to be directed toward the perpetuation of the biological stock to which we belong. Then the question will arise, on what principle should it be deemed such a fine thing for this stock to survive—or a fine thing at all?
>
> (1903, CP 5.36)

Peirce outlines the division of labor among the normative sciences in terms of these three norms. Logical reasoning in its broadest sense, including the scientific methodologies of induction and abduction, stands in service to practical reasoning—what practical hypotheses, practical maxims, will likely attain an end. Esthetics is to determine which ends are sufficiently admirable and worthy to pursue. Ethics, in turn, is concerned with what ends, among the worthy ones, to deliberately adopt, and to make sure that the ways and means of attaining ends conform to ideals of conduct. Now "the problem of ethics is to ascertain what end is possible," that is, what end among those identified by esthetics as admirable to pursue is possible (1903, CP 5.134). "It is only after the moralist has shown us what is our ultimate aim," Peirce writes, "that the logician can tell how we ought to think in order to conform to that end" (1901, CP 8.158n3). In this way, logical and scientific reasoning are provided the normative constraints that Peirce seeks.

To serve Peirce's interests here, the three norms of practical reasoning made ethical can be folded into one basic norm to consider: *What ought to be done is what is right to do that is also likely to attain what is good to pursue.* This demonstrates a certain ordering among the goals of the normative sciences, so that logical and scientific reasoning is constrained by what ethics and esthetics determine what is best to pursue and the right ways to pursue it. But it is a purely formal principle with no real content as of yet. At least, it provides some guidance to the normative sciences. The job of the normative sciences now is to flesh out that content.

There is a second way to make practical reasoning ethical. This is to employ in practical reasoning the very norms and ethical constraints present in inquiries that seek the truth. Reasonableness in Peirce's sense does entail ethical constraints. To act reasonably is to do what is most conducive to attaining one's end. But doing what is conducive to one's end requires adherence to *true* practical beliefs. Determining which practical beliefs are true is a matter of proper inquiry, a collective effort. It is "rooted in the social principle" (1878, CP 2.654). But proper inquiry, he argues, requires certain moral sentiments such as an intergenerational altruism and love of truth (1868, CP 5.354; 1878, CP 2.654). It also requires certain virtues of inquirers, honesty above all (1901, CP 8.136; 1902, CP 2.82; 1903, CP 1.49). Most importantly it requires certain norms in the practice of inquiry, such as free exchanges of ideas and criticisms without coercion or force (1896, CP 3.433; c. 1902, CP 5.546; c. 1902, CP 5.543; c. 1902, CP 2.315; c. 1908, CP 5.546). In that case, acting reasonably has certain ethical commitments that constrain means to ends. But, as just noted, if restricted to the matter of practical beliefs, it still leaves practical reasoning merely instrumental.

But what if communities at large adopt these sentiments, virtues and norms? If the norms that guide inquiry also guide the institutions and practices of a community would it transform the communities ethically? Peirce seems to think so (c. 1902, CP 7.54).

To transform communities to communities of inquiry means that they would have to adopt truth not only in service to means but also to ends. But also, if truth is to be an end, then that requires a community of inquiry to seek such truths. In this way, the two paths out of the instrumentalism of practical reasoning merge. Since the pursuit of truth, both of means and ends requires a proper community of inquiry, then both work effectively together to figure out which ends are good to pursue and what are the righteous means by which to pursue them. The advantage of their conjunction is that the norms of inquiry provide the basic norms by which such a process of inquiry can be guided.

6 Moral Realism and Moral Truth

If ethical reasoning is concerned with good ends and righteous means, how is it that ends and means will be determined to be good and righteous? For moral realists, the claim that an end is good is to assert a moral truth, and the job of ethical reasoning is to sort out which moral claims are true from those that are false. In the empirical realm, this is a task analogous to Peirce's second branch of semiotics—critical logic. It is concerned with "the theory of the conditions of truth" (1902, CP 2.93). If there is a parallel between the organization of the normative science of logic and that of ethics, then ethical reasoning should be concerned with the conditions of moral truth. Indeed, Peirce notes this parallel as "almost exact" (1903, CP 1.608).

Peirce's Moral Realism

Peirce is a realist if ever there was one, and it can be supposed that he holds to a moral realism (Mayorga, 2012). Peirce's realism developed over time and involved a move from counting only generals as real to one which, by his own lights, involved an "extreme" form of realism. Peirce had become what Max Fisch called a "three category realist" (1967, p. 195). Not only are generals real, but existents and possibilities, individuals and qualities—in Peirce's parlance, thirds, seconds and firsts, would be counted as real (c. 1906, CP 5.470; Murphey, 1993, pp. 123–150; Fisch, 1967, pp. 184–200).

As interesting as it might be to recount the intricacies of the development of Peirce's realism, it may be more fruitful for purposes of explaining his ethical theory how it is situated among contemporary positions on this matter. Moral realism is, of course, opposed to all varieties of anti-realism. These include versions of noncognitivism, such as emotive theories of truth, where moral claims are merely expressions of approval or disapproval rather than truth claims (Stevenson, 1937). But it also includes moral sentimentalism of the Humean kind, in which desire or sentiment defines what is good (Parfit, 2011, 2, pp. 378–379). This is consonant with a certain sort of subjectivism in which people have the most reason to do whatever would best fulfill what they desire (Parfit, 2011, 1, p. 1). Realism also stands against all forms of non-objectivism, such as the relativism of Gilbert Harman (1996) and David Velleman (2013), where moral truths are considered to be culture-and-time-dependent. It is also opposed to so-called error theory of J.L. Mackie, which claims that, based on the wide cultural disagreements on moral claims, and the very strangeness or "queerness" of moral properties, that the search for moral truths is misguided in the way in which search for supernatural properties might be (1977).

There are three claims that mark traditional *moral* realism. First, normative claims can be true or false. "If there were no such normative truths," Derek Parfit declares, "nothing would matter, and we would have no reasons to try to decide how to live" (2011, 2, p. 21). Second, most moral realists argue that there are "stance-independent" moral properties, objective moral properties against which claims about things are made independently of how anyone might believe it so (Shafer-Landau, 2003, p. 15). As such they serve to adjudicate between those claims that are true and those that are false. Thirdly, many moral realists argue that goodness (or badness) is a real property of actions or decisions. Moral cognitivists, such as Derek Parfit (2011) may subscribe to the first thesis but want to avoid the ontological commitments of at least the third thesis (Parfit, 2011, 3, pp. 3–4). Non-natural moral realists who commit to the third thesis are what Parfit calls metaphysical non-naturalists, who believe there are "ontologically weighty non-natural entities," which naturalists would find "mysterious" (2011, 3, p. 60). Russ Shafer-Landau argues that contractualists such as John Rawls (1971) or T.M. Scanlon (2000) are committed to moral truths, but not the second claim of stance-independence since, in a certain sense, moral truth is constituted by human agreement (2003, p. 14).

Peirce seems to stand with the three claims of traditional moral realism Peirce certainly recognizes that there is "ethical truth" as one sort of truth (1906, CP 5.570). Since the parallel between logic and ethics is almost exact, and (critical) logic is concerned with the conditions of truth, it can be supposed that ethics is concerned with the conditions of *moral* truths. As Peirce says "the same definitions [of positive scientific truth] equally hold in the normative sciences" (1901, CP 5.566). According to that definition, "truth is that concordance of an abstract statement with the ideal limit towards which endless investigation would tend to bring scientific belief." (1901, CP 5.565). This is known otherwise as his *convergence theory of truth*. And he explicitly states here that it also holds for normative claims. For example, "if a moralist describes an ideal as the *summum bonum* . . . the perfect truth of his statement requires . . . [that] the future development of man's moral nature will only lead to a firmer satisfaction with the described ideal." In that case, Peirce says, "the doctrine is true" (1901, CP 5.566). He says something similar in a letter to Lady Welby:

"that to the acceptance of which as a basis of conduct any person you please would ultimately come if he pursued his inquiries far enough . . . that alone is which I call truth" (1958, VC, p. 398). He writes elsewhere,

> now the different sciences deal with different kinds of truth; mathematic truth is one thing, ethical truth is another . . . but all those different conceptions have in common something very marked and clear. We all hope that the different scientific inquiries in which we are severally engaged are going ultimately to lead to some definitely established conclusion. . . . Agreement with that ultimate proposition that we look forward to,—agreement with that, whatever it may turn out to be, is the scientific truth.
>
> (1901, CP 7.187)

Peirce also clearly adheres to the stance-independence of truth claims, including moral truth claims as it would be supposed: "There are real things, whose characters are entirely independent of our opinions about them" (1877, CP 5.384). "The real is that which is not whatever we happen to think it, but is unaffected by what we may think of it" (1871, CP 8.12). He remarks that "it is true that the majority of writers on ethics in the past have made the root of morals subjective: but the best opinion is very plainly moving in the opposite direction" (1902, CP 2.156).

In regard to the third thesis of moral realism, Peirce adheres to a form of realism which he identifies as "scholastic," after John Duns Scotus (1903, CP 5.77n1; 1905, CP 5.423). It supposes that generals are real, as opposed to nominalists who argue that generals are simply cognitive abstractions. The only thing that is real for nominalists are individuals, as Peirce interprets them. Early in his thought, Peirce argued that only generals are real but, since generals are operative in nature, they operate in and through individuals, Peirce came to realize that individuals must also be counted as real, although not in the sense in which generals are (1903, CP 8.266; 1903, CP 5.101; 1905, CP 5.503).

Generals are manifested in the dispositions or habits of individuals things of a kind. The disposition of opium for example to put people to sleep is due to a general property ("a dormative property") operative in nature (1902, CP 4.234). Natural law in this sense is the tendency of things to take on habits. A habit "denotes such a specialization, original or acquired, of the nature of a man, or an animal, or a vine, or a crystallizable chemical substance, or anything else, that he or it will behave, or always tend to behave, in a way describable in general terms upon every occasion (or upon a considerable proportion of the occasions) that may present itself of a generally describable character" (c. 1902, CP 5.538). For Peirce, such a realism makes science possible since "habits produce statistical uniformities" (1903, CP 6.97; Feibleman, 1970, p. 193). And without such statistical uniformities induction would not be possible

(1892, CP 6.262). Without induction, as the basis of all ampliative reasoning, inquiries would fail and truth would not be known. As Peirce sees it, the possibility of truth assumes this sort of realism.

Since the formation of habits is part and parcel of human life and conduct, then if moral realism holds in Peirce's sense, then generals are also operative in the sphere of human conduct. Whether it is the conduct of individuals, the formation of practices and institutions of communities, or moral life in general, these will tend to take on habits. To the extent that these habits become more and more generalizable over time, either as "original" through instincts or "acquired" through inquiries and experiments of living, that would be an indication of its truth. The more indurate and persistent the habit, the greater likelihood of its truth. From this, it can be inferred that what is morally true is what is "generalizable" in the way of human conduct, that is, what can hold together in the long run in the form of habits of conduct developed over time. Just as "general principles are really operative in nature," it can be supposed that general rules of conduct are those really operative in the human condition and would be realized in the long run (1903, CP 5.101).

Moral realists also divide between normative naturalism and non-naturalism. Whereas naturalists argue that normative properties or facts can be described, explained, reduced to, or identified as natural properties or facts, non-naturalists argue that the normative is irreducible and primitive. The defense of non-naturalism was made famous by G.E. Moore's so-called open question argument, which claimed that all naturalist properties are descriptive and descriptive claims, such as the good is the maximization of utility are subject to the question of whether the maximization of utility is good (1903, sect. 10). Moore argued instead for the intuitive, indefinable nature of the good. Weaknesses in Moore's argument are well known. Among these is the argument that Moore's open question rests on the assumption that, in his example, goodness and maximization of utility means the same thing. But it's quite possible that they do not so that moral inquiry could come to the discoverable claim that the maximization of utility is the good, much in the way in which it was discovered that water is H_2O. The property identity of water and H_2O is found *a posteriori* (Brink, 1989).

Some moral cognitivists, such as Derek Parfit, also defend a non-naturalist account of normativity with something of a version of the open question argument. Parfit argues that normative facts are simply different *in kind* to natural facts since they provide reasons and commitments for what is good to do; natural facts describe the way the world is (2011, 2, pp. 324–325). He argues that no natural fact can provide a normative reason for action. The fact, for example, that jumping from a burning building will best fulfill the desire not to die in a fire, is still not necessarily a reason why one *ought* to jump, even if it's empirically true that it would likely save one's life (2011, 2, pp. 326–327). It's still an open question as to whether one ought to jump, even if it's factually true that doing so will save one's life. One might argue, more generally, whether one ought to do what is likely to attain what one desires. The decisive reason to jump is not that it will likely save one's life, but that one *ought to* jump because it would save one's life. Parfit claims this "normativity objection" to normative naturalism is "decisive" (2011, Vol. 2, p. 328).

Naturalists divide, further, into analytic and non-analytic camps. Analytic naturalists, such as Frank Jackson (1998) and Michael Smith (2000), hold that the identity claims between normative and natural concepts are analytical truths. Jackson in particular argues that if something is right then it has a certain pattern or organization of natural properties, much in the way in which density is a ratio of mass and volume (2012, p. 78). He argues that, if moral properties are analytically identical to natural ones, then because there is such an *a priori* connection, the open question argument wouldn't hold. Using the same analogy, just as insight into the concept of density is obtained by showing that it is nothing more than the ratio of mass and volume, then showing that the good is maximizing utility, for example, is just as insightful and not circular. Jackson argues in particular for a functionalist account of the normative, so that "what is a priori according to moral functionalism is not that rightness is such and such a descriptive property, but that A is right if and only if it has whatever property it is that plays the rightness role in mature folk morality, and it is an a posteriori matter what that property is" (1998, p. 151). Mature folk morality is what folk morality—"our present raft of intuitions"—"would turn into in the limit under critical reflection" (1998, p. 139).

Non-analytic naturalists, such as David Copp hold that the relation between normative and natural properties is empirical (2012). If a property is natural, then empirical evidence is relevant to the justification of any belief about it—the evidence established "by means of empirical observation and standard modes of inductive inference" (2004, p. 13). Most normative naturalists argue that normative properties are natural ones and, as such, they can be the subject of, and explained in the natural sciences. This was originally the account given by G.E. Moore (1903, p. 13). Russ Shafer-Landau defines normative naturalism precisely in these terms, where moral properties "would figure ineliminably in perfected versions of the natural and social sciences" (2003, p. 59). This is repeated by a number of others (Jackson, 2012, p. 70; Harman, 2012, p. 10; Parfit, 2011, Vol. 2, p. 305).

For Copp, normative facts are simply those facts that will solve normative problems. For example, one important problem for all societies is the problem of sociality, that is the problem of how to minimize conflict and maximize cooperation. The solution of "normative governance" as he calls it, is to determine which among moral codes solves that problem best. Since the best solution requires certain actions, those are the actions people are required to do (2012, p. 38). Normative commitments fall out of what is likely to attain certain ends.

Where would Peirce fit among the different categories of moral realists? Although there may be a way to infer some form of normative naturalism in Peirce, it's not entirely clear whether that is his position (Liszka, 2014b). As discussed earlier, he characterizes the normative science of ethics as both formal and positive, the latter meaning that it rests on experience. If so, does it rest on natural facts? It seems so. Peirce says of the normative sciences, "although they ask, not what *is* but what *ought to* be, nevertheless are positive sciences since it is by asserting positive, categorical truth that they are able to show that what they call good really is so; and the right reason, right effort, and right being, of which they treat, derive that character from positive categorical fact" (1903, CP 5.39).

Yet, in his classification of the sciences, he does not treat it as an idioscopic or empirical science, since it utilizes a mode of observation, coenoscopic, that appears to be more analytic in methodology, rather than empirical. Since the hallmark of normative naturalism is that ethical matters could be in principle the subject of natural sciences, then it would appear that he is not a normative naturalist of that sort, if one at all. Peirce recognizes a version of the naturalistic fallacy, in the sense that a natural disposition in acting or thinking, even if widely present, is not a sound reason to claim that it is ethically or logically good (1903, HL, p. 210). Moreover, he seems to treat the modalities of what must be, what appears to be, what ought to be and what is, as distinct, and perhaps irreducibly so. He does scold John Dewey for making logic into a naturalist study. Peirce tells him in a letter that "[y]ou propose to substitute for the Normative Science [of logic] which in my judgment is the greatest need of our age a "Natural History" of thought or of experience" (1904, CP 8.239). He continues,

> it is one of the characteristics of all normative science that it does not concern itself in the least with what actually takes place in the universe. . . . But as to particular and variable facts, no normative science has any concern with them, further than to remark that they form a constant constituent of the phenomenon.
>
> (1904, CP 8.239)

On the other hand, Peirce argues in The Fixation of Belief and elsewhere that the scientific method is the best method for fixing beliefs, beliefs that would presumably include moral beliefs. Since that is one of the principal features of normative naturalism, that would seem to push him toward that camp. Moreover, his moral sentimentalism is a naturalist theory, since it supposes that moral sentiments are the result of natural evolution, and still evolving. Since he claims that the instincts are better guides to moral conduct than ethics in its current state, this would suggest that natural evolution has a tendency to produce sound moral habits which, of course, seems to rub up against the naturalistic fallacy. Additionally, at least in some of his earlier work on practical ethics ("pragmatics"), Peirce sees a tie between pragmatics and what he calls empirics—which includes logic, metaphysics and the nomological sciences of psychology and physics. Pragmatics is characterized as "the study of how we ought to behave in the light of the truths of empirics" (1896, R 1345, p. 1). Finally, the pragmatic maxim shows that the truth of any practical maxim, any hypothetical imperative, rests on the truth of its corresponding empirical one. It is the fact that diamonds cut glass that makes it right to use a diamond cutter to cut glass if that is one's end. So, at least to that extent, ethical reasoning is dependent on scientific, that is, empirical reasoning. In other words, to the extent that people abide by the norm of reasonableness—people *ought* to do what will likely attain their ends—such a normative claim has its warrant in empirical facts as to what *will likely* attain their ends.

All of this is to say that it is unclear where Peirce would sit in the taxonomy of moral realists, at least in regard to the question of normative naturalism.

Peirce's Convergence Theory of Truth

Since ethical reasoning is not only concerned with what will likely attain ends, but whether the ends sought are good, and the means righteous, how are the truths of these claims to be determined? In general, Peirce holds to a *convergence theory of truth*. The latter, in so many words, argues that whatever is true will be the result of inquiries done rightly over time, indicated by a convergence of belief among inquirers. True claims will tend to agreement, false ones to discord. "*Where there is no real doubt or disagreement there is no question and can be no real investigation*" (1869, W2, p. 354). Can this be translated to claims about what is right and good?

The convergence theory of truth argues that inquiry done well enough and persisted sufficiently long enough would result in true claims about the matter of investigation (Hookway, 2002, p. 49; Misak, 1991, p. ix). What is true is the final result of such inquiries. "If," Peirce says, "we can find out the right method of thinking and can follow it out . . . then truth can be nothing more nor less than the last result to which the following out of this method would ultimately carry us" (1906, CP 5.553). The *locus classicus* of this statement is found in "How to Make Our Ideas Clear," where Peirce claims that "the opinion which is fated to be ultimately agreed to by all who investigate, is what we mean by the truth" (1877, CP 5.407). This is not to say that mere consensus or agreement among inquirers constitutes truth. In this context, Peirce is claiming what truth *means* by using the pragmatic maxim—which is the subject of the article. What something means is clearest when expressed in its practical, observable consequences. Peirce realized that the practical consequences of true claims are that they tend to bring inquiries to fruition and settle opinion. Consequently, consensus of opinion is an indication of a claim's truth—not the consensus of anyone, but by those engaged in its inquiry by means of the best methods of inquiry.

Peirce argues that if good methods of reasoning are utilized in the process of inquiry and "duly persisted in," then this will "lead to a result indefinitely approximating to the truth in the long run" (1902, CP 2.781; 1900, CP 8.112; 1903, CP 5.170; 1892, CP 6.40). The good methods of reasoning for science are the interconnected processes of abduction, deduction and induction. "Induction," as he says, "if . . . persisted in . . . will in the long run yield the truth, or an indefinite approximation to the truth" (c. 1897, CP 2.269). Empirical claims are tested first, in accord with the pragmatic maxim, by being formulated in terms of their observable, practical consequences; second, sufficient sampling done to observe whether those consequences occur frequently enough to warrant not rejecting that claim.

The eventual success of inductive sampling to light upon the truth, *ceteris paribus*, is guaranteed mathematically by the Law of Large Numbers. The Law of Large Numbers is an intuitive, well-established theorem at the foundation of all statistical theory. An initial proof of the law was given by Jacob Bernoulli in 1713, expanded in the 19th century by Siméon Poisson (1837), followed by refinements in the 20th century by Emil Borel (1909), among others. Simply stated, it expresses a very intuitive concept, namely, that if an inquiry is attempting to determine the proportion of a variable in a population, as the number of samples of that population increases, the mean of those samples will approach the true proportion of that variable in the population. Said more conveniently, as the samples increase, the mean of the samples will *converge* to the true value in the population. Or said a bit more cautiously, as the samples increase, the difference between the mean value of the sample and true value of the variable in the population will diminish, that is, will *approximate* to the true value. As Jacob Bernoulli noted in a letter to Gottfried Leibniz that "even the stupidest man knows by some instinct of nature per se and by no previous instruction, that the greater the number of confirming observations, the surer the conjecture (1713, Chapt. 4). As Peirce writes, "induction . . . is mathematically certain . . . that the general character of a limited experience will, as that experience is prolonged, approximate to the character of what will be true in the long run, if anything is true in the long run" (1903, CP 6.100). The French mathematician, Émile Borel, proved the Strong Law of Large Numbers in 1909, which pertains specifically to inductive sampling. Whereas the weak law of Bernoulli and Poisson cannot guarantee that, even after a large number of samples, the mean of the samples will continue to converge toward the mean of the population without aberrations, Borel's strong law does show this. As Peirce explains this simply:

> As we go on drawing inference after inference of the given kind, during the first ten or hundred cases, the ratio of successes may be expected to show some considerable fluctuations; but when we come into the thousands and millions, these fluctuations become less and less; and if we continue long enough the ratio will approximate towards a fixed limit.
>
> (1878, CP 2.650)

Peirce gives an intuitive example of this in a rather long passage, concerning a hypothesis about the distance of an observed fire:

> Let the second man, having seen the fire, ask "Would you say, now, that that fire was about three miles away?" This virtually suggests that if the first man or any other man will fill his purse, and take ship, and go to Westminster, and break into the houses of Parliament, and bring away the standard yard, and lay it down repeatedly on the ground from where the two stand to where the fire is, and utter the cardinal numbers in their order as the successive layings down proceed, or if he will perform any other experiment virtually amounting to that, then the last number uttered might be 5280, and if it should prove to be a number near to that, he might not be surprised. Extensive experience leads us to expect that if an experiment virtually amounting to that were tried a hundred times, different numbers would be obtained which would cluster about one of them, and that among a million trials the clustering would be still more marked, according to a law well-known to mathematicians. It is possible, no doubt, that if our experience were still more extensive, we should find that if the experiment were tried, say, more than a billion times, then a new phenomenon would emerge and the oftener it was tried the less marked might grow the clustering. Our hope, however, in endeavoring to make a measurement extremely precise, is that there is a certain value toward which the resultant of all the experiments would approximate more and more, without limitation. Having that hope . . . whenever we endeavor to state the distance, all that we aim at is to state as nearly as possible what that ultimate result of experience would be. We do not aim at anything quite beyond experience, but only at the limiting result toward which all experience will approximate,—or, at any rate, would approximate, were the inquiry to be prosecuted without cessation.
>
> (c. 1900: CP 8.112)

The "law well known to mathematicians" to which Peirce refers is of course the Law of Large Numbers. Since, as Peirce argues, all ampliative reasoning is from sampling, or inference from part to whole, and reasoning is the means by which truth is attained, then truth rests on such sampling and, thus, on the Law of Large Numbers (1892, CP 6.40; 1868, CP 5.346; 1868, CP 5.352), which he sometimes called "the law of high numbers" (1901, CP 7.221). "All positive reasoning," as Peirce says, is "of the nature of judging the proportion of something in a whole collection by the proportion found in a sample" (1897, CP 1.141). "Judging of the statistical composition of a whole lot from a sample is judging by a method which will be right on the average in the long run . . . . " (c. 1896, CP 1.93). "Since the method of induction must generally approximate to that truth, that is a sufficient justification for the use of that method" (1903, CP 6.100).

Besides a consensus among inquirers, there are two other observable consequences that could be inferred about any claim that would turn out to be true. One is that inquiries or inquirers, independently of one another, would come to a similar result. Peirce argues:

> human opinion universally tends in the long run to a definite form, which is the truth. Let any human being have enough information and exert enough thought upon any question, and the result will be that he will arrive at a certain definite conclusion, which is the same that any other mind will reach under sufficiently favorable circumstances. (1871, CP 8.12)

This would explain well-documented phenomena of simultaneous discoveries in science and technology, as proposed by Robert Merton:

> The pages of the history of science record thousands of instances of similar discoveries having been made by scientists working independently of one another. Sometimes the discoveries are simultaneous or almost so; sometimes a scientist will make a new a discovery which, unknown to him, somebody else had made years before. Such occurrences suggest that discoveries become virtually inevitable when prerequisite kinds of knowledge and tools accumulate in man's cultural store and when the attention of an appreciable number of investigators becomes focused on a problem, by emerging social needs, by developments internal to the science, or by both. Not only does this account for the many cases of contemporaneous but independent discoveries of similar matters, such as the calculus, but it covers the more mundane claim that independent repetitions of the same experiment with similar results tend to confirm a hypothesis over time. (1971, p. 371)

A third practical consequence can be inferred about true claims. If inquiries are employing proper methods of inquiry such as induction and given, by the Law of Large Number, that continued inductive sampling over time approximates closer and closer to the actual ratio of features in the population sampled, then it would be expected that there would be progressive approximations to the truth as inquiry proceeds. In other words, there would be a progressive convergence toward true claims over time. As Peirce explains, "the validity of an inductive argument consists . . . in the fact that it pursues a method which, if duly persisted in, must, in the very nature of things, lead to a result indefinitely approximating to the truth in the long run" (1902, CP 2.781; see also 1903, CP 5.170; 1892, CP 6.40). In more sweeping terms, if methods of inquiry are indeed truth-apt and, by their nature, approximate to the truth, then there should be visible signs of progress in inquiries—progress understood in the sense that claims that replace previous claims have improved upon earlier ones.

The Convergence Theory of Moral Truth

If the convergence theory of truth can provide an account of empirical truth, can it also provide one for moral claims? Would ethical reasoning, well-done and persisted in result in moral truths in a way that is parallel to logical, scientific reasoning? Peirce seems to think so:

> Now, just as conduct controlled by ethical reason tends toward fixing certain habits of conduct, the nature of which . . . does not depend upon any accidental circumstances, and in that sense may be said to be destined; so thought controlled by rational experimental logic, tends to the fixation of certain opinions, equally destined, the nature of which will be the same in the end, however the perversity of thought of whole generations may cause the postponement of the ultimate fixation.
>
> (1905, CP 5.430)

As he says elsewhere, "good morals are the kind of human behavior that would come to be approved if studies of right behavior were carried sufficiently far" (c. 1911, R 673, p. 12). What Peirce means by "studies" here is unclear, but as he writes elsewhere:

> we have considered positive scientific truth. But the same definitions equally hold in the normative sciences. If a moralist describes an ideal as the *summum bonum*, in the first place, the perfect truth of his statement requires that it should involve the confession that the perfect doctrine can neither be stated nor conceived. If, with that allowance, the future development of man's moral nature will only lead to a firmer satisfaction with the described ideal, the doctrine is true.
>
> (1906, CP 5.566)

This suggests that the truth of a moral claim is found in how it plays out in experiments of living, the various ways in which people organize their lives and practices. As noted in the analysis of normative sciences, Peirce claims that ethical study employs what he calls *coenoscopic* observation. It "uses the most rational methods it can devise, for finding out the little that can as yet be found out about the universe of mind and matter from those observations which every person can make in every hour of his waking life" (1905, CP 1.126), that is, in "common experience" (1903, CP 1.182). "The only solid foundation for ethics lies in those facts of everyday life" (1901, CP 8.158). In other words, just as naturalistic sciences draw on experiments with nature, so an ethical science must draw on the data concerning practical life, the ways and means by which, over time, people conduct their lives in the practices and institutions of the communities in which they live. Whatever righteous means there are, what ideals of conduct might be discovered, what ends should be pursued, would be disclosed through the study of the way in which folks do, in fact, try to figure these things out.

In this regard, if there is a parallel between laboratory experiments and experiments of living, this might support a claim that there is a parallel between the convergence theory of truth in the natural world and the practice of moral life. Inquiries into empirical truth and inquiries into moral truth should share some larger similarities. Peirce provides a good description of the framework of inquiry:

> All our knowledge of the laws of nature is analogous to knowledge of the future, inasmuch as there is no direct way in which the laws can become known to us. We here proceed by experimentation. That is to say, we guess out the laws bit by bit. We ask, what if we were to vary our procedure a little? Would the result be the same? We try it. If we are on the wrong track, an emphatic negative soon gets put upon the guess, and so our conceptions gradually get nearer and nearer right. The improvements of our inventions are made in the same manner. The theory of natural selection is that nature proceeds by similar experimentation to adapt a stock of animals or plants precisely to its environment, and to keep it in adaptation to the slowly changing environment.
>
> (1902, CP 2.86)

Philip Kitcher, who advocates what he calls a "pragmatic naturalism" (2011, pp. 5–6), characterizes ethical inquiry in similar terms:

> We make scientific experiments by trying to produce a particular change in the world, and we judge the success of our experiments by observing whether or not that change has occurred. In similar fashion, moral experiments consist in changing the social world . . . .

> We judge the outcome of these changes by trying to live with them, checking whether their consequences fit with our other habits and impulses, leaving us in a situation that is less problematic for us than that in which we began, or whether our problems have only increased, so that we find diminished opportunities for satisfying conduct.
> (2012, p. 337)

In experiments of living, through ethical reasoning, people develop habits of conduct and practices that delimit the ways and means to attain certain ends generally held provisionally to be good. They are constituted by certain practical hypotheses, constrained by certain ideals of conduct that make claims about how best to attain those ends. The ends themselves are proposed as hypotheses as well. As they are lived, they are corrected when they fall short and, in many cases, discarded if even improvements fail to satisfy. Peirce argues "Common sense corrects itself, improves its conclusions," so "we see social, political, religious common sense modifying itself insensibly in course of generations, ideas of rights of man acquiring new meaning, thaumaturgic elements of Christianity sinking, spiritual rising in religious consciousness" (c. 1905, CP 6.573).

Suppose, for example, a community is pursuing, among several ends, the end of safety. Many would claim that a safe community is a good, intuitive end. This is rather vague, and what it means to be a safe community would be realized by the means through which it is achieved. How is the end to be represented? Some might say that indication of a safe community is low crime rates. That could be further clarified in terms of the type of crimes that need to be reduced. Suppose the goal is to reduce the crime rate for property theft in the community. Practical reasoning would be engaged in formulating practical hypotheses which, if followed, would predict a reduction in the crime rate in the community. In this way, the practical hypothesis is set up like any empirical hypothesis, but where what is predicted is tied to some end. Suppose the practical hypothesis is that community policing would result in lower crime rates. But, in the context of ethical reasoning, this practical hypothesis has to be considered against ideals of conduct that are part of the existing set of standards. Suppose the practical hypothesis proposed instead is the execution of any thief, no matter what is stolen or the manner in which it is stolen. It might reduce the crime rate for theft, but say it violates a standard of conduct that has won wide approval in the community and has worked well in regulating retributive justice practices, namely, the punishment should be proportionate to the crime. How are the alternatives to be tested in these experiments of living?

If there is a parallel between logical, scientific reasoning and ethical reasoning as Peirce suggests, then the convergence theory of truth should apply also to the matter of such ethical reasoning. Recall that Peirce expresses convergence in three different but equivalent ways. One indication of true claims is approximation. Inductively, that is understood as the case where continued sampling does not appear to change the expected value (1878, CP 2.748). In more general terms, it is indicated by progressive changes in hypotheses. New hypotheses solve some of the anomalies and problems of previous ones, and people can witness a train of progressively better hypotheses and theories in that respect over time.

In applying this to ethical reasoning, it might be said that one can also witness a progression in the norms that govern institutions and practices and general principles of conduct that people adopt over time. One indication of a good ethical norm, then, is whether it has reached the limit of its improvability. Practically speaking, this means that significant changes would make matters worse and, relative to its domains, there is no known alternative that could do better. For example, Philip Kitcher notes that among the earliest known legal codes in the Ancient Near East, the *lex talionis* is interpreted rather literally. If someone causes the death of "the daughter of a senior," then "that man's daughter is to be put to death" (2011, p. 140; Pritchard, 1950, pp. 170, 175). Most would say without hesitation these days that although this is a proportionate retribution for the crime (assuming the death caused intentionally), it is unjust relative to the daughter since she has committed no crime. This interpretation seems to vanish a few centuries later so that "now it is the perpetrator of the deed who must pay in the manner, and to the extent, of the damage inflicted: his or her life must be exacted to pay for the life of the victim" (2011, p. 140). The fact that this view, that the perpetrator should be punished rather than someone innocent of the crime, seems to have persisted in most institutionalized systems of justice hence. Kitcher concludes that "more than two millennia on, we may demur at the thought that this is the final word on the matter, but it is hard to resist seeing the change as an improvement," perhaps, it could be said even more strongly, the limit of its improvability (2011, p. 141).

A second sense of convergence to the truth of a moral claim is the idea that any inquirer or any community of such inquirers with good methods should reach the same conclusion as any other community with good methods, independently of one another (1878, CP 5.407). Peirce argues in a letter to Lady Welby that truth is "something public." By that "it must mean that to the acceptance of which as a basis of conduct any person you please would ultimately come if he pursued his inquiries far enough—yes, every rational being, however prejudiced he might be at the outset" (1908, VC, p. 398). In this regard, one indication that an ethical norm is righteous would be if different communities, unknown to each other, have adopted and retained similar norms. Peirce points to prohibitions against incest as one such case but he doesn't think prohibitions against suicide meets that criteria (1905, CP 5.444–5.445).

Although incest prohibitions have been shown to be relatively universal for certain categories of kin, and with some exceptions among Inca,

Hawaiian and ancient Egyptian royal families, demonstrating ethical "universals" is a tricky, complicated business. Some have claimed, for example, those incest prohibitions are common only because they are genetically determined, therefore, not a deliberate cultural construction as other norms might be (Read, 2014). Peirce would say whether it is through biological or cultural evolution, convergence is convergence. Nonetheless, it is the ostensible variety of norms among different cultures that have given ammunition for relativists, and fodder for Mackie's error theory. It is much easier to point to normative differences than similarities among cultures.

Although this second test for convergence would be more patent if specific norms could be found to be held by a statistically significant number of cultures, that approach may reflect more the lack of sophisticated thinking among relativists. One approach to the question of normative commonalities among cultures might be something analogous to the difference between deep and surface grammar in linguistic theories. The approach of some researchers is to suggest that there are commonalities to communities, and the differences among cultures are a matter of how such commonalities get configured in the moral life of the community. Jonathan Haidt, for example, argues something in this manner. There are common "moral foundations" across cultures, but the variety of norms observed in cultures is due to how these play out in the culture's institutions and practices. But whatever norms exist can be translated back to these foundations. Among these are care/harm, fairness/reciprocity, in-group/loyalty, authority/respect and purity/sanctity (2012, pp. 123–124). Similarly, normative differences among individuals within a culture are due to differences in the configuration of these moral foundations. Even though there may be a divide, for example, between the moral beliefs and norms of liberal-leaning and conservative-leaning folks, each can be traced back to some configuration of care, fairness, loyalty, obedience to authority and purity. Based on thousands of samples across cultures, Haidt argues that conservative folks tend to emphasize all five moral foundations with roughly equal consideration, whereas liberals tend to emphasize care/harm and fairness/reciprocity as most important to moral life (2012, pp. 153–154). Thus, norms of loyalty to a group and fair treatment within that group are strong moral norms for conservatives, but loyalty is preempted by fairness for liberals.

One might also have the faith of Michael Walzer who argues for a "minimum morality":

> Minimal morality is very important, both for the sake of criticism and for the sake of solidarity. . . . It consists in principles and roles that are reiterated in different times and places, and that are seen to be similar even though they are expressed in different idioms and reflect different histories and different version of the world.
>
> (Walzer, 1994, pp. 16–17)

As James Wallace argues in reference to Walzer's thesis, "human beings are everywhere alike in that they live in communities, use language and cooperate with one another . . . and certain norms are absolutely necessary for such cultural artifacts" (2009, p. 74).

Research by Oliver Curry and his colleagues, for example, takes up this approach. They focus on those aspects of morality which positively promote cooperation, and they show that cooperation is statistically held up as a positive moral norm in most cultures. They then define cooperation in terms of seven well-established types to show that such norms as helping kin, helping one's group, reciprocation, bravery in defense of the group, deference to superiors, dividing disputed resources and respecting property, are considered morally good in the 60 societies that constituted their sample. Although these are all considered good, they are manifested differently through the institutions and practices of the society (Curry et al., 2019).

These examples certainly do not prove there are moral universals (or more accurately, a significant number of commonalities among large samples of cultures)—and that's not the intent here—but they, at least, demonstrate some plausibility to this second indication of convergence as a test of moral truth.

The third indicator is a convergence of a belief among those who have inquired into the matter over time (1877, CP 5.407). Similarly, an indication of a righteous norm would be that more and more people adopt it as a standard or best practice over time. It is something that informs the conduct of a wide swath of the community. In other words, people tend to agree that it is a good norm of conduct. Not merely agree to it in the sense in which people go along with what's popular or conventional, but have reasons for agreeing to it, or at least no good reasons for rejecting it, and are willing to live by it.

People tend, at least initially, to believe the norms in which they are raised, the norms they have inherited. A better test would be wide acceptance of a change to a norm that has been held for some time. In that case, people must choose between the norms they have inherited, and the new ones being brought to the fore. In that way, there is more deliberation and reflection and real opportunity to consider alternatives. On a global scale, the decline of monarchies in favor of republics and democracies may be one example. Granted that there are also many tyrannies that have taken the place of monarchies, still a form of government emerged and was deliberately preferred to the older, traditional monarchy, at least as indicated by the number of democracies and republics in the world in recent times. As of 2017, of 167 known countries about 96 are democracies of some kind. This has been a growing trend particularly since World War II and the fall of Soviet Union (Desilver, 2019). There are about 44 monarchies in the world, but only about 4 or 5 are considered absolute monarchies, the remainder are constitutional or ceremonial in nature.

American history, as most community histories, is punctuated by these moments where long-held norms are changed, sometimes violently, sometimes peacefully, but always with resistance. Yet once in place and lived through for some period of time, reasons to return the old ways are hard to find. Practices, such as slavery, move from morally acceptable to morally questionable, to a near consensus that it is morally wrong. Same with the case of woman's suffrage, or the more recent turnaround on moral approval of LGBTQ marriage. In 2001, 35% of the U.S. population favored same-sex marriage, by 2019 that nearly doubled to 61% (Pew Research Center, 2019). It's hard to imagine that, given the organization of practices, laws, and attitudes that the United States would return to a slave society, or force women to give up their right to vote. Once the consequences of change in practice are in place, and people live through those consequences, it becomes clearer why the old ways are no longer preferable. As Kitcher argues, although preference for the new versus the old ways is not a perfect indication of moral progress, it is at least an indication (2011, p. 175).

Preference must be at least one factor since it would be odd that people would choose norms and practices that they did not prefer in some way to known alternatives. As Peirce says, one key criterion in identifying ends was that people found it "fine" and "admirable" (1903, CP 1.608). It may also depend to some extent on whether the preferences are reason-based, or unreflective taste. But most would say, the lived experience of woman not being able to vote prior to 1920 and after 1920 might be sufficient grounds for the preference. All of the standard reasons for objecting to women suffrage have been proven doubtful through the actual experiments of living with woman's suffrage.

For example, J.B. Sanford (1911), Chairmen of the Democratic Caucus, prepared a list of reasons against women's suffrage in 1911. Among these are that a woman's place is in the home, and her absence would be to the detriment of the children. Her place in the home has been set by God. Womanly women oppose suffrage. Women are exalted by men and having them mix in with men in the political arena would cause them to lose that respect and regard. Divorce has greatly increased in those states where equal suffrage has been enacted. Pseudoscientific claims were also prevalent. William Sedgwick, professor at MIT, claimed in 1914 that the mental exertion of voting could jeopardize reproductive health. Too much thinking would shrink the ovaries. Women had inferior brains. Menstruation would produce a temperament unsuited for politics. Women were hypersensitive and unreasonable. Civilization as people knew did not collapse as predicted, once women got the vote (Koren, 2019).

Each of these indicators of convergence, precisely because they are only indicators, might be challenged as the measure of moral truth. The presence of cross-cultural norms alone would not be sufficient to warrant moral truth. This would commit a naturalistic fallacy. Just because norms that value and celebrate aggression may be present in many cultures does not thereby sanctify such norms. Just because war seems to be a persistent feature of nearly all cultures does not make war right. Relative to all known cultures, the fact that polygamy, marriage with multiple partners, is the predominant does not thereby make it morally preferable to monogamy. As noted, Peirce points to a naturalistic fallacy in this sense in regard to moral sentiments (1903, HL, p. 210). The fact that many people may believe in a norm does not make it morally right.

Second, a norm may persist because it is imposed rather than elected for reasons. Norms may persist because a society has an effective, oppressive, authoritative regime that disallows consideration of alternatives. The collapse of the Soviet Union in 1988–1991 is a good example. With the collapse, East German peoples celebrated reunion with the democratic republic of West Germany. The lived experience under an oppressive, Stasi-enforced regime provided sufficient reasons to run to an alternative once that was possible. Or, imagine if the scale of censorship managed by North Korea were lifted, what would change in terms of people's preferences.

Peirce addresses these matters in his 1877 article, "The Fixation of Belief." Here Peirce uses the term "fixation" in the sense of the removal of doubt sufficient for beliefs to persist. It certainly has a family resemblance to the idea of the convergence of belief. It turns out to be a rather uncanny use of the term. Even though the science of genetics is yet to be developed, "fixation" of belief is consistent with its modern genetic sense. Fixation occurs when an allele on a gene locus, more adaptive than its variants, begins over generations to spread through a population to the point where it excludes its alternatives, so that every member of that population has that allele (Hartl and Clark, 2006). What matters, Peirce says in this famous *Popular Science Monthly* article, is not just that beliefs become fixed, but the *method* by which such beliefs are "fixated."

One could manage to do something like North Korea and attempt to censor all other beliefs contrary to what a population is allowed to believe, but the effort it takes to realize what he calls the "method of tenacity" would be a cost that might not be able to outpace the "social impulse against it." "We shall necessarily influence each other's opinions" (1877, CP 5.378).

The method of state or religious authority would also fail in this regard. Consider a state, Peirce writes, that has institutions that "keep correct doctrines before the attention of the people," disseminates them "perpetually," teaches them to the young and has the "power to prevent contrary doctrines from being taught, advocated, or expressed." "Let their passions be enlisted," so that unusual opinions are treated with hatred, and "let all the men who reject the established belief be terrified into silence." "When complete agreement could not otherwise be reached, a general massacre of all who have not thought in a certain way has proved a very effective means of settling opinion in a country" (1877, CP 5.379). History is replete with such methods of fixing belief, Peirce says, and though they have accomplished many things that could not be accomplished otherwise, such oppressive authority fails in the long run. It's not that they have not been successful, but the success is not for long, nor is it progressive. There will always be some people compelled to think through what they've been taught or have been indoctrinated to believe. Doubt is consequent to doubtful claims (1877, CP 5.381).

Peirce also rejects a third method. "Let the action of natural preferences be unimpeded, then, and under their influence let men, conversing together and regarding matters in different lights, gradually develop beliefs in harmony with natural causes." "The most perfect example of this," Peirce says, "is found in the history of metaphysical philosophy." It is a method of adopting propositions that seem "agreeable to reason" (1877, CP 5.382). But, if metaphysics or philosophy generally is the model, its history shows a vulnerability to intellectual fashion; it does not seem to achieve consensus, but a seemingly endless pendulum swing among positions. "These minds do not seem to believe that disputation is ever to cease." "Philosophers have been less intent on finding out what the facts are than on inquiring what belief is most in harmony with their system" (1878, CP 5.406).

Each of these methods enjoins a certain kind of inquiry, but also a certain sort of community of inquiry, with norms, virtues and sentiments that are conducive to the method. People should expect that the method of authority, for example, would promote virtues of blind obedience, respect and loyalty among its members. As Peirce writes, in such communities "loyalty replaced that of truth-seeking" (1878, CP 5.406). Its norms would be reflective of imposed authority and hierarchy, law and order. Sentiments that serve the apotheosis of authority would be cultivated.

Since these methods fail in the long run, to fix beliefs, then, the method cannot be based on what people want to believe, or already tend to believe, or what authorities say people should believe, or the interests of those in power, or what appears to be reasonable, but it should be based on something stance-independent, one of the hallmarks of realism (1877, CP 5.384). Peirce makes no bones that science is the best method in this respect precisely because its method of inquiry—induction-based experimentation—is most conducive to realism, to stance-independence—the laboratory is to be preferred to the seminary (1905, CP 1.129; 1905, R 320, p. 25). The history of the practice of science shows all the indications of convergence—progressive inquiries that reject erroneous hypotheses in favor of improved ones, independent discovery of truths and a wide consensus of belief among scientists on fundamental claims. But all because of the right method. As Peirce says, science "has had the most wonderful triumphs the way of settling opinion" (1877, 5.384).

But, most importantly, science engenders the right sort of community and promotes in its members the sorts of sentiments and virtues most conducive to inquiry, as well as a set of norms that are most likely to lead to a convergence or fixation of belief that is most conducive to truth-getting. As Peirce goes on to show in several different writings, scientific method promotes certain sorts of moral sentiments, such as intergenerational altruism, cooperation with others, love of truth (1878, CP 2.655; 1902, CP 7.87). Indeed, the logical sentiments are exactly those that endear thinkers to "an indefinite community of inquiry" (1868, CP 5.354; 1878, 2.654). Scientists must have certain virtues to ensure proper inquiry, honesty above all (1901, CP 8.136; 1902, CP 2.82; 1903, CP 1.49). More importantly, there are the norms of science, the public nature of inquiry, so that what one proves can be proven by others (1893, CP 5.380 n1); openness to inquiry, obligations to defend what one asserts and the right of others to make assertions about someone's assertions (1896, CP 3.433; c. 1902, CP 5.546; c. 1902, CP 5.543; c. 1902, CP 2.315; c. 1908, CP 5.546).

In advocating the scientific method as the best method for fixing belief, Peirce is not just advocating for science or a method but also a particular *community* of inquiry. What distinguishes the likelihood of genuine convergence on moral truths, a fixation of moral beliefs, is the normative structure of the community of inquiry it engenders. And that is why authoritative or censorious communities will not be successful in the long run. It is these moral sentiments and norms that account for much of the success in fixing belief as do the logical methods by which it does its work (1902, CP 7.87).

Convergence of belief is an indicator of the truth of a moral claim, but only under the condition that it is the result of an inquiry with the right method and in the right sort of community of inquiry. Under those conditions, moral truths will "consist of those which, at a time sufficiently future, the community will always continue to re-affirm; and of those which, under the same conditions, will ever after be denied (1868, CP 5.311). To repeat an earlier claim: "good morals are the kind of human behavior that would come to be approved if studies of right behavior were carried sufficiently far" (c. 1911, R 673, p. 12). "If . . . the future development of man's moral nature will only lead to a firmer satisfaction with the described ideal, the doctrine is true" (1906, CP 5.566), that is, *morally* true.

True to Peirce's brand of realism, the reality is that which is operative in the practice of living in the sense that it acts as a constraint on what can turn out to be generalizable in the conduct, practices and institutions of practical life, that is, what tends toward convergence of belief, conduct and sentiment. "The only effect which real things have is to cause belief" (1878, CP 5.406), but also all that follows from those beliefs.

If beliefs are that upon which people are prepared to act, then beliefs tend to form habits of action, whether in nature or the human sphere and, in regard to the latter, in individuals, practices, or institutions. Habit is "a specialization, original or acquired, of the nature of a man, or an animal, or a vine, or a crystallizable chemical substance, or anything else, that he or it will behave, or always tend to behave, in a way describable in general terms upon every occasion (or upon a considerable proportion of the occasions) that may present itself of a generally describable character" (c. 1902, CP 5.538). "[Readiness] to act in a certain way under given circumstances and when actuated by a given motive is a habit" (c. 1906, CP 5.480). "Under given conditions," Peirce says, a person "will have formed the habit of acting in a given way whenever he may desire a given kind of result" (c. 1906, CP 5.491).

Because Peirce's claim is that what is good and right is what turns out to be generalizable in the way of human conduct, this may be considered to be some version of Kant's categorical imperative: "Act only according to that maxim by which you can at the same time will that it should become a universal law" (1785, p. 39). Because false promises, once made universal, create a formal contradiction and reduce to absurdity, then it cannot pass the test of what is morally right.

But Peirce's sense of generalizability does not rest on formal contradiction, but actual concrete, empirical manifestation. Peirce is forced by the pragmatic maxim to be a moral consequentialist. The meaning of promising is found in its practical consequences and the purposes it entails; correspondingly the meaning of false promising is found in its practical consequences and the purposes it entails. But the latter conduct could not be generalizable in Peirce's terms. It can be exceptional in that a few, statistically speaking, can conduct themselves in that manner, but it could never become widespread enough so that the ends and goals of promise-keeping could be attained. Promise-keeping, among other things, ensures the stability and purpose of contracts. If the greater trend in a society was to break agreements, then contract-making would be a silly enterprise. A society without some form of promise-keeping or truth-telling as a norm would hardly attain many of the ends needed to retain some modicum of social stability or cooperation.

Peirce makes it clear that he is wary of Kant's signature principle. "Kant, as you know, proposes to allow that categorical imperative to stand unchallenged—an eternal pronouncement. His position is in extreme disfavor now, and not without reason" (1903, 5.133). Peirce's reason for rejecting the categorical imperative is his analytic methodology. He argues that ethical matters cannot "be reduced to a mere formalism" (1903, HL, p. 214).

The categorical imperative employs an analytic method, essentially a mathematical *reduction ab absurdum*, to show which actions, if universalized, would create a contradiction or absurdity. The hallmark of the categorical imperative is consistency of action under universalization. Lying, if universalized, would lead to an absurdity, since no one could deceive if everyone lied (Kant, 1785, p. 40). As suggested by John Rawls (1980), when operationalized, Kant's imperative (using the universal law of nature formula) suggests the following test for right action:

1. Form a hypothetical imperative: I am to do X to bring about Y.
2. Make (1) into a maxim of action.
3. Generalize the maxim: Everyone is to do X to bring about Y.
4. Imagine the generalized maxim in (3) as a law of nature, that is, a law that must be followed.
5. Consider the result when (4) is combined with other existing natural laws and human conditions and dispositions.
6. If the result is inconsistent or absurd, then one should not act on (1).

Peirce argues that the methodology must be based, instead, on a "*synthetical*" process, one garnered from experience, and "not to be settled by an appeal to the principle of contradiction":

> Almost everybody will now agree that the ultimate good lies in the evolutionary process in some way. If so, it is not in individual reactions in their segregation, but in something general or continuous. Synechism is founded on the notion that the coalescence, the becoming continuous, the becoming governed by laws, the becoming instinct with general ideas, are but phases of one and the same process of the growth of reasonableness.
>
> (1902, CP 5.4)

In drafts to his 1903 Lowell Lectures, Peirce outlines "three kinds of considerations [that] go to support ideals of conduct" (1903, CP 1.608) and, as such, serve more reliably as practical criteria for the improvement or persistence of norm, ideals and ends. First, "the conduct seems fine in itself." People must find the norms or conduct or ends attractive in some sense. Even though slavery was normalized in early America, its repulsion grew over time, leading to the ultimate confrontation of norms in the Civil War (Davis, 2014, pp. 5–13). People are attracted to the practice or conduct and disgusted or angered with its contraries. For example, thievery has not been much admired and, in fact, generally condemned across cultures (Curry et al., 2019). To be called a thief is not a term of endearment in most cultures.

Second, the conduct should be "consistent," presumably consistent with other indurated practices, and thievery is inconsistent with property ownership (1903, CP 1.608). How is it possible to be both a good neighbor and a thief who robs one's neighbors? As Peirce says, "an aim which cannot be adopted and consistently pursued is a bad aim" (1903, CP 5.133). Can it be the case that "all men are created equal," yet some not so? If justice is "blind" yet, racial injustice exists, how is that satisfying?

Third, there should be a consideration of "what the general effect would be of thoroughly carrying out our ideals" (1903, CP 1.608). This would be the place at which perhaps the most important three tests of convergence come into play. If thievery were to become the ideal of conduct, then what would be the practical effects of its predominant exercise by any population, could it achieve some level of convergence, generalizability? Could it achieve some consensus of belief in an economic system based on private ownership of goods? How common are norms against theft in a variety of cultures? If norms against theft were abandoned, would it make things better or worse?

The convergence theory of truth requires an ongoing process of inquiry, an experiment of living through which moral norms evolve and change for the better. Moral truths are not something decided once and for all by formal contradiction, but in the struggle of lived inconsistencies and problems that must be worked out. Just as science progresses through problems and anomalies with existing hypotheses, so moral life progresses in a similar fashion.

For the same reason that Peirce seems antithetical to the analytic approach of Kant, it could be inferred that he would not favor contractualist or constructivist approaches to ethics as well. Principles that are decided all at once through thought experiments, such as Rawls's device of the Veil of Ignorance in the Original Position might be suspect for reasons that all constructivist approaches are suspect (1971, p. 118ff). In such approaches, the principles that are derived are the result of how the agents are constituted, and the conditions under which they must make their decisions. For example, constitute the agents as rationally self-interested, but without a veil of ignorance, and one ends up with something like David Gauthier's more libertarian set of principles (1986). Robert Nozick can come up with principles contrary to Rawls by changing the conditions under which he imagines original positions are constituted (1974). T.M. Scanlon's decision-makers are constituted as reasonable rather than rational, and so the search is for principles that reasonable agents could not reasonably reject (2000, pp. 191–192). Contractualist theories seem suspiciously like those methodologies Peirce criticizes as "agreeable to reason."

For Peirce, what counts as generalizable is the sorts of habits that have *actually* become indurated, both individual and in the collectivity of practices and institutions, so that there is something like a convergence of sentiment, action and belief, based on the continuum of experiences. It is to what has worked out over time that one looks for the test of what is right, but still with the hope that whatever operates presently is an improvement over what has come before.

Wiggins's Convergence Theory of Moral Truth

Both David Wiggins and Philip Kitcher acknowledge a debt to Peirce's convergence theory of truth in their own accounts of moral truth

(Wiggins, 1998, p. 340ff; Kitcher, 2011, p. 246). Their differences and disagreements with aspects of Peirce's theory can also serve as an interesting foil to the account provided here, as well as seeing how it fits in contemporary thinking.

In *Needs, Values, Truth* (1998) and in *Ethics: Twelve Lectures on the Philosophy of Morality* (2006), Wiggins lays out what he considers to be five "marks" of what he calls "plain truth." As Wiggins claims, convergence is one critical "mark" of truth, and he outlines four others. As he defines the mark of convergence, if x is true, then, "if conditions are fully hospitable to inquiry, those who understand x will tend to converge upon x, and the best explanation of this convergence will be inconsistent with the denial of x" (2006, p. 360). The other marks are, first, if something, whether a proposition, belief, concept, is true, then it passes muster by being assessed on the basis of the sort of thing it is. For example, if beliefs were assessed as if the falsehoods in them were not a matter of its assessment, then there would appear to be no way in which the correctness of the belief could be determined, that is, how things would have to be for the belief to succeed in being correct (1998, p. 148). Next, if x is true, "then x has content and x says something about something. Also, if x is true, "then x is true by virtue of something. Finally, "if x is true and y is true, then their conjunction is true. In other words, what is true is consistent with all other truths" (2006, p. 360).

In regard to the mark of convergence, as he says simply, if something is true, "how can there help but be a tendency for thinkers to arrive at similar conclusions?" (2006, p. 362). Wiggins acknowledges his debt to Peirce's notion but, at the same time, begs to differ with it in some significant ways:

> For me the main interest of convergence is this: by the use of this idea, which is one of several that animate the search for the marks of truth, I arrive at a necessary condition for a subject matter's being one that admits of truth . . . a subject matter that admits of truth will need to have the wherewithal to create and sustain (in the favourable cases) the beginnings of principled agreement. . . . Truth is in jeopardy unless things are like that. For Peirce, on the other hand, our convergence in a belief that will in fact stand up and will thereby end the discomfort of doubt is constitutive . . . of our actually attaining truth.
>
> (1998, p. 340)

Additionally, Wiggins argues that, contrary to Peirce, this mark of truth does not provide any "clear effective test (palpably sufficient condition) of truth." Nor is this mark of truth, along with others he lists, provides any "method for finding truth" (1998, p. 340).

Wiggins also disagrees with Peirce's claims in The Fixation of Belief as to which method would be most effective for inquiries into matters of *moral* truth. He thinks that the flaws of the third method—being "agreeable to reason"—are fixable and that the scientific method proposed as the remedy would impose standards on moral truth that would not be practically attainable:

> What is demanded is only a principle that cures the deficiencies of Peirce's third method without committing us to the more stringent peculiarities of Peirce's characterization of the fourth. And *ad hominem*, I would point out that Peirce himself provides precisely the materials that we need in order to find such a stopping place. What we need is the distinction between states of mind proper to idle supposition, wishful thinking, telling a good story or whatever, for which the third method seems perfectly appropriate, and propositional attitudes like belief that are proper to active inquiry and have, on pain of extinction, to see themselves as answerable to something.
>
> (1998, p. 344)

Pointing to the way in which it is presented in The Fixation of Belief, Wiggins believes that Peirce's account of truth in terms of a predestinate opinion is related to *absolute* truth versus "plain truth." The insistence on absolute truth as the criterion of truth can sacrifice those claims which deserve to be believed and those that do not for a higher exacting standard (1998, p. 343). "Both plain truth or truth for the working day and absolute truth make a demand for objectivity. But the second demands it in a way leading to a restriction of vocabulary so stringent as to raise altogether new questions about meaning" (1998, p. 343n34). Wiggins is also wary of Peirce's realism, particularly as it is cast as something that affects every inquirer in the same way regardless of his history or acculturation," so that in quoting Peirce, "any man if he has sufficient experience and he reasons enough about it will be led to the True conclusion" (1998, p. 344).

Wiggins interpretation of Peirce's convergence theory of truth as one concerned with *absolute* truth seems puzzling given a number of Peirce's known positions. First, as interpreted here, Peirce's convergence theory of truth rests on probability theory. Although the Law of Large Numbers is *mathematically* certain, there's an important difference for Peirce between that sort of certainty and absolute truth. There is no absolute certainty, Peirce emphasizes (c. 1902, CP 7.108), but there's enough warrant to call certain claims "established truths" (1898, CP 5.589), so that there is a "practical certainty" (c. 1906, CP 5.494), something that might be comparable to Wiggins's notion of "plain truth." Second, Peirce's fallibilism would ensure the same sorts of things that Wiggins worries about in terms of "truth for the working day." Fallibilism allows for the acceptance of beliefs sufficient to cast off doubt, even if they cannot prove themselves absolutely true (c. 1897, CP 1.13).

Wiggins account of convergence as a mark of truth here is really no more than what is said in The Fixation of Belief and can serve to distinguish false from genuine convergence. If some belief, x is p, is true, Wiggins says, *and* conditions are hospitable to inquiry *and* people understand the claim, *and* the best explanation of the convergence hinges on the fact of p—that is, something stance-independent—rather than some other stance-dependent reason, *then* such a claim will tend to converge. Convergences that result from stance-independent inquiry will tend to be genuine convergences. Those that result from tenacity, authority, or convention will not be genuine markers of truth. As he writes, "in so far as we want to settle opinion and end the irritation of doubt, what we have to want is for our belief that p not to be determined 'by circumstances that are extraneous to the facts' but come about precisely *because p*" (1998, p. 344). "The question that Peirce could have insisted we should ask," he continues, "is precisely the same as the second mark of truth directs us to ask, namely: is the best explanation of such consensus as we achieve independent—or is it not independent—of the content of that consensus" (1998, p. 345). The best explanation of a consensus achieved in an authoritarian state is not that the beliefs are true based on the content of the beliefs, but because authorities want the population to believe such matters to maintain order and stability, or to maintain their power, or to serve their interests.

For example, if the road of inquiry as to whether x is p is true is inhospitable, as in the case of the method of tenacity, then it is unlikely that even if x is p is true, it will attain some level of convergence. Also, in a community governed by tenacity, if there is any convergence of belief, the best explanation is the pervasiveness of tenacity, not its truth. Similarly, if the best explanation of a convergence in the belief that x is p is false, is that it is contrary to what authorities in a community believe to be the case, then the convergence does not rest on the fact of p, but some other explanation. This would also be the case with counting x is p as false based on it being inconsistent with what is presupposed by some set of inquirers. Thus, as Peirce says, the only method that would guarantee a genuine convergence, one that would persist over time, would be one that is independent of what people tend to think and has an externality, which is not affected by what people think about it (1877, CP 5.384). A genuine convergence is one in which the best explanation of the convergence is that believers tend to believe that x is p because of p.

Consider, for example, the theory of evolution. There is a convergence of belief among scientists, in the relevant fields, that the theory is true in the main, and it is true in the main because the claim is based on stance-independent facts. A statement by the National Academy of Sciences says:

> "scientists . . . use the term "fact" to refer to a scientific explanation that has been tested and confirmed so many times that there is no

> longer a compelling reason to keep testing it or looking for additional examples. In that respect, the past and continuing occurrence of evolution is a scientific fact. Because the evidence supporting it is so strong, scientists no longer question whether biological evolution has occurred and is continuing to occur.
>
> (National Academies of Sciences, 2020)

One can find similar statements by American Association for the Advancement of Science, American Anthropological Association, National Association of Biology Teachers, among other scientific organizations.

On the other hand, a significant portion of the American population, about 30% according to the Pew Research Center, do not believe in the fundamental claim of evolution, that humans and other living things have evolved (2015). By the standard of Peirce and Wiggins, which convergence is more genuine, the scientists or the non-believers? Certainly, the convergence among non-believers may be explained by a lack of understanding of the theory. Indeed, the Pew Research data shows that about 56% of non-believers have only a high school diploma or less. A better understanding might be achieved at the college level, and that is perhaps why most believers in evolution are also college-educated. Denials of the truth of the theory may also be based on reasons "accidental" to what should be, independently, the basis of the claim. For example, the theory of evolution contradicts literal biblical creationist claims. A segment of nonbelievers in the theory of evolution subscribes to the creationist thesis. Given that the denial of the creationist thesis would seriously refute the belief in the inerrancy and literalness of the Bible—the core of certain religious beliefs—this would explain some of the reasons for the convergence among non-believers in evolution theory.

Wiggins may come closer to Peirce's sense of convergence than he thinks. As noted, he disagrees with Peirce that convergence is constitutive of truth. But this may be a misreading of Peirce. As argued here, Peirce's convergence theory of truth is certainly not constitutive in any Kantian sense. Peirce makes it clear that he is not the sort of philosopher to run to a transcendental apothecary to address a particular philosophical issue (1902, CP 2.113). There is a proof of the possibility of convergence, but it is a mathematical proof, based on the Law of Large Numbers, and not based on some *a priori* presupposition or transcendental proof. Since the mathematical proof is hypothetically necessary, it proves possibility, but it does not guarantee any actual historical realization.

As interpreted here, like Wiggins, Peirce sees convergence as a mark or indication of truth. Since the *meaning* of truth, as analyzed through the pragmatic maxim, is that it would tend to converge toward agreement, as would be expected in any determination of true claims. True claims tend to converge belief, false ones tend to create a diversity of opinion. As Wiggins says, convergence would be expected of a true belief. Cheryl Misak notes, "what is being offered [by Peirce] is more like a specification of the chief symptoms or expectations of truth." As she continues,

> We can expect true hypotheses to have certain properties, such as being the sort of hypothesis which would figure in the final opinion, being the sort of hypothesis which would not fall to recalcitrant experience, etc. These are properties that true hypotheses typically have, not accidentally but essentially. Just as it is essentially typical of cats to have four legs (but not all do), it is essentially typical of true hypotheses to have the property of being those that would figure in the final opinion (but not all have it).
>
> (1991, p. 157)

In a footnote to this passage, Misak notes that "David Wiggins encouraged me to put the point this way" (1991, p. 157n35), which suggests that this is the way Wiggins understands Peirce. But this sounds like the interpretation of Peirce proposed here: since the expectation is that true claims would converge beliefs, then convergence of beliefs would be an indicator, a mark of truth. Indicators of convergence, such as the limit of improvability, common cross-cultural norms, and consensus about norm-changes, are *indications* of moral truth, not *constitutive* of truth.

Misak goes on to argue that in this passage that since convergence of beliefs is an indicator of truth, "the pragmatic project is less formal and less ambitious than that standardly undertaken by a 'theory of truth'. But, as we shall see, it is ambitious enough to provide us with a substantial account of truth" (1991, p. 157). She comes to the conclusion that Peirce's theory is a *regulative* theory of truth, that is, not constitutive, but presumably in Kant's sense of regulative (1991, p. 157, 2000, p. 69). For Kant, a regulative idea, is something that unifies a practice, such as the search for knowledge, by acting "as if" the world forms a well-ordered system governed by laws. That cannot be proved ahead of experience, yet it informs the practice of science (1781, A666/B694; 1790, sect. 4.2). As argued elsewhere, Misak's conclusion that Peirce's convergence theory of truth is regulative would also be inconsistent with the interpretation of his theory presented here (Liszka, 2019).

To explain, Peirce is asking three important questions about truth. Is it *possible* for inquiry to converge to the truth? If possible, *will* inquiries converge to the truth? If they will, what is reasonable to hope for? The possibility that inquiry rightly conducted will converge to the truth is guaranteed mathematically by means of the Law of Large Numbers. But whether it is realized in any one inquiry or on any subject matter is difficult to say given so many contingencies, but, given, a number of "established truths" (1898, CP 5.589), there is certainly a reasonable likelihood that truths will be discovered (1878, CP 2.664). And because of the successes of inquiry to date, people can hope that more truths will be established in the future. Can people be absolutely certain that so-called established truths are truly established? No, since the principle of falliblism prohibits claiming anything so. Yet, at the same, time, the principle argues there is no reason to cast doubt on such claims until there is a reason.

Kitcher's Convergence Theory of Moral Truth

Philip Kitcher is another philosopher who acknowledges a debt to Peirce's convergence theory as an account of moral truth. Like Wiggins, Kitcher is wary of classical moral realism. In his analysis of turning points in the advance of morality, such as questioning the morality of slavery as a practice, Kitcher doubts that abolitionists engaged in some "novel apprehension of 'ethical reality'" (2011, p. 180). Changes in moral beliefs in these historical situations are not comparable to those one sees in the changing of beliefs in the history of science (2011, p. 180). "What could encounters with external constraints be like? Some philosophers have supposed we can have contact with something deserving the name of "ethical reality," and that people have psychological capacities enabling them to arrive at well-grounded ethical judgments" (2011, p. 181). A "challenge for the thesis that ethics is a form of inquiry responding to external constraints" is to explain "how those external constraints play some substantive role in the evolution of the ethical project" (2011, p. 186).

Kitcher poses an ethical naturalism, a "pragmatic naturalism" in place of classical realism, to explain these transitions. It is a position that views morals as evolved out of the natural progression of conflicts in social life, experiments of living. In accord with this view, morals should be understood functionally as solving problems of social conflict and maintaining cooperation. "The original function of ethics is to remedy *those altruism failures provoking social conflict*" (2011, pp. 223, 225, 239).

The real problem in ethics is to figure out what moral rules and codes people should keep and which they should change or discard, and that boils down to a matter of what is progressive and what is regressive. Although moral realists would argue that progress is the result of substituting false moral claims for true ones, Kitcher sees no evidence in historical transitions out of slavery or in woman's suffrage, or in the institution of gay marriage for this claim: "factual knowledge and social exchange are prominent in this important ethical advance, but I find no place for apprehension that same-sex love has a simple and irreducible property with which the conventional wisdom of the 1950s failed to credit it" (2011, p. 196).

Instead, "ethical progress is prior to ethical truth, and truth is what you get by making progressive steps (truth is attained in the limit of progressive transitions" (2011, p. 210). In direct reference to Peirce's convergence theory, he argues that

> descriptive counterparts of ethical rules count as true just in case those rules would be adopted in ethical codes as the result of progressive transitions and would be retained through an indefinite sequence of further progressive transitions.
>
> (2011, p. 246)

As he elaborates, "progress is the prior notion, and descriptive counterparts of rules *come to count as true* in virtue of the fact that they enter and remain in ethical codes that unfold in progressive sequence" (2011, p. 246).

The key question, then, is what counts as progressive? It is whatever refines and makes more efficient the function of ethics, namely, those codes and norms that reduce social conflict and maintain cooperation in a society (2011, p. 239). What sorts of codes and norms would do that? Although there are many causes of conflict, fundamental conflicts occur when goods or desires that are "endorsable," are denied some group. "Desires are endorsable just case there are possible environments in which they could be satisfied for all our fellows." Having adequate food, for example, is endorsable, but monopolizing reproduction in only a few is not (2011, p. 223). Codes that would "expand the circle," such that more people can be included in what counts as endorsable goods are progressive (2011, p. 215). The abolition of slavery, the enfranchisement of women, and the legalization of marriage for LGBTQ are all examples of progress in that sense. Second, progress occurs when there is an expansion of endorsable goods (2011, p. 217).

For example, in the matter of chattel slavery, codes such as not treating people as property, or prohibitions on buying and selling people, forcibly separating family, prohibiting wanton acts of cruelty are all norms that are generally approved during the run-up to the civil war. It's that the slave population did not count as subjects of these norms. Indeed, David Brion Davis demonstrated very forcefully that the animalization of the slave population was a dominant social perception. As such, they were treated as subhuman, not animals, but not quite humans and, as such, had little moral standing. Davis goes on to show how, even after emancipation, this categorization of the African-American population dominated the Reconstruction landscape and continued into the Jim Crow era. Much of the categorization was based on false empirical claims of characteristics attributed to African-Americans (2014, p. 15ff).

Kitcher seems to be right about how much of the slavery issue was an altruism problem in the sense of "expanding the circle," so that slaves would be given the moral standing of others.

However, Kitcher's picture of the transition from slavery is not the whole picture. There are also efforts to establish slavery as a moral good or an immoral evil, depending on the side of the issue, to make claims that slavery is a moral good or a moral evil. There were also factual claims that attributed certain characteristics to the slave population and certain claims about their conditions and the benefits or harms from slavery. These were proposed, it can be supposed, as stance-independent truths.

For example, Kitcher ignores the famous 1837 speech of John Calhoun justifying slavery as a moral good. The normative claim of Calhoun is that slavery is a positive good (1837, p. 225). He justifies this claim on a crudely consequentialist basis, namely something like the following: Because there are a number of consequences of practices of slavery that people would count as good, then slavery is good. First, since peace is a good and happiness is a good, and since the continuing practice of slavery will maintain the peace and happiness of both races, then slavery is a good in that respect (1837, p. 224). The slave population was treated better than most European laborers (1837, p. 225). The Africans were brought to America in a "low, degraded and savage condition" but, "in the course of a few generations, it has grown up under the fostering care our institutions. . . . This, with the rapid increase of numbers, is conclusive proof of the general happiness of the race" (1837, p. 224). Moreover, the white race has at the same time prospered under the institution of slavery (1837, p. 224).

Since consequentialism of this sort, based on reasons proclaiming facts, is refutable to the extent that the empirical claims can be refuted, it holds the posture of stance-independence. Kwame Appiah argues for two types of racism—*extrinsic* and *intrinsic*. Extrinsic racism is based on certain supposedly stance-independent beliefs that the racial essence of a group entails certain morally relevant qualities, for example, the belief that African-Americans are hypersexual (1989, p. 45). Appiah argues that to extent that such beliefs can be refuted, then this loosens the evidence for such beliefs. To the extent that people are reasonable in Peirce's sense, then this sort of racism has much less grounding in people's minds. Appiah holds that people who hold false beliefs about races, once recognizing such falsehoods, should yield their racist beliefs. Intrinsic racism is another matter. It is visceral and tied to group identity and loyalty. Neo-nazis may believe in the negative moral characteristics of Jews and Blacks, but not for stance-independent reasons, but simply because they are a member of that group so identified (1989, p. 45). They are tenacious in their beliefs, in Peirce's sense of the term.

This may not detract from Kitcher's larger claim that what is morally true are the norms that will continue to persist in historical transitions. Although extrinsic and intrinsic racisms still exist, what doesn't persist is slavery or the claim that slavery is a "positive good."

One can see a family resemblance between Peirce and Kitcher in that a moral truth is one that persists over time and has reached the approximate limit of improvability, that is, it does not appear to be vulnerable to further criticism. It is something that has survived criticism to the point that there are few if any who see the point of its criticism. It is further confirmed by that fact that it continues to be adopted by communities as they go through various transitions of their codes and practices and, it would be supposed, that it is adopted by a wide variety of communities. Since such norms must be adopted with the fallibilist attitude, the danger that norms are accepted merely on their basis of popular approval or the imposition of authority is avoided.

Peirce would seem to agree with Kitcher's functionalism. Peirce would also approve of Kitcher's pragmatic naturalism which, unlike what we would find in constructivist or contractualist normative theories, argues for no pre-ordained set of principles true once and for all, but rather a tentative future that may or may not achieve moral clarity, nor a clarity ahead of the evolutionary process as to what will be those norms that endure. In Peirce's eyes, the best that can be hoped for is that if inquiry is structured around certain norms, and that inquirers have certain sentiments and exhibit certain virtues, then the results of such inquiries are more likely to result in moral truths. Peirce is still committed to the notion of inquiry, inquiry in the moral realm, and that the ultimate end of inquiry is the truth about its subject of inquiry.

7 Ethical Community

For Peirce, moral truths are the result of inquiries done rightly and sufficiently long enough through experiments of living, so that the norms and ideals appear to have reached the limit of their improvability. Changing them would only make things worse and returning to what has preceded it is no longer desirable. There is sufficient consensus about these truths; they have appeal so that people tend to adopt them as guides to their conduct and recognize their value. The experiments of living, the practices of everyday life, the ends people pursue, the ways and means by which people conduct the pursuit of these ends is their testing ground. However, like any experimental result, like any induction, the judgment that norms and ends are morally true is a fallible judgment, and what seems settled could still become doubted in the future.

If this is how moral truths are to be measured, then proper inquiry is key to their determination. Communities must be so designed that their experiments of living can bear fruit. Their design must be such that they are conducive to inquiry into moral truths. Communities poorly designed in this respect would only inhibit the search for moral truths. In the discipline of logic or semiotic, Peirce thought that his universal rhetoric would take on the task of laying out the conditions for good inquiries (1870, W2, p. 539; 1896, CP 3.430; 1902, CP 2.106–110; 1902, R L75; 1902, CP 2.207; 1903, CP 1.191; 1903, R 478; 1903, R 452, p. 9; 1905, R 606, p. 15; c. 1907, R 320–327; Liszka, 1996, 2000, 2010). If there is a parallel in the organization between the normative science of logic or semiotic and the normative science of ethics, then there should also be a study of proper inquiry conducive to the determination of moral truths.

The great insight of Peirce was that proper inquiries themselves require certain moral sentiments, ethical norms of conduct and direction toward certain ends that already lay down an ethical framework. Adopting them makes it more likely to determine which claims are morally true. As such the *community* of inquiry can serve as a model for an ethical community generally. As Richard Atkins notes, in Peirce's later years, "inquiry itself is a way of realizing the greater good" (2018, p. 142). This idea that inquiries into what is right and good, or inquiries of any sort for that matter, make truth claims and such claims involve implicit norms and commitments, has been an inspiration to the ethical theories such as Karl-Otto Apel (1980), Jürgen Habermas (1990), Cheryl Misak (2000), Robert Brandom (1994, 2000) and Robert Talisse (2005), among others.

Since inquiry is inquiry, the normative features of an inquiry into empirical truths and moral truths should have many similarities. Hilary Putnam puts this succinctly: "*if* there are ethical facts to be discovered, *then* we ought to apply to ethical inquiry just the rules we have learned to apply to inquiry in general. For what applies to inquiry in general applies to ethical inquiry in particular" (1995, p. 223).

Inquiries are, first, not solitary affairs, but done collectively in a community of inquiry. "We individually cannot reasonably hope to attain the ultimate philosophy which we pursue; we can only seek it, therefore, for the *community* of philosophers" (1868, CP 2.265). Peirce eschewed the Cartesian method of solitary, monologic, intuition-based, deductive reasoning, in favor of public, communal, dialogic, experimental and inductive reasoning. Science as the exemplary practice of inquiry was something public in these respects (1878, CP 5.384). Claims are to be "determined in a public and methodical manner" (1893, CP 5.380n1). Good inquiry requires an open process. "The next most vital factor of the method of modern science," he argues, "is that it has been made social." It is public in the sense that the investigations and their results "must be something open to anybody to observe" (1902, CP 7.87). Above all, they must have certain normative features. "The most vital factors in the method of modern science," he says, "have not been the following of this or that logical prescription—although these have had their value too," says Peirce but, "moral factors" (1902, CP 7.87). Communities of inquiry must abide by certain norms; inquirers must exercise certain virtues, and be motivated by certain moral sentiments in order to be successful in such an endeavor.

To achieve an operative, working community of inquiry, Peirce recognizes that the task is one similar to the task of rhetoric, traditionally understood as an effort to create a *solidarity* among members of the community for the sake of acting on some end. Peirce claims "It is quite true that the success of modern science largely depends upon a certain solidarity among investigators" (1902, CP 2.166). He defines solidarity as "harmonious cooperation" (1902, CP 2.166; 1896, 3.425).

Peirce's modified desire-belief model of human conduct might serve as the way to explain how such solidarity might be achieved. If people intend to act on what they believe will likely attain what they desire, then to create solidarity among inquirers, people must aim for similar ends, and believe that the same means will likely attain those ends. If there are alternative means that will achieve the same ends, these too must be recognized and appreciated. People must have as their end a similar sense of the good, and similar beliefs about the morally best, most likely means to attain that good. Cooperation and solidarity would be maximized under those conditions, since most would be rowing in unison toward the same destination. Without a sense of the common good, conflicts, clash and the diminishment of cooperation is likely. There is also likely to be discord if there is disagreement about the righteously prudent way to attain those ends. Consensus about the ends and means is likely to create a more stable, cooperative community. Settling those beliefs about best means and good ends is key.

Peirce recognized that fostering solidarity required an appeal to the whole person, sentiment, resolution, as well as reason. Peirce is likely influenced by George Campbell's rhetorical theory in this respect, one he studied at an early age (c. 1906, CP 5.13). Campbell makes the case for this approach. He makes a distinction between conviction and persuasion. Conviction is achieved by proving some position disbelieved or doubted by the hearers; persuasion is accomplished by convincing the judgment, interesting the passions and fixing the resolution (Campbell, 1776, I, p. iv). In other words, persuasion follows the logic of practical reasoning and appeals to both head and heart. "The first is, to excite some desire or passion in the hearers; the second is, to satisfy their judgement, that there is a connexion between the action to which he would persuade them, and the gratification of the desire or passion which he excites" (1776, I, 200). As he continues,

> In order to evince the truth considered by itself conclusive arguments alone are requisite; but in order to convince me by these arguments, it is moreover requisite that they be understood, that they be attended to, that they be remembered by me; and in order to persuade me by them, to any particular action or conduct, it is further requisite, that by interesting me in the subject, they may, as it were, be felt.
>
> (1776, I, pp. 186–187)

Indeed, this interplay of sentiment, virtue and belief in certain rules of conduct reflects the traditional understanding of the role of rhetoric. It is reminiscent of Aristotle's three modes of rhetorical persuasion: *pathos, ethos* and *logos*, and shows the connection between ethics and rhetoric (*Rhetoric*, 1356a1–25). Indeed, for Aristotle, rhetoric is a combination of logic and ethics (*Rhetoric*, 1359b9–10). Kenneth Burke expresses the same sense of it in his definition of rhetoric: "the classical principles of persuasion are put to the task *of inducing cooperation in beings that by nature respond to symbols*" (1950, pp. 22, 43). Cicero also emphasizes the importance of rhetoric in moving us toward an understanding of the common good (c. 87 B.C.E., *De inventio*, I.ii.3). Francis Bacon says "the duty and office of Rhetoric is to apply Reason to Imagination for the better moving of the will" (1605, III, p. 409). Charles Bazerman says much the same thing: "the study of how people use language and other symbols to realize human goals and carry out human activities" (1988, p. 6).

If solidarity is achieved by a common good articulated in terms of ends and means, Peirce operated on the working hypothesis that the end of inquiry is truth, whether empirical or moral. Common sense would dictate that the righteous means, the ideals of conduct by which such inquiries would be pursued would be honesty above all, fairmindedness, humility and the like. How could the truth be discerned if inquirers are dishonest and unfair to those who may have legitimate criticisms of received views? Communities of inquiry must also abide by certain norms: above all, do not block the road of inquiry, the responsibilities of providing reasons and justifications for assertions, free, open and public discussions of those assertions, and the authority of reason in the form of the better argument, case or evidence of claims. Peirce identifies scientific practice as the exemplar of inquiry precisely in these terms, as having a definite end and means:

> Science is to mean for us a mode of life whose single animating purpose is to find out the real truth, which pursues this purpose by a well-considered method, founded on thorough acquaintance with such scientific results already ascertained by others as may be available, and which seeks cooperation in the hope that the truth may be found, if not by any of the actual inquirers, yet ultimately by those who come after them and who shall make use of their results.
>
> (c. 1902, CP 7.54)

The Pathos of Inquirers: Intergenerational Altruism

For Peirce, addressing the sentiments of inquirers, their *pathos*, is essential to foster solidarity in any community of inquiry. Peirce is one of the earliest philosophers of science to recognize the importance of the cultivation of certain sentiments in inquirers as fundamental to the process of inquiry (Liszka, 1996, 86ff). Christopher Hookway makes this clear: "Peirce claims that sentiment has an ineliminable role even in reflective deliberation and scientific inquiry" (2002, p. 224).

Peirce discusses the sentiments related to inquiry and communities of inquiry principally in two places. The first is in "The Doctrine of Chances," published in the 1878 *Popular Science Monthly* series—which restates some of the themes ten years earlier in "Grounds of Validity of the Laws of Logic," published in 1868 in *The Journal of Speculative Philosophy*. The second is "Evolutionary Love," published in *The Monist* series in 1893, some years after he began his study of ethics, and certainly after he studied the British moral sentimentalists.

In the "Doctrine of Chances," Peirce attempts to show how the logician, in reasoning inductively, is committed to something larger than self-interest, namely an interest in a community of inquiry. In "Evolutionary Love," Peirce argues that growth and progress, including progress in inquiry and the growth of ideas, requires that people have an impulse to make things better, even for that which is "hateful." This must be combined with an impulse to cultivate what is best and pass it on (1893, CP 6.289). This is possible through a general sympathy and communion with others (1893, CP 6.294). As noted earlier, it is in this piece that he makes one of the earliest mentions of his moral sentimentalism, which is to become a topic in the first of his Cambridge lectures in 1898, "Philosophy and the Conduct of Life." He connects moral sentimentalism to evolutionary love, defining it as the doctrine that "great respect should be paid to the natural judgments of the sensible heart," (1893, CP 6.292).

The combination of interest in something greater than self, an impulse to make things better, and a drive to cultivate what is best, characterizes different facets of an intergenerational altruism. It is a willingness to contribute to present and future communities, to make things better and pass it on to those that follow, even if one does not benefit oneself from such contributions. In fact, it is the essence of what makes a community, a community. As Peirce explains it in the context of scientific inquiry, "the individual strives to produce that which he himself cannot hope to enjoy. One generation collects premises in order that a distant generation may discover what they mean." He continues,

> When a problem comes before the scientific world, a hundred men immediately set all their energies to work upon it. One contributes this, another that. Another company, standing upon the shoulders of the first, strike a little higher, until at last the parapet is attained.
> (1902, CP 7.87)

Obviously, the contrary of intergenerational altruism is a selfish impulse to attain ends and gain what one can in the present for oneself or one's community, regardless of whether it harms prospects for the future. Certainly, the two impulses are on display in the current climate crisis, but their conflict has marked human history in many instances over and over again.

The Disinterested Inquirer

Consider the first aspect of intergenerational altruism—an interest in something greater than self. For inquirers, Peirce claims this is manifested as an "identification of one's interests with those of an unlimited community" (1878, 2.654). In "The Doctrine of Chances," he explains the most important sentiments for inquirers:

> I . . . put forward three sentiments, namely, interest in an indefinite community, recognition of the possibility of this interest being made

> supreme, and hope in the unlimited continuance of intellectual activity, as indispensable requirements of logic.
>
> (1878, CP 2.655)

He thinks the first essential, the other two corollaries (1878, CP 2.655). If inquirers are to identify their interests with the interests of such a community of inquiry, what are the interests of a community of inquiry? Ostensibly, the interest of a community of inquiry is to determine the truth or falsity of the subject of the inquiry. In other words, inquirers must identify with an interest in truth.

Peirce attempts to show in "The Doctrine of Chances" that interest in a wider community of inquiry falls out of the very nature of inductive reasoning. Peirce argues that, to the extent that inquirers are committed to using inductive reasoning to discern the true from the false, they are also committed to some sort of community of inquiry. "The social principle," as he calls it, "is rooted intrinsically in logic" (1868, CP 5.354; 1878, 2.654). How is that? Peirce employs what might be called a *pathetic proof*, one that uses reasoning, appeals to common values, thought experiments and stories to promote a certain sentiment in the audience.

Induction rests on the Law of Large Numbers which, as discussed, also grounds Peirce's convergence theory of truth mathematically. To show that a hypothesis is true, one must show that *in the long run*, continued sampling of what it predicts shows a convergence to a fixed ratio of positive outcomes. To do this, the sampling must be *extended in time*, presumably by many samples, thus, many samplers. To be effective, the inquiry must establish a *continuity* of investigation over time, for the inquiry to build its way to the truth. What one contributes helps the contribution of others who follow.

People cannot sufficiently secure the truth of a hypothesis alone, nor in a person's lifetime: "death makes the number of our risks, of our inferences, finite and so makes their mean result uncertain. The very idea of probability and reasoning rests on the assumption that this number is indefinitely great" (1878, CP 2.654). This requires a cooperative inquiry, a community of inquiry. To conduct inquiries and maintain this continuity, it would be assumed that people would communicate with one another, share results publicly, engage in the give-and-take of genuine inquiry and other forms of cooperation necessary to further the inquiry.

However, this sort of cooperative inquiry wouldn't necessarily lead to the "identification" of any one inquirer's interests with the interests of the community. Inquirers could cooperate with other inquirers purely out of self-interest and mutual benefit. For example, if the inquiry was a matter of discovering which drug best cures a disease then, to the extent that people have interest in having such a cure, they would certainly cooperate in such an inquiry, assuming they have the capability of doing so. Some inquirers might be interested in discovering the drug because it will be profitable, or it will promote their careers. In other words, there could be a number of self-interested reasons for cooperating with others in an inquiry that doesn't necessarily lead to the identification of one's interests with the community of inquiry.

Yet, Peirce insists some 30 years later in 1910 that among the points "that were worth making" in "The Doctrine of Chances," was "no man can be logical whose supreme desire is the well-being of himself or any other existing person or collection of persons" (1910, R 701, pp. 1–2). This a repeat of the claim in 1878 that an inquirer "cannot be logical so long as he is concerned only with his own fate, but that that man who should care equally for what was to happen in all possible cases of the sort could act logically" (1878, CP 2.654).

There are a couple of things to note about this claim to get at what Peirce means. First, he emphasizes in each of these iterations, that one cannot be *logical* if one is concerned only with oneself in such inquiries. Peirce cannot mean by this that inquirers shouldn't be concerned with their own well-being generally, only that it should not be the *supreme* interest, *relative to inquiries.*

If "self-interest" is substituted for "well-being" this might bring his point out better. It has to be supposed that if the purpose of the inquiry is to determine the *truth* of a claim, then to be a truly *logical* inquirer, inquirers would have to forego self-interest, that is, they would have to be *disinterested* in this sense. Consider the case of inquiries into the effectiveness of a drug to cure a disease, the dilemmas of which are well-depicted in Sinclair Lewis's *Arrowsmith*. Suppose the inquirers are self-interested, in that their goal in the inquiry is to make money from the drug. In that case, they have a vested interest in demonstrating that the drug is effective and would be more prone to biasing the inquiry and foiling the search for truth. Of course, people who have the disease would have a self-interest in getting a drug that would cure the disease, but only if the drug *truly* cured the disease. For that reason, they have an interest in the disinterested inquiry. As Peirce writes, people should regard their own inferences "so far . . . as they would be accepted by the hero," that is, the logical inquirer (1878, CP 2.654).

Peirce gives some substance to this notion of logical disinterest in his first Cambridge lecture, "Philosophy and the Conduct of Life." Peirce holds that "the scientific man is not in the least wedded to his conclusions. He risks nothing upon them. He stands ready to abandon one or all as soon as experience opposes them" (1898, CP 1.635). Peirce goes on to rail against the use of science for practical purposes: "The point of view of utility is always a narrow point of view" (1898, CP 1.641). Here he is contrasting theoretical with applied science. But, regardless of whether the inquirer is aiming to find the truth about something for its own sake, or to find out what will cure cancer, the inquirers must be disinterested in their hypotheses to find the truth, whether it is about rare elements or about what will cure cancer.

In his account of induction, Peirce is keen to devise methodologies that ensure this disinterest in a very practical way. After all, Peirce insists that there has to be a method that judges the truth "by something upon which our thinking has no effect" (1878, CP 5.384), meaning that the truth is not what people tend to believe, or what they want to believe. Peirce's method of predesignation is one tool in the toolbox to prevent researcher influence on experimental results since it inhibits the hunting and snooping for data that could bias evidence in favor of the hypothesis, and to ensure that reliability of induction (1878, CP 6.413). Peirce is also the first to introduce the method of randomization into the experimental process, in a published experiment in 1884, done with his student at Johns Hopkins, Joseph Jastrow (1884, CP 7.21–7.48). Predesignation, randomization and double-blind testing are now standard methodologies to ensure the bias and self-interest do not seep into scientific studies (Hacking, 1988, p. 430; Stigler, 1986, p. 248).

As discussed earlier, Peirce seems especially concerned about how inquiries into moral truths can be easily corrupted by self-interest in this respect, and inquirers engage in sham reasoning and rationalizations for what they already believe ethically. Reasoning no longer "determines what the conclusion shall be, but it is the conclusion which determines what the reasoning shall be" (c. 1896, CP 1.57). If inquirers into moral truths act like ideologues and end up simply being apologists for the dominant moral conventions, then such inquiries become suspect. Ethical inquiry must be practiced in a disinterested manner that allows the possibility of inquirers to detach themselves from moral conventions to evaluate those norms at some level—as hard as that might be to do.

Since the interest, the common good of communities of inquiry is truth, then to identify one's interest with the community of inquiry is to adopt an interest in the truth. But, to identify with that interest, one must vacate all self-interest and become a disinterested inquirer. This perhaps explains better what Hilary Putnam calls "Peirce's puzzle" in "The Doctrine of Chances."

Peirce supposes a gambler has a choice between selecting a card from a pack of 24 black cards with 1 red card, or a pack of 24 red cards with 1 black. If the card selected is black, the gambler is visited by everlasting woe; if red, the gambler is rewarded with everlasting felicity. Thus, it is a one-and-done bet. Peirce asks "what *consolation* would he have" if he chose the single black card out of the red pack? (emphasis added) (1878, CP 2.652).

Hilary Putnam interprets Peirce's point to this example in the following way: "it is only because I care about what *might* happen to people in similar situations that I do what has the best *chance* in my own situation" (1987, p. 83). He characterizes this as a motivation based on rule-utilitarianism. People should follow a rule which most likely benefits the most in the long run, even if it may not benefit a few, including oneself, in the short run. Thus, one's altruism comes out of the recognition that, even if one does not achieve the good for oneself, following actions that are likely to achieve certain ends will, at least, benefit most everyone, if everyone follows the rule. So, the gambler who happens to choose the one black card from the red pack can be reconciled on that basis (1987, pp. 83–84). However, Putnam is skeptical that it is this sense of altruism that motivates the gambler to choose the card from the red back. Rather, it is just plain old self-interest. The gambler is concerned about his own weal, not anybody else's, and chooses what he believes will attain everlasting felicity.

Christopher Hookway also expresses skepticism about Peirce's claim that altruism would fall out of the gambler example. He interprets Peirce's reasoning in the following way, similar to the idea of Putnam's sense of rule utilitarianism:

> "although *I* can carry out only one inference of the sort described, *we* can carry out lots; and so, by relying on probabilities I adopt a policy which, although it may not benefit *me* ought, if consistently carried through, to benefit *us*. The conclusion then drawn is that if I care about how well the community at large will do, the inferential policy which may condemn me to everlasting woe can be rationally endorsed.
>
> (2002, p. 227)

Hookway thinks that Peirce's derivation of altruism from this example is "crazy" (2002, p. 227). Instead, he argues that Peirce would better off just positing certain sentiments that promote inquiry:

> My conjecture is that an appeal to sentiment is required . . . we require a kind of acceptance of fundamental commitments which is neither grounded in non-scientific inquiry, nor detached and tentative, nor undeserved. This is possible only if these commitments enjoy a sort of secure immediacy, and my claim is that, in Peirce's view, an appeal to logical sentiments is intended to provide this.
>
> (2002, pp. 234–235)

But Peirce seems to want to show here why people should adopt these sentiments, rather than arguing that people already have them. The goal of rhetoric is to address the heart through speech, and this is what Peirce seems to be doing here. To use the language of Thomas Nagel, Peirce is attempting this sort of pathetic proof to motivate desires by instilling certain beliefs in people (1978, p. 29). Moreover, the sort of argument that Hookway puts forward as an appeal to a natural inclination is unsatisfying since it does not provide a reason for why people should adopt an interest in truth if they do not already have such an inclination. Peirce's argument seems more akin to the rhetor arguing for his audience to take up a *cause*, and thereby stirring the passions to action. In this case, it is the *cause of truth*.

To see Peirce's point more clearly, suppose that people are so unlearned that nobody knows what will likely happen when a card is picked. This would simulate a case of choosing to do something in the context of uncertainty—which is often the case when figuring out which practical hypotheses will attain the ends-in-view. Suppose there are two types of gamblers, based on their motivations. One is purely self-interested in getting eternal felicity, and the other is interested in finding out what choice, will in the long run, get *anyone* eternal felicity. The latter is reasonable in the sense of having an *interest is in what is generalizable*. The interest is in the truth of the practical hypothesis, "if people want eternal felicity, they should select a card from the red pack." The self-interested gambler is only interested in the one-time event, what will get *him* eternal felicity.

Suppose the self-interested gambler, on a hunch, selects a card from the predominantly red pack, yet unfortunately picks the only black card from the deck, and is sent to perdition. As he sits in hell, he regrets his choice and thinks he has chosen poorly and cannot be reconciled. At this point, he is no longer interested in what might happen to others who choose, since he was concerned only with his own fate.

Suppose now the logical, truth-interested gambler, interested in what is generalizable, acts on a hunch, selects a card from the predominantly red pack, yet unfortunately picks the only black card from the deck, and is sent to perdition. Of course, the gambler being only human regrets the choice and her own fate. But since she is interested in the truth, she is concerned about what happens to the fate of others. However, it is more of a Spockian sense of concern for the truth, than one generated by sympathy for others. Putnam, for example, assumes that the gambler already has a sympathy for what happens to others, whereas Peirce's logical gambler "cares equally for what was to happen *in all possible cases of the sort* . . ." (emphasis added) (1878, CP 2.654). The concern for the fate of the gamblers is only in the context of an interest about whether their practical hypotheses are true or not. They function as samples in the cause of truth, as does the truth-seeking gambler. There's no mention of concern for the fate of future gamblers *personally*.

Now, since people have no knowledge of probability and statistics, others having observed the fates of the two gamblers might conclude from this small sample that there is some order to things such that black cards tend to be picked more frequently from red packs, while red cards more frequently from black packs. Of course, the only way to figure that out is to perform a sufficient number of experiments. Since the original gamblers cannot select again, it is now up to others. What should the next person do—pick from the red or black deck? Over time, as more and more selections are made, people would be quickly disabused of that hypothesis. It would become clear that people are more likely to pick a red card from the red pack than the black pack. Reasonable people would tend to correct their original belief. If that becomes habituated and passed on, then countless people will be rewarded with eternal felicity, even though a certain percentage (about 4% of the population) will not.

With this established, the original truth-interested gambler is now *consoled* that her sacrifice has contributed to the collective enterprise of the search for truth—and that she did choose wisely after all. Remember that Peirce asks what *consolation* the gambler would have. The self-interested gambler, only interested in his own fate, is never consoled. Whether he likes it or not, the self-interested gambler has engaged in a kind of non-voluntary altruism, since others that follow will use the results of that decision to inform their own. The self-interested gambler has adopted a Darwinian attitude in this respect. Peirce says elsewhere, the Darwinian attitude is that "ruined gamesters leave their money on the table to make those not yet ruined so much the richer" (1893, CP 6.304). However, the truth-interested gambler is acting in an intentionally altruistic way, realizing that her decision will contribute to the collective results of the inquiry for future generations. The quest for truth leads to a sort of Spockian, impersonal altruism in this respect, an altruism directed to something larger than self.

The Greater Altruism of Evolutionary Love

Peirce's disinterested inquirer is altruistic in the sense of willing to forego self-interest for the sake of something greater than self—the cause of truth. Because such a pursuit cannot be done solely but requires a community of inquiry, disinterested inquirers identify their interests with the interest of such a community in its pursuit of truth. But as characterized in "The Doctrine of Chances," it is a cold-hearted altruism, in that the inquirers as purely logical agents see each other as instrumental means to the end of truth. By the 1890s, Peirce had expanded this notion of altruism to one that included a more sentimental picture, one that included a sense of sympathy and *solidarity* among people as they endeavor to find their place in the order of things:

> Long ago. In the *Journal of Speculative Philosophy* . . . I pointed out that a person is nothing but a symbol involving a general idea; but my views were, then, too nominalistic to enable me to see that every general idea has the unified living feeling of a person.
>
> (1892, CP 6.270)

As Max Fisch points out, it was around this time in the publication of the *Monist* series, that Peirce had expanded his realism to include individuals as real (1967, p. 195). This may explain the turn from viewing the individual as logical fodder for the cause of truth to an empathic solidarity with others in its pursuit. He continues, "all that is necessary, upon this theory, to the existence of a person is that the feelings out of which he is constructed should be in close enough connection to influence one another" (1892, CP 6.271). This explains the possibility of such feelings of solidarity as *esprit de corps*, national sentiment, and a genuine *community* of inquiry who, through sharing a sense of the common good, are sympathetically connected with one another (1892, CP 6.271). In this change of heart, Peirce's sentimentalism leans into, perhaps, some of the insights of the ethics of care (Baier, 1987).

In 1898, in the first of the series of his Cambridge Lectures, "Philosophy and the Conduct of Life," Peirce picks up this theme again of cause greater than self but refreshes it from the viewpoint of a moral sentimentalism. In the lectures, as in previous positions throughout his writings he champions altruism over self-interest. There, in his closing remarks, he identifies so-called "vitally important topics" with self-interest. The attitude of self-interest is that "the only vitally important matter is my concern, business, and duty—or yours." But what is "vitally important" is "of all truths the veriest trifles." After all, "you and I—what are we? Mere cells of the social organism. Our deepest sentiment pronounces the verdict of our own insignificance." To pursue self-interest as one's highest interest leads to two alternatives. One, in reference to the Gilded Age of the time, the fierce, competitive and cut-throat world of business, "Americanism" as he calls it, where "the fertilizing stream of genial sentiment dries up." Or it could be the withdrawal from the world, a sort of "monasticism," a life of "sleepwalking" (1898, CP 1.673). Neither one leads to the sort of intergenerational altruism that passes on what is best and improves on what is worst.

Peirce proposes, instead, that "the very first command that is laid upon you, your quite highest business and duty, becomes . . . to recognize a higher business than your business." Peirce is reinforcing the exhortation to adopt an interest in something greater than self, echoing here his first ethics teacher, Theodor Jouffroy. He argued that it is only when human beings elevate themselves from the pursuit of self-interest to something greater than self that true morality emerges (1840, p. 42). It is only when our interest is a universal interest—"not our good alone—the good, the end of every creature," that we've achieved the moral stance (1840, p. 45). This is not to be "merely an avocation after the daily task of your vocation is performed," Peirce proclaims, but "a generalized conception of duty." Peirce likens this to the "good mother," presumably "good" in the sense of someone who nurtures the family so that the best comes out and the worst is constrained (1898, CP 1.673).

However, although much of this sounds like the earlier logical altruism, what is important to point out is that Peirce no longer sees this higher interest as solely the outcome of logic, but "the very supreme commandment of sentiment" (1898, CP 1.673). By 1898, Peirce had engaged in his study of ethics for about 15 years. He had surely by now encountered the British and Scottish moral sentimentalists—Shaftesbury, Hutcheson, Hume and Reid in particular, and he had already introduced his own version of moral sentimentalism in 1893, in "Evolutionary Love."

Peirce characterizes the adoption of something greater than self in "Philosophy and the Conduct of Life," in ecstatic terms, as the "commandment" to "generalize," to "become welded into the universal continuum," such that "distinct individuals weld together" (1898, CP 1.673). It would be interesting to see the reaction of the audience to these claims, and how many would return for the remaining lectures, perhaps perceiving Peirce as a bit off, as his student Christine Ladd-Franklin thought during this period in his life (Houser, 2010, p. xcvi). The way in which Nathan Houser interprets Peirce's zealousness and ecstatic fervor is due to the worsening of Peirce's life situation and his expulsion from the Academy. These events "intensified his realization that we must approach our quest for knowledge with humility. None of us alone can make progress or ever know if we have reached the truth. Our greatest contribution is our dedicated participation in the quest for truth along with our fellow searchers" (2010, p. xcvii).

Peirce's change of heart from a Spockian altruism to one motivated by solidarity with other individuals may have been a confluence of a number of things. Among these, as noted, a theoretical change in his realism so that individuals are recognized as real, the influence of the moral sentimentalists, such as Shaftesbury, Hutcheson and Reid, and Peirce's own miserable condition undoubtedly made him more sympathetic also to the suffering of others. His own misfortunes during this period had to have a profound effect on his thinking. There was the loss of his father in death, his first wife in a divorce, the loss of his academic career at Johns Hopkins, the threat of losing his home, and the loss of his status at the Geodetic Survey, with the resulting poverty and stress. All of this in the midst of one of the worst economic depressions in the U.S. in 1893. Victor Hugo was one of Peirce's favorite authors and, in reference to *Les Miserables*, thought he had "written the least foolishly" about "the world of misery" (1897, W8, p. 28). As Peirce writes to James in the same year: "I have learned a great deal about philosophy in the last few years, because they have been very miserable and unsuccessful years,—terrible beyond anything that the man of ordinary experience can possibly understand" (Brent, 1998, pp. 341–342).

However, the task here is to bring Peirce's ecstatic claim in "Philosophy and the Conduct of Life" down to earth and make some sense of what it means to be "welded to a universal continuum." To do that it's necessary to go back to the development of this thought in the early 1890s, particularly as it is expressed in his *Monist* series. These include. "The

Architecture of Theories" (1891), "The Doctrine of Necessity Explained" (1892), "The Law of the Mind" (1892), "Man's Glassy Essence" (1893) and "Evolutionary Love" (1893). There Peirce develops his doctrine of synechism based on, as many of his metaphysical theories are, the best mathematics and physics of the day, particularly the study of topology as he knew it (Murphey,1993, pp. 391, 405). Perhaps an intuitive sense of the doctrine and its relevance to the notion of intergenerational altruism will be helpful here.

Peirce's reflections on Zeno's classic paradox of Achilles and the Tortoise, his study of the mathematical concept of the continuum and topology, all lead him to argue that continuity in time or change, or anything else, could not be explained in terms of any collection of discrete units. A line, for example, is not a collection of discrete points (1902, CP 1.276; Murphey, 1993, p. 285). In Zeno's classic paradox, Achilles can run twice as fast as the Tortoise. Even if the Tortoise is given a head start of half the length of the racecourse, Achilles will never catch up so long as he must pass through discrete points in the racecourse. Peirce argues that to say Achilles's position is determinate is to impose a metric construct that has discrete units onto a continuous line that is not discrete. As Murphey notes "the fact that Achilles' path can be measured in this way relative to a given metric does not mean that it has this character relative to any metric or that the path itself has this character" (1993, p. 285). In fact, change in time, or, for that matter change in anything, including growth would not be possible without some continuum. Just as Achilles never catches the Tortoise, nothing would change in a world of discrete units.

Peirce extrapolates this principle, claiming that it applies to anything (Murphey, 1993, p. 400). "I carry the doctrine so far as to maintain that continuity governs the whole domain of experience in every element of it" (1893, CP 7.566). As far as Peirce was concerned, continuity made generalizability possible and generalizability could explain things like the spread of ideas or feelings, essential for the possibility of intergenerational transmission (1891, CP 6.21; 1892, CP 6.103). This principle of continuity serves as the basis of his "law of mind," presented in his third paper of that title in *The Monist* series. "The one primary and fundamental law of mental action consists in a tendency to generalization." Feelings tended to spread; ideas become disseminated and adopted. It can explain the possibility of evolution (1903, CP 6.101).

Most relevant to his ethical theory, is that it characterizes personality not discretely but continuously. "It has to be lived in time," such that "this reference to the future is an essential element of personality" (1892, CP 6.156). It also explains the possibility of communication between minds:

> the recognition by one person of another's personality takes place by means to some extent identical with the means by which he is conscious of his own personality. The idea of the second personality,

> which is as much as to say that second personality itself, enters within the field of direct consciousness of the first person, and is as immediately perceived as his ego, though less strongly. At the same time, the opposition between the two persons is perceived, so that the externality of the second is recognized.
>
> (1892, CP 6.160)

To the extent that one's own personality can be extended in time in the future, such that one can recognize one's future as oneself, so others can be recognized as oneself in this respect. The principle of synechism results in a view of personality in which,

> your neighbors are, in a measure, yourself, and in far greater measure than . . . you would believe. Really, the selfhood you like to attribute to yourself is, for the most part, the vulgarest delusion of vanity. In the second place, all men who resemble you are in analogous circumstances are, in a measure, yourself."
>
> (1892, CP 7.571)

This is an argument similar in many ways to Thomas Nagel's argument for the possibility of altruism (Nagel, 1978). Nagel argues that practical reasoners must see themselves temporally extended in time and, as such, they could in principle, see themselves impersonally, as anyone when they reason as such. What they would choose to do in that practical situation is what they think anyone would do. In that case their action is generalizable (1978, p. 71). Following Robert Lane, Richard Atkins interprets this welding as the possibility that people can share the same beliefs and feelings. To the extent this rings true, then people slipstream into the continuum. False beliefs fall out of this continuum. They fail to get passed on, they are the ones changed (Lane, 2009, p. 10; Atkins, 2018, pp. 154–160).

This same idea applied to personality can be applied on a larger scale to generational communication. When one thinks of the influence of one generation on another, it is continuous in this sense. Generations are not discrete, although one can mark them artificially by decades, like generation X, in the manner in which a metric can be imposed on a line. They are intermixed at the points of transition. At any place along this generational continuum, one can show how previous ideas, feelings and actions came to bear on the woe or weal of people moving forward; and how ideas, feelings and actions at that point, influenced the weal and woe of those who came next, and many generations to come. It is in this mix that, in Peirce's words, people "become welded into the universal continuum," such that "distinct individuals weld together" (1898, CP 1.673).

There is a certain transitivity in generational change that allows the possibility of growth. Thus, at any point in the generational continuum one can see how the present is benefitted or harmed by the previous and the actions of the present, in turn, will benefit or harm what is yet to come. If benefitted, then the present is better off than it would be if it were not for what came previously; if harm has been passed on, then its task is to make it better. Since any place on the generational continuum is transitive then the responsibility of people's actions for the future can be mind-staggering. To be self-interested is to treat oneself and one's interests as discrete. To treat oneself as a discrete individual is to dissociate oneself from this continuum just as one might dissociate the present self from a future one, as Nagel suggests (1978, p. 99).

This theme gets more clearly expressed in the culminating work of *The Monist* series, "Evolutionary Love." As he defines it, evolutionary love has two aspects: one is an impulse to make things better, the other is to cultivate and pass on what is best. This applies to both communities and persons: "love is not directed to abstractions but to persons" (1893, CP 6.288), it is "an ardent impulse to fulfill another's highest impulse" (1893, CP 6.289), to work toward the perfection of others (1893, CP 6.288). On the other hand, it is manifested as an impulse to improve on what is even "hateful" (1893, CP 6.289), to even embrace what is hostile and negative to oneself (1893, CP 6.287).

Peirce wants to show in this piece that the intergenerational continuum cannot be explained on the basis of self-interest. His foil is the Social Darwinists of his day, who advocate for progress and betterment by means of self-interested agents working for their own good (1893, CP 6.290). He holds up his nemesis, Simon Newcomb, as an exemplar of such thinking. He bemoans what he observes as "the conviction of the nineteenth century . . . that progress takes place by virtue of every individual's striving for himself with all his might and trampling his neighbor under foot whenever he gets a chance to do so" (1893, CP 6.294). He also mentions Bernard Mandeville in this camp, bane of the Cambridge Platonists, as the advocate of this position, but he could have easily used Adam Smith's "invisible hand" theory as its basis (Smith, 1776, Bk IV, Chapt. II, par IX). It is the idea that it is through each individual pursuing self-interest that the greater good is promoted.

Some contemporary thinkers such as David Gauthier argue similarly. He claims that a community of rational, self-interested agents would, in fact, have to adopt moral constraints on their behavior to maximize their interests, where everyone is trying to maximize their self-interest (1986, p. 9). Even Kant made a similar claim in *Perpetual Peace*, arguing that it is possible to establish a constitution even for a "race of devils," "in such a way that, although their private intentions conflict, they check each other, with the result that their public conduct is the same as if they had no such intentions" (1795, p. 112) As Gauthier argues, mutual cooperation requires, for example, keeping promises, doing no harm and helping others when there is no significant harm to oneself, and rarely is it the case that people can achieve their interests without some form of cooperation with others. However, in this case, the reason for cooperation is self-interest, not interest in something greater than self, such as the good of the community.

As Peirce writes sarcastically about these theories: "Intelligence in the service of greed ensures the justest prices, the fairest contracts, the most enlightened conduct of all the dealings between men, and leads to the *summum bonum*, food in plenty and perfect comfort. Food for whom? Why, for the greedy master of intelligence." Peirce is chagrined that people might think "greed is the great agent in the elevation of the human race and in the evolution of the universe" (1893, CP 6.290). Peirce is refighting the fight of the Cambridge Platonists and the British sentimentalists. But, instead of Hobbes, his foe is the Social Darwinists. It is a dispute between two types of community, and two types of social contract as Peirce sees it. One is a community governed by self-interested rational agents, who are only interested in others to the extent that they serve their interests, and are led into moral constraints on their conduct, only on the basis of maximizing their interests. The other that looks to a sympathetic connection of members of a community that seeks the common good. As applied to inquiry, that common good is the truth.

Peirce's principal argument against the Social Darwinists—similar to Hutcheson's argument against Hobbes—is that Darwinian types of evolution cannot explain certain observed phenomena in cultural evolution, such as the widespread sympathy needed for the spread of ideas, the sense of the common good, national identities and other collective goods. He thinks it's hard to see how one gets from self-interested agents to such collective phenomena purely through Darwinian models of evolution (1893, CP 6.307). As Peirce characterizes it, Darwinian evolution is primarily stochastic and mechanical. Random variations occur and natural selection is the mechanism that sorts out those that are adaptive from those that are not. This can't account for intentional acts of improvement and learning from those improvements (1893, CP 6.299).

Peirce thinks the model of Lamarckian evolution provides a better explanation (1893, CP 6.300). Peirce describes Lamarckian evolution as "evolution by the force of habit" (1893, CP 6.300). For Peirce habits are the results of ways of living, feeling, or thinking that tend to reinforce themselves or change for the better as the results of experiments of living. They are acquired and can be modified over time, and improved upon, and the more positive ones passed on. Fruitful habits catalyze cultural evolution. Habits play a double role, establishing "new features," but also bring things "into harmony" with what remains (1893, CP 6.300). Thus, habits exemplify the notion of a continuum. This is characteristic of learning, growth and improvement, and consistent with his principle of synechism and "the Law of Mind" (1893, CP 6.301; 1893,

CP 6.289). Lamarckian types of evolution are linked to Peirce's notion of evolutionary love. "The good result is here brought to pass, first, by the bestowal of spontaneous energy by the parent upon the offspring and, second, by the disposition of the latter to catch the general idea of those about and thus to subserve the general purpose" (1893, CP 6.303).

"The agapastic development of thought is the adoption of certain mental tendencies, not altogether heedlessly, as in tychism, nor quite blindly by the mere force of circumstances or of logic, as in anancasm, but by an immediate attraction for the idea itself, whose nature is divined before the mind possess it, by the power of sympathy, that is, by virtue of the continuity of mind." It can happen in its collective personality "a powerfully sympathetic connection with the collective people" (1893, CP 6.307).

This is probably not the place to discuss all of the intricacies around various theories to explain altruistic behavior on a Darwinian basis, such as kin-selection and group-selection (Hamilton, 1964). Suffice it to say that Peirce would have to reconsider his dismissal of Darwinian forms of evolution as the basis for some types of altruistic behavior. For example, Philip Kitcher argues that psychological altruism, altruism that involves the promotion of the interests of other people, can follow from an extension of kin selection, that includes non-kin relations such as juvenile friendships and larger coalitions (2011, pp. 64–65).

Peirce might have been better served by adopting the Baldwin effect as an alternative to the Lamarckian model. This was a theory developed by James Baldwin, a contemporary of Peirce, whom Peirce knew quite well, since he wrote voluminous entries for his *Dictionary of Philosophy and Psychology*. Surprisingly, Peirce does not seem conversant with his theory, which is a more plausible account of Larmarckian-like mechanisms that still work within the Darwinian model.

Daniel Dennett explains the Baldwin mechanisms nicely. Suppose a population in which people's brains are wired up with considerable variation. Among the variants, suppose there is one or a few genotypes that make the organism very adaptive, while the others are more run-of-the-mill adaptive. As such, that genotype is more likely to be passed on than the others. Suppose that the genotype is such that it gives some capacity to phenotypes to adjust its wiring, depending on what they encounter in their life experience. In other words, it can learn from its experience sufficient to change its behavior. Clearly, these organisms would have much more adaptive capacity than those whose phenotype is set in stone. Consequently, they would tend to reproduce at a greater rate, leading to genetic drift in the population (1995, pp. 77–78).

Still, many anthropologists, biologists and social scientists tend to think that cultural evolution is based more obviously on a Lamarckian model rather than a Darwinian one, since acquired cultural traditions and habits are transmissible (Ayala, 2010, p. 9021; Simon, 1981; Freeman, 1992;

Metcalfe, 1993; Hodgson, 2001; Kronfeldner, 2007). As the eminent paleontologist, Stephen Jay Gould, noted:

> I am convinced that comparisons between biological evolution and human cultural or technological change have done vastly more harm than good—and examples abound of this most common of intellectual traps. . . . Biological evolution is powered by natural selection, cultural evolution by a different set of principles that I understand but dimly.
>
> (1991, p. 63)

Peirce seems to have the same concern that Gould has in using Darwinian models to frame social and cultural evolution as the Social Darwinians do (1893, CP 6.291). However, still, if Darwinian evolution is at the basis of all evolution, then it would have to be supposed that the possibility of culture and the sort of cultural transmission it entails evolved originally out of Darwinian type of evolution, so something like a Baldwin effect may have happened. On the other hand, the thinness of Richard Dawkins and Daniel Dennett's "meme" theory of cultural transmission to explain the richness of culture is testimony to the inadequacy of Darwinian models and prompts a search for some alternative to explain cultural evolution (Dennett, 1995, p. 345ff).

Disinterested Love

In "Evolutionary Love," the altruism of the disinterested inquirer of "The Doctrine of Chances" is broadened to include not only the adoption of an interest greater than self, but a sympathy with others in a quest to make things better. How does Peirce's disinterested inquirer compare with other models of disinterest?

There are four different models of disinterest that might be helpful in sorting this out. One is the notion of the *impartial spectator*, proposed by Adam Smith (1759) and David Hume (1739), but also more recently advocated by Roderick Firth (1952) and R.M. Hare (1981). The second is the disinterested agent under Rawls's *veil of ignorance* (1971). The third is the *impersonal standpoint* of Thomas Nagel (1978). The fourth is Shaftesbury's notion of *disinterested love*.

As Adam Smith argues, each person is self-interested. But since each person is so disposed, no one other than that person could tolerate that particular person's interest as supreme. Consequently, each person must view their actions from the standpoint of an impartial spectator who is not self-interested. The spectator, having no particular interests and, thereby, being impartial, can judge what is right for anyone. But the impartial spectator also has a sympathy for others that allows the spectator to disapprove of actions that unjustly harm others, and approve of actions that do not harm or benefit others (1759, pp. 162–163). As a result, Smith links the impartial spectator with the voice of conscience (1759, p. 232).

Peirce's disinterested inquirer doesn't quite seem to fit this model. Peirce's disinterested inquirer and Smith's impartial spectator seem to play different roles. The latter serves as a judge to take on the voice of others who might be affected by another's action. It serves, like a conscience as Smith suggests, to chasten those who know better than what they are about to do.

Disinterested inquirers do not act as judges, but seek moral truths, truths about what are good ends to pursue, including the highest ends, and the righteous means by which they can likely be attained. To do this rightly, inquirers must forego self-interest. Inquirers are disinterested in order not to bias the inquiry; they do not know already what is right or wrong. Smith's spectator is impartial in that it does not take anyone's side but is sympathetic to those who might be unjustly harmed. On the other hand, disinterested inquirers work in sympathy with others for the cause of truth. The disinterested inquirer is also different from variants of the impartial spectator, such as Roderick Firth's *ideal observer*. But Firth's observer is in a state of perfect knowledge as well, and Peirce's inquirer is not, and is most certainly fallible (1952).

As John Rawls points out in his discussion of the Original Position, an agreement about the ends and the rules by which the pursuit of such ends should be constrained would be unlikely so long as people were self-interested (1971, pp. 136–137, 140). Hence the necessity for the veil of ignorance (1971, p. 19). Since under the veil of ignorance, people do not know what their self-interests might be, they would literally be disinterested. Rawls is keen to point out some of the differences between his concept of the disinterested deliberator and the impartial spectator of Hume and Smith, as well as Firth's ideal observer (1971, pp. 184–185). For one thing, the impartial spectator leaves vague what the fundamental rules of justice are to be, whereas Rawls's deliberator can deduce these rather clearly (1971, p. 185). Secondly, the fact that the impartial spectator is sympathetic could lead to utilitarian-based principles that require the sacrifice of a few for the betterment of the many. Rawls insists that the agents under the veil of ignorance are *mutually disinterested*, meaning that although they do not know what their self-interests are, they do not care about any particular interests of others (1971, p. 187)

From the standpoint of this sort of disinterested deliberator, the selection of ends (goods) and rules (of justice) pertaining to their means would have to have two features according to Rawls. First, since they couldn't be biased toward their own interests, deliberators would select rules and norms that are *general*, in the sense that they would apply to people no matter what their interests might be (1971, p. 131). Second, according to Rawls, whatever ends and norms, rules of conduct are selected, it would have to universalizable. To be universalizable according to Rawls is "to assess principles on the basis of their being intelligently and regularly followed by everyone." (1971, p. 132). As Rawls argues, this is consistent with Kant's notion of the categorical imperative under a certain interpretation (1971, pp. 133, 251).

Peirce's disinterested inquirer seems to be disinterested in a different way than Rawls's agents. Peirce's inquirers are interested in the truth, empirical or moral, which requires that they refrain from self-interested biases in their inquiries. This engenders a sort of altruism on their part—the sacrifice of their self-interests in favor of the truth, unless their interests align. Rawls's agents remain self-interested throughout the deliberation process, but they are just not aware of what those particular self-interests might be. But, constrained by the veil of ignorance, they want to select ends, means and the rules pertaining to them that will fulfill their interests best, whatever those might be.

Peirce's account of ethical reasoning and ethical truth would agree with Rawls that the right sorts of rules of conduct must be generalizable. However, this generalizability, whether empirical or normative, is a matter of inquiry, leading to a convergence of belief over time. What is empirically true or morally right cannot be grasped hypothetically in ideal thought experiments, but in inquiries based on actual experiments of living over time.

Thomas Nagel's *impersonal standpoint* is a third model. Thomas Nagel wants to show how the practical reasoning of individuals, even if it is based on norms of rational self-interest, can lead to the possibility of altruism, understood as an interest in others' interests (1978, p. 79). As mentioned, altruism is possible, according to Nagel, because people can put themselves in the place of others. "You see the present situation as a specimen of a more general scheme, in which the characters can be exchanged" (1978, p. 83). The recognition that others are persons as oneself allows any person to think in terms of the ends and desires of persons *in general*. There is a way to view one's own end simply as *someone's* needs and desires (1978, p. 84). "To recognize others fully as person requires a conception of oneself as identical with a particular, impersonally specifiable inhabitant of the world, among other of a similar nature" (1978, p. 100). This, as Nagel argues, is the ability to adopt *general* principles of action (1978, p. 82).

Nagel argues that for practical reasoning to make sense, it has to be assumed that such reasoners see themselves as temporally extended in time. Unless one is acting instantaneously, practical judgments are based on temporally extended circumstances. Consider, for example, that one ought to learn some Italian because one will be traveling to Italy in six weeks. The practical judgment that one ought to learn Italian now is based on the reason that one will be in Italy in six weeks. But this could be true of any time in which one is traveling to Italy in the future, and with any difference in time between now and the time proposed for such travel. Instead of finding out now that the traveler will go to Italy in six weeks, the traveler could have found this out some other time in the future, and the time of arrival could only be three weeks past receiving that information instead of six. Nagel argues that in these cases "prudence depends on a belief in the reality of the future, and on a conception of oneself as temporally extended" (1978, p. 71).

For that reason, Nagel argues there are *tenseless* beliefs in practical judgments that are temporally neutral, that is, at any time, no matter what the present time and the distance to the future time, certain judgments about what to do would hold. "Just as a change from a tenseless to a tensed factual judgment does not alter what is believed, but only the standpoint from which one views it, so the change from a tenseless to a tensed practical judgment does not alter what one accepts as a justification for wanting, but only the standpoint from which one wants it (1978, p. 71). To treat personality as tensed is to treat it as dissociated from itself (1978, p. 72). All of this is possible because people must perceive themselves as temporally extended in time.

Nagel argues that the practical judgment that any one person makes must be viewed by that person as holding for any other such person. As Nagel characterizes it, the formal principle underlying altruism will "be closely analogous to the formal principle of timelessness, in that it will deny the possibility of restricting to one *person* the derivative influence of a reason for action, just as the formal principle which underlies prudence denies the possibility of restricting such derivative influence to one *time*. The principle underlying altruism will require, in other words, that all reasons be construable as expressing objective rather than subjective values" (1978, p. 88). As Nagel explains,

> the conception underlying altruism is that of oneself as merely one person among others, and of others as person in just as full a sense. This is parallel to the central element in a conception of oneself as temporally extended: that the present is just a time among others, and that other times are equally real.
>
> (1978, p. 88)

Peirce's principle of continuity matches many of Nagel's points, as pointed out. In his concept of personality in "The Law of Mind" and "Man's Glassy Essence" (1892, CP 6.268), the principle of synechism argues that "reference to the future is an essential element of personality," and the welding of people in the continuum is a metaphor for a sympathetic connection of personalities, ideas and feelings (1892, CP 6.157). The recognition of another's personality takes place by means similar to the consciousness of one's own personality (1892, CP 6.160), such that others "are, in a measure, yourself" (1893, CP 6.571).

Also like Rawls, Nagel focuses on the generalizability of action as a key marker in what is morally right, as Peirce does. But, again, Peirce is not suggesting that the disinterested inquirer is capable of determining what is right for others simply on the basis of being able to identify with the interests of others. Peirce's expanded sense of altruism is still tied to a cause larger than self rather than the interests of others. Inquiries are not seeking ways to satisfy a certain set of human interests, but to find out what interests *ought* to be satisfied and how to satisfy them in the best way. For Nagel, the objectivity of ends is expressed in the following way, "in any situation in which there is reason for one person to promote some end, we must be able to discover an end which there is a reason for anyone to promote should he be in a position to do so" (1978, p. 90). For Peirce, discovering the right ends is a process of inquiry, such that "we consider what the general effect would be of thoroughly carrying out our ideals" (1903, CP 1.608). This cannot be determined merely by means of a sympathetic connection with others, or in thought experiments but, in conformity with the pragmatic maxim, through the practical effects following that end has on ways of life and experiments of living.

The last model to consider is Shaftesbury's notion of *disinterested love*—one of Peirce's favorites among the British sentimentalists. Recall, that for Shaftesbury, people who are *interested* seek ends and goods, whether it is truly their real good or not (1711, p. 170). Disinterested love, on the other hand, "has no other object than merely the excellency of that being itself." Disinterested love is such that "we shall find it of a kin which relates not in the least to the private interest of the creature, nor has for its object any self-good or advantage of the private system" (1711, p. 268). As E.E. Kleist notes in regard to Shaftesbury, "one's "true interest" emerges out of the attitude of disinterestedness" (2000, p. 118). The admiration, joy, or love turns wholly upon what is exterior and foreign to ourselves (1711, pp. 202–203). Disinterest is a non-instrumental appreciation of the object, sparked by the perceived beauty in the object (1711, pp. 318–320). This in effect links the good and beautiful. In turn, Shaftesbury links disinterested love to *enthusiasm*: "all sound love and admiration is enthusiasm" (1711, p. 320), something which elevates people to something greater than self, and the good of the whole (Grean, 1967, pp. 20, 33–34). Peirce often uses the term *admiration* to characterize attitudes toward the highest goods.

After 1883, Peirce certainly speaks about "love of truth" in these terms, as one of the characteristics of the true scientist, the genuine inquirer (1903, CP 1.49), the "scientific *Eros*," (1898, CP 1.620) and "man's capacity for loving the truth" (1889, CP 6.183). "The genuine love of truth" is the first, among the moral factors that make up science (1902, CP 7.87). But there's no textual support showing any direct influence of Shaftesbury on Peirce on this matter.

There may also be an echo of influence from Shaftesbury's idea of the *sensus communis*, a sense of the common good and love of community

(1711, pp. 48–53; Gadamer, 1975, p. 24). Self-interest is bound up with one's private good, but one's real good is the harmonization of private with the common good. The moral person is one who is moved by affection for the common good of the whole, as opposed to those who address the common good out of self-interest (1711, p. 169).

Kant is also influenced by Shaftesbury's notion, but gives it a somewhat different interpretation in *The Critique of Judgment*. For Kant, the *sensus communis* is a faculty of judgment by which one compares one's judgment "with the collective reason of humanity." "It is done by comparing our judgment with the possible rather than the actual judgments of others, and by putting ourselves in the place of any other man, by abstracting from the limitations which contingently attach to our own judgment." This makes possible three kinds of thinking: first, the ability to think for oneself, to think autonomously, as opposed to adopting what others think, that is, thinking heteronomously; second, to put ourselves in the place of everyone else, that is, to "enlarge our thought"; third, to think reasonably, that is, in accord with reason (1790, pp. 136–137).

Peirce shares some features with all of these models of disinterest, but the disinterested inquirer strikes out a rather unique template compared to these others. The sort of altruism that the disinterested inquirer has is one of foregoing self-interest for a cause greater than self, namely the truth—whether empirical or moral. The very nature of logical reasoning commits the inquirer to a community of inquiry, which is necessary to accomplish such a task. Peirce broadens this altruism in a way that exhorts a solidarity with fellow travelers on this road to inquiry. A disinterested love of truth imbues inquirers with a desire to improve on what is lacking and pass on what is best and, through this, develops an intergenerational altruism, a "welding to the universal continuum."

The Ethos of Inquirers

Besides the sentiments needed for inquiry, inquirers must have the right sort of epistemological virtues and character for inquiry to be successful. They must conduct inquiry not only with the best scientific methodologies but virtuously as well. No criminals have ever advanced science, Peirce argues (1902, R 433, p. 5), including, it can be supposed, scientists who have falsified data or findings. Peirce makes it clear in several places that the virtues are prerequisite for good reasoning and the conduct of inquiry "A scientific man must be single-minded and sincere with himself. Otherwise, his love of truth will melt away, at once. He can, therefore, hardly be otherwise than an honest fair-minded man" (1903, CP 1.49). The scientist must have humility: "he is keenly aware of his own ignorance, and knows that personally he can make but small steps in discovery" (1901, CP 8.136). Honesty itself is essential to scientific practice: "Intellectual honesty and sincerity and a real love of truth" are "absolutely necessary" to reason properly (1902, CP 2.82). To do good induction, the reasoner must be "a man of honor," and have the virtues of "probity, industry is essential" (1902, CP 1.576). Indeed, probity and industry are needed for good induction (1902, R433, p. 4). The scientist cannot be vain and must have a sense of something greater than self, and for this reason "good reasoning and good morals are closely allied" (1902, CP 1.576).

Robert Talisse provides a list of the virtues he thinks are required for inquirers and deliberators that are similar to the list Peirce insists on. These include honesty, modesty, charity and integrity (2005, pp. 112–113). Honesty is "the disposition to follow evidence and weigh various factors relevant to a problem, and a willingness to base decisions upon such considerations . . . . The . . . honest deliberator follows reasons and arguments, not bare interests or preference" (2005, p. 112). The modest deliberator understands proposals "not as ultimate resolutions, but as hypotheses to be tried and evaluated in terms of their effects." Charitable interlocutors "accept as a default position that their opponents are not simply stupid or misguided or corrupt, but possibly correct." Talisse defines integrity in an odd way. It usually means that people will publicly declare their principles, and stand-up for those principles, especially when there is some risk to doing so (Carter, 1996, p. 7). Talisse defines it in a way that sounds more like what might be called fairmindedness—"he . . . strives to be fair to his opponents; he tries to place himself in the position of others to better understand their concerns; he seeks not only to refute or disprove opposing views, but to rationally persuade others and, when persuasion fails, strike a reasonable compromise" (2005, pp. 112–113). Corruption, as noted, is another concern Peirce had about any inquiry. If inquirers are paid to prove a certain position or paid to serve as an advocate or mouthpiece for others, this inherently corrupts the inquiry (1898, CP 1.619; 1.642).

How does a virtuous character come about? Peirce talks about "ideals of conduct" in drafts to the Lowell Lectures in 1903. Consistent with his conservative sentimentalism, these ideals of conduct are "imbibed in childhood," and shaped by their "personal nature" and by their "circle of society." People develop certain rules of conduct from these ideals. These are modified as time goes on and experience warrants (1903, CP 1.592). When the occasion arises to employ them, there is a certain resolve and determination to follow them (1903, CP 1.593). If successfully followed, they are accompanied by a feeling of pleasure (1903, CP 1.594). In any case, the action is reviewed and evaluated, so that "whether the man is satisfied with himself or dissatisfied, his nature will absorb the lesson like a sponge; and the next time he will tend to do better than he did before" (1903, CP 1.598). There will also likely be, over time, review of the ideals or standards themselves, as to their fitness. This is the essence of self-control, and the core part of purposive, goal-directed behavior. Such self-correction lies at its heart and self-correction implies comparison of one's actions with some standard or ideal. "Ethics," as he says, is in part the study of "what the *fitness* of an ideal of conduct consists in, and to deduce from such definition of fitness what conduct ought to be" (1903, CP 1.600).

Peirce discusses the virtues in Chapter 4 of *The Minute Logic*, in the context of his analysis of Plato's various concepts of the good. He discusses Plato's four cardinal virtues as expressed in *The Republic*. Peirce is reading Plato in Greek, and makes his own translations, As Peirce calls them, they are wisdom, courage, self-control and righteousness (*The Republic*, 428a). Peirce translates *dikê* as "righteousness," although it is usually translated as "justice." *Sophron* is usually translated as "temperance," but Peirce translates it as "self-control" (1902, R. 434, pp. 89–90). In other places, he calls it "self-command" (1902, R 434, p. 90). In the context of *The Republic*, Peirce interprets Plato's notion of righteousness (justice) of the state as the proper division of labor in the state among the three classes (philosophers, guardians and merchants) in accord with the three goods of wisdom, honor and gain (R434, p. 82). In regard to the individual, righteousness "consists in each part of the soul doing its part" (R434, p. 92).

However, in other places, Peirce seems to characterize righteousness as temperance or self-control: "the righteous man is the man who controls his passions" (1903, CP 5.130). Generally speaking, self-control is thought to be the core element in the virtues, whether it is self-control in regard to pleasures as in temperance, self-control in regard to fear, as in courage, or self-control in wants, desires and needs, as in justice. Based on these texts, it's reasonable to assume that righteousness is another term for the virtues in Peirce.

Peirce's account of how ideals of conduct are acquired is not much different than an account given by Julia Annas. Annas considers virtues as habits, dispositions to act in certain ways and not others (2006, p. 516). As Annas has it, virtues are built up primarily through the exercise of the agent's practical reasoning (2006, p. 516). Practical reasoning involves "doing the right thing for the right reason, in the appropriate way—honestly, courageously, and so on" (2006, p. 516). Similarly, for Aristotle, virtues are habits of action that are perfected by habituation (*Nicomachean Ethics*, 1103a20–25). It is by actions in the context of transactions with others that people become just, or in repeated dangerous situations that people become brave, or in the face of desires that they become temperate (*Nicomachean Ethics*, 1103b 15–20). Annas adds a dimension to this, missing in Peirce. She points to degrees of self-control as an indication of how well the virtue is habituated in the person. The more self-control that is needed, the less habituated the virtue, so that a temperate person, for example, is disposed to act temperately "effortlessly and with no internal opposition" (2006, p. 517).

Annas emphasizes that people are not blank slates receptive to a theory of right action, but that "begins from our embedded lives" (2006, p. 525).

"We start our moral education by learning from others," by adopting some people as role models or teachers. At first, these are adopted on the basis of authority, and what is adopted is fragmented at first. But, as children acquire experience and practice and begin to think for themselves, they begin to "detect and deal with inconsistencies, and will try to make . . . judgments and practice coherent in terms of a wider understanding" that enables them "to unify, explain and justify" decisions (2006, p. 517). Acquiring virtues are like acquiring practical skills. "Ethical reflection begins from what you have learned in society . . . . Virtue begins from following rules or models in your social and cultural context," but then is taken over by self-reflection and deliberate adjustment. Reflection about ethical views will often reveal them to be inadequate as to the way people want to be followed, consequently, by an effort to improve oneself (2006, p. 524). People consider virtues "as an *ideal*" and that ethics "involves "aspiration" to an ideal (2006, p. 525).

The Norms of Inquiry

In addition to sentiments and virtues needed for successful inquiry, Peirce also points out that there are certain norms of conduct implicit in inquiry that ought to be followed. As Peirce says rather blandly, such norms are "convenient and serve to minimize the effects of future inadvertence" (1903, CP 1.592).

The goal of inquiries is the truth of the matter investigated. Yet there are communities that are regulated by norms that are not conducive to that end. Peirce makes this clear in his 1878 article, "The Fixation of Belief." To discover which beliefs are true and right, a community cannot close its ears and eyes to beliefs that oppose its own. Communities must be open to criticism Communities cannot be tenacious in their beliefs and still hold out hope that they will be right in the long run (1877, CP 5.377–5.378). To discover the truth requires self-criticism and self-correction. Science, for example, progresses precisely because it is a master of self-correction that does not rely on what inquirers tend to think is true, but accepts that there is something independently of such beliefs that can sort out which to retain and which to reject. As Peirce says, "reasoning tends to correct itself, and the more so, the more wisely its plan is laid." (1898, CP 5.575). Communities that impose beliefs by authority and fiat cannot also hope to discover what is right and good, even if they are able to stabilize communities in the short term by such methods (1878, CP 5.379). Asserting that a claim is true solely *ex cathedra* is to violate a duty of assertion, namely, to provide reasons for the assertion. To claim that something is right simply on the basis that it is issued by some authority is to fall into the fallacy already noted by Plato in *The Euthyphro*. Even if a supreme, all-good authority, such as God, were to issue some rule as morally right, surely it is right not because God issues it but, because it is right, a good God would issue it. Thus, there must be a reason behind its issue, and this is what counts it as good. Dogmatism in any form is another folly that is not conducive to inquiry (1878, CP 5.382). To claim that something is true but cannot be questioned, or must be presupposed, is to also cut off the possibility of inquiry. Fallibilism is the cure for dogmatism.

Peirce expresses these criticisms by one motto: "Do not block the way of inquiry." It is as he says, "one corollary which itself deserves to be inscribed upon every wall of the city of Philosophy." "To set up a philosophy which barricades the road of further advance toward the truth is the one unpardonable offence in reasoning" (c. 1905, CP 1.135–1.136). Dogmatism, the assertion that one's assertion is absolutely true, is an attitude that blocks inquiry (c. 1905, CP 1.137). Asserting that something can never be known is also a block to inquiry (c. 1905, CP 1.138). Contrariwise, asserting that something is finally proven, also blocks the road to inquiry (c. 1905, CP 1.140).

If these are the basic norms of a community of inquiry, there are also norms that regulate the discursive practices of co-inquirers. These are articulated by Peirce in his analysis of the speech-act of assertion. The practice of inquiry involves, above all, making assertions that certain hypotheses or claims are true. Indeed, the point of an inquiry is to come away with some assertion about the hypothesis under investigation. Peirce analyzes the features of assertion to show that there are certain implicit norms, commitments and expectations in the speech act that inform the practice of inquiry. As proof to its normative character, Peirce notes that failure to these commitments is often met with sanctions by those affected by the assertion (1903, CP 5.30). "In case the substance of what is asserted should be proved untrue," then, "it would be followed by very real effects" (c. 1902, 5.546).

Peirce asks, "What is the difference between throwing out the word *speaking monkey*, and averring that *monkeys speak*, and inquiring *whether monkeys speak or not?* This is a difficult question" (1893, R 409, p. 94). Anticipating speech-act theory, Peirce argues that there should be a distinction between a proposition and the assertion of a proposition, mirroring the familiar distinction between locution and illocution (c. 1902, CP 5.543). He likens the assertion to taking an oath, and emphasizes that "it is not mere saying, but is *doing*" (c. 1902, CP 5.546). Peirce also notes the perlocutionary aspect of assertion. A judgment, Peirce says "is the mental act by which the judger seeks to impress upon himself the truth of a proposition." But "while the judgement is only intended to affect oneself," asserting the proposition is "intended to affect others" (c. 1897, CP 2.252).

In analyzing such illocutions, Peirce notes first that every assertion implies a speaker and a listener:

> When an assertion is made, there really is some speaker, writer, or other sign-maker who delivers it; and he supposes there is, or will be, some hearer, reader, or other interpreter who will receive it. It may

> be a stranger upon a different planet, an aeon later; or it may be that very same man as he will be a second after. In any case, the deliverer signals to the receiver.
>
> (1896, CP 3.433; Bellucci, 2018, p. 157)

This, as Kenneth Boyd emphasizes, characterizes assertion as "an inherently social act," so that an assertion assumes the presence of speakers and hearers in the context of a communicative situation (2016, p. 24).

Second, the assertor makes certain kinds of commitments when making the assertion. "To assert a proposition is to make oneself responsible for it, without any definite forfeit, it is true, but with a forfeit no smaller for being unnamed" (c. 1902, CP 5.543). Peirce likens this to going before a notary and taking a binding oath, with consequences should the assertion prove untrue (c. 1897, CP 2.252; 1903, CP 5.30). Peirce continues:

> This ingredient, the assuming of responsibility, which is so prominent in solemn assertion, must be present in every genuine assertion. For clearly, every assertion involves an effort to make the intended interpreter believe what is asserted, to which end a reason for believing it must be furnished. . . . At this point, the reader should call to mind . . . that even solitary meditation every judgment is an effort to press home, upon the self of the immediate future and of the general future, some truth . . . Consequently it must be equally true that here too there is contained an element of assuming responsibility, of "taking the consequences."
>
> (c. 1908, CP 5.546)

As Kenneth Boyd notes in the interpretation of this passage, it

> suggests that by taking responsibility for the truth of a proposition one undertakes a commitment to provide reason to believe the proposition one is asserting. This commitment is rooted, in part, in the fact that asserting a proposition one tries to convince someone . . . of its truth.
>
> (2016, p. 23)

This is similar to Robert Brandom's conclusions in his theory of *normative pragmatics* (Keeler, 2004). Normative pragmatics argues that speech practices contain norms concerning how it is correct to use speech, and under what circumstance it is appropriate to perform those speech acts, and what appropriate consequences such performances entail (1994, p. xiii). Assertions, if genuine, imply that assertors believe in some way, on some basis, that the assertion is true. "The attitude of taking-true," Robert Brandom argues, "is just that of acknowledging an assertional commitment." It is an "attitude that grounds consequential undertakings of such commitments" (1994, p. 202). "What is it that we are doing when we assert, claim or declare something? The general answer is that we are undertaking a certain kind of commitment" (1994, p. 167). He writes, "the characteristic authority on which the role of assertions in communication depends is intelligible only against the background of a correlative responsibility to vindicate one's entitlement to the commitments such speech acts express" (1994, p. xii). Cheryl Misak, in interpreting Peirce, says much the same. "First, when I assert or believe that p, I commit myself to certain consequences—to have expectations about the consequences of p's being true. She continues:

> These will be specified in terms of actions and observations: 'if p, then if I do A, B will be the result'. And, as Peirce stressed, some of these consequences will be consequences for belief. When I assert or believe that p, I find myself bound up in a web of inferential connections. If, for instance, I believe that p, and p entails q, then I am committed also to q.
>
> (2000, pp. 73–74)

Third, as Boyd points out, since assertions assume the presence of a speaker and hearer in the general sense, then the commitments of the speaker are directed to that partner or partners in the context of the discursive practice (2016, p. 24). Of course, for co-interlocutors to assert what they know to be false has significant consequences for any interlocutor in the mix, and certainly in the public domain, as in the courtroom. In fact, Peirce implies that a condition of sincerity—believing what one asserts—is a necessary condition for counting anything as an assertion. Otherwise, it's just a lie or a ruse, which is another type of speech act (Boyd, 2016, p. 25). An assertion "supposes that . . . a person performs an act which renders him liable to the penalties of the social law (or, at any rate, those of the moral law) in case it should not be true" (c. 1902, CP 2.315).

Fourth, assertions call up the presence of a community of inquiry. Misak argues that, additionally, in asserting a claim, people are committed to what Habermas emphasizes—that people are arguing that anyone should believe the claim as they do (2000, p. 74; Habermas, 1990, p. 65). This is the basis for Misak's assertion that the illocutionary force of speech acts of belief and assertion not only commit people to inquiry, it also commits people to communities of inquiry (2000, p. 95). After all, making assertions to others enjoins them to make their own inquiries about what is asserted. An assertion, as Habermas insists, is a call by the assertor for all to believe as the assertor does. In that regard, it is an address to some community of inquirers. As Peirce argues, "no sensible man will be void of doubt as long as persons as competent to judge as himself differ from him. Hence to resolve his own doubts is to ascertain to what position sufficient research would carry all men" (1869–1870, W2, p. 355). Misak concurs:

> Belief involves being prepared to try to justify one's views to others and being prepared to test one's belief against the experience of others. Thus, the differences of inquirers—their different perspectives, sensibilities and experiences—must be taken seriously. If they are not, reaching the best or the true belief is not on the cards.
>
> (2000, p. 94)

Robert Talisse summarizes Misak's argument nicely:

1. To believe p is to hold that p is true.
2. To hold that p is true is to hold that p "is a belief that cannot be improved upon, a belief that would forever meet the challenges of reason, argument, and evidence.

   (Misak, 2000, p. 49)

3. To hold that a belief would forever meet these challenges is to engage in the project of justifying one's belief, what Peirce called "inquiry."
4. One cannot determine on one's own when all the best reasons and evidence have been considered, so the project of squaring one's beliefs with the best available reasons and evidence is an ongoing and essentially social endeavor that requires what Peirce called a "community of inquiry."

   (2005, p. 103)

Of course, Karl-Otto Apel had earlier argued much the same thing, claiming that those who assert truth claims or moral claims must defend those claims publicly, through the use of reasons that co-interlocutors can accept or reject. This calls up a community of inquirers. As Apel clarifies this broadly:

> Everyone who philosophizes, and that means everyone who argues seriously, must already—at least implicitly—have recognized an ethical fundamental norm. If one is prepared to reflect on the implicit meaning of one's argumentative acts, then one must see that one already presupposes, together with the possibility of linguistic meaning and truth, that all claims to meaning and truth must in principle be resolvable through arguments—and through arguments alone—in an unlimited community of communication. That means that one has already recognized that as arguer one presupposes an ideal community of communication composed of all human beings as equally entitled partners, a community in which all differences of

> opinion—also those which involve practical norms—should be solved in principle only through consensual arguments.
>
> (1996, pp. 196–197)

Altogether, Peirce and his interpreters provide a picture of the ideal community of inquiry. It is one that could also serve as a model for an ethical community, generally, since a community that abides by the basic norms of inquiry is more likely to light upon what is good and right than one that abjures these tenets. The implicit norms of assertion commit those who make claims about what is right and good to provide reasons for such claims. If the goal of such assertions is to have co-inquirers believe as the assertor, they must allow the interlocutors opportunities to seek clarification, ask questions, make criticisms and the like. If people sincerely attest to their assertions and believe they have good reasons to believe they are true, then they ought to be willing and, indeed, are committed to their test in a robust community of inquiry. Commitment to what is asserted, is commitment to the truth, and the commitment to truth is finding out if what one asserts will survive the test of time and endure criticisms over time—and that is a commitment to a community of inquiry.

8 Esthetics

To make the practical reasoning that informs people's purposive conduct ethical, communities must engage in inquires as to what counts as good ends to pursue. Peirce sees the working together of the normative sciences of ethics and esthetics as help in this regard.

In his early days, Peirce thought little of esthetics since he was "lamentably ignorant of it" (1902, CP 2.120) and, like many others, he believed that esthetics was the study of beauty, and beauty was a matter of taste. But, as he recounts his thinking, he later changed his mind and realized its importance and understood it in a broader sense. If deliberate action was directed to ends, then esthetics would have something to do with the study of those ends, completing the goals of the normative sciences (1903, CP 5.111). Indeed, by 1906 he proclaims that "[i]t is in esthetics that we ought to seek for the deepest characteristics of normative science, since esthetics, in dealing with the very ideal itself whose mere materialization engrosses the attention of practices and logic, must contain the heart, soul and spirit of normative science" (1906, CP 5.551).

This sense of esthetics comes around 1902 where, in a letter to William James, he chides himself for not seeing how logic rests not only on ethics but also that ethics rests on esthetics (1902, CP 8.255). In his application to the Carnegie Foundation in that same year, he states this clearly: "I show that Ethics depends essentially upon Esthetics and Logic upon Ethics" (1902, R L75, Memoir 9). He repeats this hierarchical ordering of the normative sciences in the first and fifth of the 1903 Harvard Lectures: Esthetics is "the basic normative science upon which as a foundation, the doctrine of ethics must be reared," and logic in turn is founded in ethics (1903, HL, p. 119).

In 1902, Peirce was working on his *Minute Logic* with this hierarchy in mind. He began a chapter on ethics, which he did not complete, and indicates that he intends to write another chapter devoted to esthetics. But he warns the reader that the chapter will have more questions than answers (1902, CP 2.197; 1902, R 432–434). He makes the *raison d'etre* of the study of esthetics clear in the second chapter of the proposed book. There, he addresses two fundamental questions about logic: What validates the principles of reasoning on which logic is based and why study logic? In regard to the first question, Peirce asks, "what it is that justifies that faith" in reasoning? (1902, CP 2.147). The second question is made plainly: "O Reader . . . why is it that you have undertaken the study of logic? (1902, CP 2.123; 1902, CP 2.153). The answer to the second question hinges on the first, because good, sound reasoning tends to lead to true beliefs and tends to avoid error, which is why people desire to study it (1902, CP 2.125). Thus, there is a hypothetical imperative, an implicit prudential norm, in the answer to why one should study logic: If one wants to attain true beliefs and avoid error, then one ought to study logic.

But because this is only a hypothetical imperative, a prudential norm, it leads to another, more fundamental question: Why should one seek truth at all? Peirce thought that ethics could answer that question since it determines what is good to do and, presumably, why it is good to seek the truth (1902, CP 2.198). But even if ethics answered that question satisfactorily, it still left an even more fundamental question: Why should one seek the good or, for that matter, any worthy end? This raises the question of what makes an end worthy of pursuit, what makes something a worthy ideal? (1902, CP 2.199). In this way, Peirce sees esthetics, the study of ends, as the most fundamental of the three normative sciences.

Peirce did not reveal all of the thinkers who may have influenced his effort to build his science of esthetics. But based on the textual evidence, there seem to be three principal ideas which shaped his thinking. One is Friedrich Schiller's concepts of the living shape (*lebende Gestalt*) and the play impulse (*Spieltrieb*), as that which brings reason and feeling into harmony. A second is Plato's and Aristotle's notion of *to kalon*, understood as form fit for a beneficial function and pleasing for that reason. The third is Kant's idea of the architectonic, as reason manifested in the systematic unity and organization of the sciences.

Schiller and the Reconciliation of Reason and Sentiment

Given the goal of a systematic study of logic, Peirce feels he must answer the fundamental questions pertaining to its study—if logical reasoning makes it more likely to attain true claims, why pursue truth? If it is good to pursue truth because it is good to do, why pursue goodness? Based on the tradition in philosophy, Peirce can answer these questions by taking one of two more common paths: love or duty. In the first, one should pursue the good because of its lovability, desirability, or attractiveness. In the second, it is pursued because of the command to do good, in one or more of the various forms of the natural law. The latter answer requires no other discipline than ethics to articulate that response. The first requires understanding a class of phenomena in addition to thought and action—feeling and sentiment.

The first path of duty is the path of the Stoics, Cicero, Thomas Aquinas and Immanuel Kant, and appeals to various versions of the natural law in order to short-circuit this bottomless questioning. The natural law, perhaps most simply expressed by Aquinas, commands us by the force of reason to do good and avoid evil (1265–1274, *Summa Theologica*, Q.94. Art 2). If we should pursue truth for the sake of goodness, then the reason for pursuing goodness does not lie in another hypothetical imperative but a categorical one, as Kant argues. For him, the ground of ethics lies in the command of moral law, respect (*Achtung*) for the law (1785, p. 5).

On the other hand, the moral sentimentalists, Hutcheson, Hume and Reid, saw the "why" of goodness in the moral sense, the way of the heart. Indeed, Peirce's *sentimentalism*, as he calls it, is "the doctrine that great respect should be paid to the natural judgments of the sensible heart' (1893, CP 6.292).

Peirce seems conflicted about these two paths. He advocates for moral sentimentalism on the one hand. Yet, on the other, he upholds the importance of logic, reasoning and reasonableness. Like his hero, Friedrich Schiller, Peirce senses that esthetics can reconcile these two opposing ethical stances.

Schiller attempted to reconcile Kant's reason-based ethics with sentiment and inclination. Understanding the role of esthetics is key. Having witnessed the spectacle of the Reign of Terror as a product of the Enlightenment's overemphasis on reason, Schiller thinks reason has to be balanced with the human capacity for feeling and sentiment. The capacity of feeling needs to be developed without compromising reasoning ability (1795, p. 50). How is reason and sentiment to be reconciled?

In *The Aesthetic Education of Man*, Friedrich Schiller addresses this issue (Barnouw, 1988, pp. 616, 619). Impressed and influenced by Kant's philosophy, still he cannot completely accept the dominance of reason in the matter of morals. No, sentiment must also play a role. Cold-hearted duty is not sufficient to explain people's attraction to the good:

> Reason has accomplished all she can, in discovering and expounding Law; it is the task of courageous will and lively feeling to execute it. If Truth is to gain the victory in the struggle with Force, she must first become herself a force, and find some impulse to champion her in the realm of phenomena; for impulses are the only motive forces in the sensible world.
>
> (1795, p. 48)

As Alain Locke expresses it, "Beauty as a motive has been taken out of morality, so that we confront beautiless duty and dutiless beauty" (1923, p. 178).

Peirce read Schiller's *Letters* as a young man, and it appears to have influenced him for a lifetime (1906, CP 5.402n3; 1903, R 310, p. 4).

Jeffrey Barnouw thinks that "it is reasonable to conclude that the influence of Schiller was active at the end as well as at the inception of Peirce's philosophical development, spanning more than fifty years of his life" (1988, p. 607). As Peirce writes in drafts of *The Minute Logic* in 1902 in preparation of a chapter on esthetics:

> It is now forty-seven years ago that I undertook to expound Schiller's *Aesthetische Briefe* to my dear friend, Horatio Paine. We spent every afternoon for long months upon it, picking the matter to pieces as well as we boys knew how to do. In those days, I read various works on esthetics; but on the whole, I must confess that, like most logicians, I have pondered that subject far too little. The books do seem so feeble. That affords one excuse. And then esthetics and logic seem, at first blush, to belong to different universes. It is only very recently that I have become persuaded that that seeming is illusory, and that, on the contrary, logic needs the help of esthetics. The matter is not yet very clear to me; so unless some great light should fall upon me before I reach that chapter, it will be a short one filled with doubts and queries mainly. (1902, CP 2.197)

Peirce thought Schiller's book "a very good book for an infant philosopher" (1903, R 310, p. 4). It is difficult to summarize Schiller's *Aesthetic Education of Man*. Thomas Goudge thought it "turgid" (1950, p. 334). Peirce gives some sense of how Schiller's work may have influenced him in a youthful essay written as a student at Harvard in 1857 (1857, W1, pp. 10–12). Indeed, the general tenor of Schiller's work seems congenial to Peirce (1906, CP 1.573; 1906, CP 5.402n3).

Schiller reasons concentrically rather than linearly, circling around some central themes by adding a bit more depth each time he surveys them. But it is clear that Schiller strives to explain how it is possible through "esthetic culture" to "desire more nobly" (1795, p. 112). If the moral attitude can only inspire us to duty through the command of law, the esthetic attitude can enable human beings to go beyond duty to nobility (1795, pp. 48, 111n1).

So how does Schiller integrate inclination and duty, sentiment and reason? An earlier work, *The Kallias Letters*, attempts to expand the thinking of Kant. Its title stands in reference to the Greek notion of *to kalon*, which Peirce adopts in lieu of 'beauty.' Schiller sees a relation between esthetics and practical reason in Kant's sense of the term. With Kant, he argues that the principle of practical reason is freedom, understood as autonomy or self-determination. When practical reason is applied to such free actions, it makes moral judgments. But when it is applied to experience, to appearances it produces esthetic judgments. Since the principle of practical reason is freedom, then Schiller defines beauty here as the "freedom in appearance," a sense that if something is beautiful, it is not heteronomous, determined by something outside of itself, but is self-determined (1793b, pp. 152, 154). A horse whose gait is imposed heteronomously by the work of pulling a wagon is not beautiful as compared to one, unburdened by such imposition, freely expresses its form (1793b, pp. 163–164). In variants on the theme of the "Good Samaritan," Schiller imagines the one who acts as if the duty to help the victim fell gracefully from the very core of the person, is an act of moral beauty, someone who acts with the ease of instinct, as opposed to those who act with calculation or ulterior purpose (1793b, p. 159).

Indeed, in *On Grace and Dignity*, Schiller describes grace as the influence of freedom on form (1793a, pp. 133–134). With Kant, Schiller argues that acting from the moral law defines the moral worth of actions. But grace is the result of a moral attitude based on moral sentiments and instincts, part of people's character. When the two are combined, a disposition to do the right thing combined with reasons for doing the right thing, then the action comes naturally and gracefully—marking a "beautiful soul" (1793a, p. 138). It is in grace that one finds "harmony" between "sensuousness and reason, duty and inclination" (1793a, p. 153). It is witnessing this harmony in a person that is admirable and gives expression of approval (1793a, p. 165). The dutiful person does what is right out of duty, but something special happens when reason and inclination align, when they harmonize to produce this grace and nobility. If Schiller were to use the language of the Greeks, he would call such a person *kalos k'agathos*, someone who is not only good but also *kalos*—beautiful or noble. This is a person, as Aristotle says, who does actions that are "good absolutely" and who does not do them for one's sake but "for the sake of others" (*Rhetoric*, 1367b35–39).

In *The Aesthetic Education of Man*, Schiller tells a just-so story of human beings caught in the tension between two impulses. The impulse of sensuousness, founded in the state of nature, wrapped up in physical materiality and experienced as a multiplicity of sensations. In sensation, one feels subjectively, momentarily in the present state (1795, p. 64). This is contrasted with the formal impulse, stemming from the rational nature of human beings, to bring harmony and unity to the diversity of manifestations and experiences, through the notion of law and universality (1795, pp. 65–66). Through sensuousness, human beings *apprehend* more and more of the world; and through reason, they *comprehend* more and more of the world (1795, p. 69). The task of cultivation is to train both the sensibility and reason in order to balance and harmonize their drives (1795, p. 69). The object of the sense impulse is life in its widest sense, and the object of the form impulse is called shape, "a concept which includes all formal qualities of things and all their relations to the intellectual faculties" (1795, p. 76).

But there is a third impulse, the *play impulse*, that is manifested in beauty, that unites and balances the sense and forms impulses in an equilibrium. Its object is the *living shape*, "a concept which serves to denote all esthetic qualities of phenomena and—in a word—what we call Beauty in the widest sense of the term" (1795, p. 76). As a sculpture created from a block of marble illustrates, form and matter are integrated in a living shape:

> so long as we only think about . . . shape, it is lifeless, mere abstraction; so long as we only feel . . . life, it is shapeless, mere impression. Only as the form of something lives in our sensation, and its life takes form in our understanding, is it living shape, and this will everywhere be the case where we judge it to be beautiful.
>
> (1795, p. 76)

Indeed, the concept of play suggests, as the ordinary sense of children's play does, the freedom to rearrange the rules, order and form of existing things into new ones, to go beyond what is present to what could be, to fantasize and dream. Play engenders pure autonomy in this respect. It is the possibility not only to think of something different than what is, but the possibility of something better than what is. Thus, play could be interpreted as this realm where the shape of life can be transformed, all the better to bring shape and life into harmony. In morality, this could mean creating one's own living shape, a pure expression of autonomy. As such, because it is one's own, the inclination to follow one's moral shape flows organically. The beautiful is the self-determined, a product of complete freedom and autonomy. The good person is one who does his duty, even without inclination to do what is right; but the noble person is one where there is an inclination and ease with doing one's duty, a grace, a harmony between duty and inclination, reason and instinct. Duty gives shape to the moral life, but sentiment and inclination give life to it. It is when the two are balanced that a living shape to moral life emerges.

It is clear from Peirce's youthful essay on Schiller that this is much of the way in which he thinks of the poet and philosopher:

> Man consists of person and condition . . . from these elements of humanity arise two impulses: from Person the impulse which produces form . . . from Condition, the sensuous impulse. . . . The first impulse gives laws, the second creates cases. . . . At first sight these impulses, because contrary seem contradictory, but this is not the case. It is true no third fundamental impulse reconciling the two is possible, but since they do not conflict in the same objects they can easily coexist, and in perfect harmony, whence arises a third impulse, the result of the perfect balance of the other two, which . . . may be regarded as the impulse which creates beauty. Schiller calls it the play-impulse, because play, that which is neither internally nor externally

> constrained and, while we are in the esthetic state, the balance of the two fundamental impulses, produces perfect freedom.
>
> (1857, W1, p. 11)

In response to his professor's comments, Peirce further elaborates on this balance:

> On the one hand, the two impulses can, and must be, *balanced*, because, since the function of the formal impulse (and, as it seems to me, the peculiar of mortals is to reduce to form matter which is furnished by the sensuous impulse for no other purpose, the preponderance of either would give a surplus of faculty which would be either unemployable or of no ultimate advantage).
>
> (1857, W1, p. 534)

If beauty is that which can balance reason and feeling, how does it relate to morality. The title of Peirce's Harvard essay is after Ruskin's famous saying that "the sense of beauty never furthered the performance of a single act of duty." Peirce agrees in part with Ruskin. Peirce concludes his essay by noting that "now it will be observed that beauty gives the mind no particular direction or tendency—hence it can have no result either for the intellect or the will and can help us to perform no single duty. On the other hand, it places the mind in a state of "infinite determinableness" so that it can turn in any direction and is in perfect freedom, hence, beauty in the highest degree is fruitful with respect to knowledge and morality" (1857, W1, p. 12). This would suggest that the role of beauty, particularly Schiller's play-impulse, is to open up possibility, to "turn in any direction." Because play is "neither internally nor externally constrained" and, while "in the esthetic state," "produces perfect freedom" (1857, W1, p. 11). This would suggest that as Schiller avers, in play, one can rise above what is, to think of what ought to be.

Indeed, many years later near the end of his life, Peirce discusses the notion of "pure play" in "A Neglected Argument for the Reality of God," a piece many scholars find quite enigmatic. There he says it "involves no purpose save that of casting aside all serious purpose."

"Pure Play has no rules, except this very law of liberty. It bloweth where it listeth. It has no purpose" (1908, CP 6.458). He notes that "it can take the form of aesthetic contemplation or that of distant castle-building (whether in Spain or within one's own moral training). . . . I will call it "Musement" on the whole" (1908, CP 6.458). As he further characterizes it,

> There is no kind of reasoning that I should wish to discourage in Musement; and I should lament to find anybody confining it to a method of such moderate fertility as logical analysis. . . . I should say,

> "enter your skiff of Musement, push off into the lake of thought, and leave the breath of heaven to swell your sail. With your eyes open, awake to what is about or within you, and open conversation with yourself; for such is all mediation." It is, however, not a conversation with words alone, but is illustrated, like a lecture, with diagrams and with experiments.
>
> (1908, CP 6.461)

Peirce ends this article by showing a connection between the scientific reasoning around discovery—*abduction*—and this play of musement. The "play of musement" comes about in the confrontation of a problem to solve (1908, CP 6.460). "Every inquiry whatsoever takes its rise in the observation . . . of some surprising phenomenon, some experience which either disappoints an expectation, or breaks in upon some habit of expectation of the *inquisiturus*" (1908, CP 6.469). Peirce's point seems to be that just as this play of musement takes place in the scientific realm to produce plausible hypotheses, so it can take place in the esthetic realm and the moral realm to produce new, though hypothetical ideas. In the theological realm, for example, the hypothesis of a God as an ultimate reality is attractive by its very beauty. The muser "adoring his strictly hypothetical God," desires "to shape the whole conduct of life . . . into conformity with that hypothesis" (1908, CP 6.467). Of course, just as abduction is followed by induction in the scientific realm, to provide a reality test to any plausible hypothesis, so those moral or theological ideals generated through the play of musement must get their test in the experiments of living.

Plato and *To Kalon*

If Schiller's notion of the living shape provides a path to the reconciliation between reason and moral sentiment, the Greek notion of *to kalon* assists with clarifying the role between esthetics and ethics. As Peirce refines his sense of esthetics as a science of ends, he realizes that its association with artistic beauty may be a hindrance. In fact, he says, "that science has been handicapped by the definition of it as a theory of beauty" (c. 1902, CP 2.199). Instead, Peirce goes back to the Greeks and adopts *to kalon* as his preference, a concept used by both Plato and Aristotle to mean something broader than just the artistic sense of beauty (c. 1902, CP 2.199; 1903, CP 1.586). Scholars, such as Rachel Barney, agree that Plato also wanted to dissociate *to kalon* from artistic beauty (2010, p. 363). It is a complex concept indicated by a variety of plausible translations, certainly as "beautiful," but also as "noble," "honorable," or "fine." Its antonym *to aischron*, is often translated as "ugly," "base," or "shameful" (Hoerber, 1964, pp. 151–152). The adoption of this term suggests Plato's influence on Peirce's sense of esthetics. Indeed, drafts of the fourth chapter of *The Minute Logic*—which were planned as the chapter on ethics—are mostly preoccupied with a study of Plato. Peirce's aim was to give a review of various candidates for the good—28 in number as he says—and he starts with the Greeks (1902, R 434, p. 28 (draft B)). He begins his quest for notions of the good with the pre-Socratics but gets as far as Plato.

Peirce declares that for the "classical" period in Greece, the beautiful "alone" is recognized as good (1902, R 434, p. 30). He notes that among such thinkers as Heraclitus and Pythagoras, the beautiful was understood as "harmony" (1902, R 434, p. 31). Once he considers Plato, he becomes involved with the chronology of the dialogues since he believes that they are "the record of the entire development of the thought of a great thinker," so that "everything depends upon the chronology of the dialogues." After his own study, he's convinced of the correctness of Lutoslawski's ordering (1902, R 434, p. 34). In this manuscript, Peirce provides a synopsis of nearly all the dialogues, with an eye toward Plato's thought on the good and *to kalon*.

Peirce's interpretation of *to kalon* focuses on two dialogues, the *Symposium* and the *Philebus*. Plato scholars agree that, besides these two dialogues, the more substantial discussions of *to kalon* occur in the *Gorgias, Greater Hippias* and *The Republic*. Peirce gives a brief synopsis of the *Gorgias* but doesn't discuss the parts relevant to the discussion of *to kalon*. Lutoslawski rejected the *Greater Hippias* as authentic, so that's probably why Peirce doesn't consider it (Hoerber, 1964, p. 143n2). Most Plato scholars now agree to its authenticity, and it's unfortunate that Peirce ignored it since it is the one that is most relevant to his struggles with sorting out the roles of ethics and esthetics.

In regard to *The Symposium*, Peirce writes that "Socrates says that love is not beautiful; but simply has Beauty for its object; and that this is the *summum bonum*." "Love is desire for the everlasting possession of the beautiful, which is the good." He concludes that the message of *The Symposium* is that "the higher mysteries of love require us to forsake the individual for the general, for the spiritual universe of truth and beauty" (1902, R 434, p. 57). "Whoever perseveres along that path will at last suddenly perceive a wonderful beauty, eternal, absolute, unmixed" (1902, R 434, pp. 57–58).

Peirce characterizes the *Philebus* as an issue around whether pleasure or knowledge can be accepted as the ultimate good. And the final answer is "not simple" (1902, R 434, p. 153). Neither without the other is good, but the life of wisdom without pleasure is better than a life of pleasure without wisdom. The good is to be sought in the mixed life. The question is what mixture is to be preferred (1902, R 434, p. 154). "What there is in this mixture which makes it good. But what makes any mixture good?" "Evidently proportion and measure." He then quotes Plato at this point in which Socrates notes that "the good has taken refuge in the character of the beautiful," since the measure and proportion are what constitutes the beautiful (1902, R 434, p. 156).

However, Peirce is critical of Plato here:

> It is not Plato's best self who has this confused and not very elevated notion of the Good. The result is due in part to the imperfection of the method of investigation employed and in part to a little violence being done to the method so as to force it to this conclusion.
>
> (1902, R 434, p. 158).

Most Plato scholars would agree with Peirce that one of the key features of *to kalon* is the notion of form, understood as proportion, symmetry, harmony, order, measure, among other cognates (*Philebus*, 64e-65a; Barney, 2010, p. 364; Grube, 1927, pp. 273–274). "Plato apparently saw aesthetic beauty in proportion and harmony" (Hoerber, 1964, p. 154). Scholars, such as R. L. Nettleship would seem to agree with this interpretation of *to kalon* as constituted by measure and proportion:

> "Proportion, in one form or another, is the single source to which he [Plato] refers all artistic excellence, in the musical relations of time and tone no less than in those of place in the arts of form and construction. . . . Plato was in earnest with the idea that there is some real connexion between character and artistic form, and that the common element in both is found in the rightness of proportion which is essential alike to beauty in art and to goodness in conduct . . . . To Plato the laws of proportion, which are the condition of beauty in art, seemed to betoken the presence of the same mind as is revealed in the immutable order of the universe, and more imperfectly in the moral order of human life.
>
> (Nettleship, 1955, pp. 70, 72, 74;
> cited in Hoerder, 1964, p. 155)

These are the neo-Platonic themes that, as noted, Shaftesbury promotes. This is also clearly argued in *The Gorgias*: "it's due to organization (*taxis*) that the excellence of each thing is something which is organized and has order. . . . So it's when a certain order (*kosmos*), the proper one for each thing, come to be present in it that it makes each of the things there, good" (*Gorgias*, 506e; Barney, 2010, p. 365). "Measure and proportion manifest themselves in all areas as beauty and virtue" (*Philebus*, 64e). In *The Timaeus*, that which lacks symmetry also lacks beauty (*Timaeus*, 87d).

However, it appears that some Plato scholars would disagree with Peirce's interpretation of Plato on two accounts. First, in terms of identifying *to kalon* with the good; the second in terms of a broader sense of *to kalon* than just proportion and measure. Rachel Barney sees Socrates as claiming, both in the *Symposium* and in *The Republic*, that all good things are *kalos* (*Symposium*, 201c; *Republic* 508e-509a, 452d-e), but it is not clear whether he counts all fine things as good (Barney, 2010, pp. 363–364). If, as Peirce says, the good is *to kalon* this would have a certain implication for the role of esthetics and ethics if he were to follow the lead of Plato in sorting out the different roles of esthetics and ethics. If everything that is fine is also good, then esthetics would supersede ethics in determining ultimate goods. One would only need the determination of which ends are fine and admirable to determine that they are good to pursue. Ethics might be relegated to determining the best moral means, the righteous means, to attain those ends—something Peirce hints at this in at least one formulation (1903, CP 5.130).

On the other hand, if not everything that is fine is good, then this would suppose that ethics has the job of sorting out, among fine things, those that are good—those that people would be "prepared to adopt" (1903, CP 5.130). As discussed earlier, this seems to be the position that Peirce most often takes on the matter. The role of ethics is in determining *good* ends (1902, CP 1.575; 1902, CP 2.198–2.199).

But, furthermore, mostly based on the discussion of *to kalon* in the *Greater Hippias* and the *Philebus*, there is a significant consensus among Plato scholars that Plato argued for other features of *to kalon* in addition to proportion and measure. The *Greater Hippias* suggests three definitions of *to* kalon as what is fitting, what is useful and beneficial, and what is pleasing (Grube, 1927, p. 272). Although, the definition of *to kalon* is not settled here, as G.M. Grube argues, "it clearly enunciates three aspects of beauty which Plato, in all his further discussions of aesthetic experience, will attempt to reconcile" (1927, p. 272).

In regard to the first feature, Socrates characterizes *to kalon* as "fitting" or as suitability to function, that is, to a purpose (*Greater Hippias*, 290c-291d; Barney, 2010, pp. 364–365; Grube, 1927, p. 273). Grube thinks that by "fitting" Plato means harmony of design and function (1927, p. 273). This is also reiterated in *the Republic:* "the virtue or excellence, *to kalon* and correctness of each manufactured item, living creature and action is related to nothing but the use for which each is made or naturally adapted," that is, something adapted to its end (Republic, 601d; Barney, 2010, p. 365; Grube, 1927, p. 273). For example, Socrates argues that something as lowly as a ladle made of fig-wood is *kalos*, compared to one of gold, since its form is adapted well for its purpose in that it gives a better flavor to the broth and wouldn't damage the pot (*Greater Hippias*, 290e). But there is a difference between the functional and the good, since things can function well to produce both good and bad. Plato seems to suggest that for the function to be *to kalon* it also has to produce some good (*Greater Hippias*, 296c). But then it would seem, the account of what is beautiful requires the filter of what functions count as good.

Barney argues that Plato's point in this characterization of *to kalon* was to reject "shallow aestheticism . . . to recognize it wherever we find appropriate order and adaptation to purpose" (2010, p. 366). Something would be *kalos* if its order or design is conducive to fulfilling a certain end, purpose, or function. For example, Xenophon's Socrates argues that a dung basket is fine (*kalos*) and a golden shield ugly (*aischron*), if the one is made right for its work (*ergon*) and the other badly (Xenophon, *Memorabilia*, Bk 3, Chapt 8, 6; Barney, 2010, p. 366; Grube, 1927, p. 273). But it would also suppose that the functions of shields and dung baskets are good ones. As Robert Hoerber argues, "Although beauty and good are not necessarily interchangeable terms, identical in essence, there is no need to deduce, as Socrates does, that each may not have the other as an attribute—beauty may be a good thing and the good may be *kalos* (1964, p. 154).

The third feature of *to kalon* mentioned in the *Greater Hippias* is that of the pleasant. But the dialogue leaves the status of this feature uncertain, since Plato can't quite figure out what distinguishes beautiful pleasures from others. Grube thinks the problem is solved in the *Philebus*. where Plato argues for "pure" pleasures as those that count as beautiful. These are pleasures that are free from pain, are caused by things that are beautiful in themselves, and are moderate (*Philebus*, 51; Grube, 1927, p. 280). As Aristotle says in the *Rhetoric* something that is *kalos* is pleasant "because it is good" (*Rhetoric*, 1366a34–35). In other words, it involves proper pleasures because they are the pleasures that come from being good. Peirce's reading does discuss Plato's account of pure pleasures, but it's not clear whether he thinks this is a feature of *to kalon* (1902, R 434, p. 155).

Barney thinks that understanding *to kalon* as harmony and proportion of form, and, as fitness for function are "two paths of connection." She argues they "are really one, since appropriateness and order are themselves tightly related." She continues,

> Something comes to be appropriately adapted to its function by possessing the right kind of order: health in the case of bodies, ethical virtue in the case of human souls, the right kind of shape and other physical properties in the case of fig-wood soupspoons. In acquiring the appropriate order, each becomes at once fine and good: and whatever actions induce such order are fine and good by extension.
> (2010, p. 365)

It is a good insight to say that these two properties of *to kalon*, form (shape) and fit, work together to produce something that would count something as *kalos*: When the form or shape of something is conducive to its function, that would seem like a necessary but not sufficient condition for counting something as *kalos*. It is another thing to say that it is *both* fine *and* good for that reason. There is still the question of whether, even if form fits the function, the function is good. There seems to be a subtle layer of analysis here. The fig-wood spoon is *kalos* because its design is conducive to its function *and*, presumably, its function is good because it helps in the attainment of something beneficial, namely, food. A gold spoon would damage the pot and spoil the taste of the food, and so is not *kalos simply* for that reason, not because its function is bad. In other words, for something to count as *kalos*, its form has to fit (harmonize) with its function *and* the function is good. As Hoerber argues, Useful things are "beautiful only when they produce good instead of evil. *To kalon*, in other words, must be judged on the basis of a moral standard, which must underlie any utilitarian standard" (1964, pp. 151–152).

Barney argues "Plato's concern is to claim that whatever is good is fine, rather than the other way around" (2010, p. 365). This does not seem quite right. Rather, it would seem that something cannot be *kalos* without being good, that is, good relative to its end or function. Again, this seems consistent with Aristotle's definition of *to kalon* in *The Rhetoric* which, whatever other characteristics *to kalon* has, it is also good (*Rhetoric*, 1366a, 34–35). Conversely, it's quite possible that something could have a good function or end yet be poorly designed to fit that function, that is, its form does not harmonize with its end. In that case, it would also not be *kalos*. This would infer, as in Plato, two conditions in determining whether something counts as *kalos*. One is whether its form fits or harmonizes with its function and, second, whether its function is good. It might be helpful to avoid confusion by calling the first aspect, what is *right—orthos* to use a Greek term. For example, someone may be the right person for the job, or a situation in which something is going right, that is, as it should; or the sense of right as in a carpenter's square fitting a piece of work. This would be right in the sense of what is best or most suitable for a purpose. The contrary would be *parekbasis*, as Aristotle uses it to describe constitutions that do not fit the purpose of government (*Politics*, 1279a30). In that case, something is *kalos* if it is both right and good. These two aspects would generate four possible permutations:

(A) The form fits the end (*orthos*) and the end is good = *kalos* (noble, admirable)
(B) The form fits the end (*orthos*) and the end is bad = *aischros* (base, ugly)
(C) The form does not fit the end (*parekbasis*) but the end is good (*achristos*, useless)
(D) The form does not fit its end (*parekbasis*) and its end is bad (*avlavis*, harmless)

If this were translated to Peirce's concern with the roles of esthetics and ethics, it would suggest that the primary role of esthetics is to determine what design, form, or organization of things would best fit its end, and ethics has the role of determining which ends are good. In that case, the study of esthetics would be essential to finding which forms or organizations are critical to the realization of a good end.

Consider one example in Plato and one in Aristotle that illustrates this ordering. In *The Republic*, Plato gives a well-known criticism of the different musical modes or *harmonia* of his time, including the Lydian, Dorian, Ionian, Phrygian, Mixolydian and Syntonolydian (Mountford, 1923, p. 125). Each, it could be said are musical modes whose form fits their function well of producing certain feelings, emotions and conduct, and this is why they are called *harmonia* as such. The Mixolydian and the Syntonolydian are threnodic and the Ionian and Lydian are convivial (*The Republic*, 398d-e).

Once that is established, Socrates then argues that the mixolyudian and syntonolydian should be "done away with" in the republic, since they are "useless" (*achristos*) and do not serve the right purpose or function for the guardian class (*The Republic*, 398e). These modes also encourage drunkenness and sloth and so are "unbefitting" (*aprepestaton*) for the guardians. The Ionian and Lydian modes are too "convivial" and would make the guardians soft and sympathetic. Thus, there is a layer of filters here: there are the different *harmonia*, all of which fit their ends, but then there is an assessment of those ends based on what is beneficial to the guardian class in the republic. One would say that the Dorian and Phrygian are *kalos* relative to this assessment of ends for the guardians of the republic. There are two ways of interpreting why the Lydian and Ionian modes are not. One could say that the form does not fit the desired function, or one could say that the end is not beneficial to the guardians. But the latter seems the better interpretation.

Another example is in *The Politics* of Aristotle. In Book III he discusses different forms of government. The constitution of each is essentially its arrangement or order (*Politics*, 1278b10). Aristotle identifies the end or purpose of governments, namely, to attain a measure of well-being for its members (*Politics*, 1278b20–25), that is, the common good or justice (*Politics*, 1282b15). This is followed by an explanation of how the constitutions of monarchies, aristocracies and constitutional republics are each designed with the common good in mind, even if they have different constitutions. Tyranny, oligarchy and democracy are considered *parekbaseis* ("perversions") of these three *orthai politeia* ("right" polities) because they are not well-designed to achieve the proper end of government. Rather than ruling for the end of common good, they "rule with the purpose of private interest" (*Politics*, 1279a30). As he says in the *Rhetoric*, the end of oligarchy is wealth, and the end of tyranny is the protection of the tyrant (*Rhetoric*, 1366a1–10). "Perversion" is a felicitous translation. *The Oxford English Dictionary* gives one of its principal senses as "the action of turning aside from what is true or right;

diversion of something from its original and proper course" (*Oxford English Dictionary*, 2005). Here it is opposed to *orthos*, "right" or "true" in the carpenter's sense of square, that is, well-measured. Monarchies, aristocracies and polities *fit* the purpose of government; they are right in the sense that they square with the end. Aristotle goes on to address the merits and problems with each constitutional type to figure out which form of government would be the *best* relative to its end.

Aristotle is addressing two questions here that show the relation between the right and the good. First, there is the question of what is right: which among the different designs of constitutions fit the end or function of government. But then there is the question of the goodness of the end. Governments are good that function to achieve the common good. Governments are base—perversions—if they function to achieve private interest. At least here, Aristotle does not address the question why the common good is good and private interest bad. He seems rather to assume that this is intuitively so. But there is still the question as to which among the constitutions that are conducive to the end of government will likely *fulfill* that function. As is well known, Aristotle thinks the best is a mixed constitution or polity, that takes the best design of each of the better forms of government.

This division of labor between questions of the rightness of design and questions of the goodness of ends is further illustrated in Aristotle's criticism of Plato's republic. Aristotle criticizes Plato's *Republic* on two counts: the purpose is wrong and the design is wrong. The end to make all citizens alike would rub against the natural tendency toward the division of labor and differentiation of functions. The design of the republic in terms of the abolition of property and communalism of wives and children would destroy natural affection (*Politics*, 1260b28–1264b25).

In the *Rhetoric*, Aristotle discusses *ethos*, good character, as one means of persuasion besides *logos* and *pathos*. In this context, he discusses the difference between virtue and vice and between *to kalon* (often translated as "noble" here) and the base (*aischron*) as they apply to character (*Rhetoric*, 1366a 23). "*To kalon* is that which is both desirable for its own sake and also worthy of praise; or that which is both good and also pleasant because good" (*Rhetoric*, 1366a33–35). Clearly, then, to be counted as *to kalon* something must also be good. Virtues are *kalos* because they aim at some good, and they are excellences of character, that is, a character well-designed, one might say (*Rhetoric*, 1366a, 35–38). Virtues are right in the sense, as he says in the *Nicomachean Ethics*, they have the right measure and proportion and stand as a mean between two extremes (*Nicomachean Ethics*, 1106a14-b35). By implication, vices are base since they tend to focus on extremes, the disproportionate and produce the shameful (*aischron*) (*Rhetoric*, 1367a7–9; *Nicomachean Ethics*, 1106a14-b35). The base character is one who aims at what is in self-interest as opposed to the interest of others, and who practices the vices well-suited for that purpose (*Rhetoric*, 1366b 35–1367a5).

A third aspect of *to kalon* is its relation to pleasure and feeling. Aristotle makes it clear that the noble man (*kalos k'agathos*) is admirable and noble, that is, pleases others in the sense that his actions are not done for his own benefit, not for something ulterior, but as something beneficial to others and the community, without regard to the consequences for himself (*Rhet*oric, 1366a33–1367a33). As such, the noble person or the noble thing is a natural object of praise or admiration (Barney, 2010, p. 370). As Barney notes, *to kalon* in Aristotle is "simply what appropriately elicits the disinterested approbation of a spectator as having positive value in itself." It is "complete as it stands" (2010, p. 370).

In the *Greater Hippias*, the third account of *to kalon* as something pleasing is considered. But here Plato rejects this as a good account of the beautiful. However, the relation between to *kalon* and pleasure is developed more in the *Philebus*. He divides pleasures into "pure" and "impure." Pure pleasures are those that are not associated with pain. For example, drinking is a pleasure that results from the pain of thirst. But visual pleasures are pure, since the absence of seeing a natural beauty is not painful. The cause of pure pleasure is an object that is *kalos*. This is its second feature. They also are moderate, measured—which constitutes their third feature (*Philebus*, 50d; Grube, 1927, p. 280).

The pleasure and admiration experienced in things *kalos* is motivational in the sense that one wants to be what one admires. In *The Symposium*, Plato sees *to kalon* as motivational as something erotic or lovable (Barney, 2010, p. 375). What is *kalos* is lovable in this respect, much in the way in which a worthy friend is lovable, someone to whom one is attracted, and would choose as a companion in life. It is lovable in the way in which the philosopher is attracted to wisdom, understood precisely as the systematic understanding of all things.

As G.M. Grube interprets Plato, the philosopher attempted in his work to reconcile the three aspects of *to kalon* proposed in *The Greater Hippias*. It has something to do with its fit with its end, its design. It has to do with what is good or beneficial, and, it has to do with certain kinds of pleasures (1927, p. 272). If an end is to be *kalos*, it must be something that is useful, in the sense that its design fits its function. It must be something that is good and beneficial, and it must be something that is pleasing and attractive, lovable and admirable.

Kant's Architectonic of Reason and Peirce's System of the Sciences

There appears to be some family resemblance between Kant's notion of the architectonic and Plato's sense of *to kalon* as harmonious, symmetrical order. "By an architectonic," Kant writes, "I understand the art of constructing systems" (1781, A832; B860). "By a system I understand the unity of the manifold modes of knowledge under one idea." This idea, he says, is provided by reason, as an understanding of how the parts occupy relatively to one another and the whole. "The unity of the end to which all the parts relate and in the idea of which they all stand in relation to one another, makes it possible for us to determine from our knowledge of the other parts" (1781, A832; B860). "The whole is thus an organized unity, and not an aggregate" (1781, A833; B861). Reason, as he urges, demands "systematic unity" (1781, A840; B68). In an allusion to Plato's use of *kosmos* in *The Gorgias*, Kant claims that philosophy can be conceptualized as a *conceptus cosmicus*. On this view, "philosophy is the science of the relation of all knowledge to the essential ends of human reason" (1781, A839; B867). Any system of knowledge would require an understanding of the relation of particular sciences to one another, and the result of those sciences working together to produce knowledge.

As Nathan Houser notes, Peirce became interested in systematizing his philosophy after the publication of his 1891 piece for *The Monist*, "The Architecture of Theories" (Houser, 1998, p. xvii). Peirce writes in the article, "that systems ought to be constructed architectonically has been preached since Kant, but I do not think the full import of the maxim has by any means been apprehended." Peirce thought then that such an effort should begin with "a complete survey of knowledge" (1891, CP 6.9). It is shortly after the *Monist* article that Peirce also revives his interest in the classification of the sciences, perhaps in part for this reason. Although he started making classifications as early as 1866, there is a rather long gap after that, and he started again around 1892, after which he produced a classification just about every year or so, ending by 1902–1903 (Kent, 1987, p. ix). In his article on the architectonic of theories, Peirce imagined, as he says, not only an order to knowledge, but to "the world" that eventually "becomes an absolutely perfect, rational, and symmetrical system" (1891, CP 6.33).

As Peirce was developing his classification of sciences, Peirce may have started to make a connection between architectonic, understood as a coherent system of parts and wholes and, esthetics, as having to do with the principles of the design of systems, understood as relations among parts and wholes. Indeed, Peirce's characterization of esthetic goodness in the Harvard Lectures as a multitude of parts so related to one another as to impart an immediate quality to their totality, hints at this idea (1903, CP 5.132). In Peirce's mature classification of the sciences, esthetics is, after all, the third science in the hierarchy of the sciences, following mathematics and phenomenology (1902, R 1339, pp. 5–12). That would make sense if esthetics was about proper, systemic design. Richard Atkins picks up on this and argues that "aesthetics plays a crucial role in the systematicity of knowledge" (2008, p. 20).

In expounding on the idea of an architectonic, Peirce refers to Kant's use of the term 'cosmic'—which, as noted, alludes to Plato's use of *kosmos* in the *Gorgias*. Peirce uses it to explain the core feature of systematizing knowledge in his attempts at the classification of the sciences (c. 1896, CP 1.176). As Peirce describes the system of sciences in his mature classification, there is a certain hierarchy among them, the formal sciences the first among them, and mathematics the first among the formal sciences, since it is the study of necessary relations. Phenomenology is second since it is the study of the form of things as they appear. This is followed by the normative science as the study of what ought to be. Metaphysics comes next as the study of what is. In this way, the formal sciences cover all modalities: what must be, what appears to be, what ought to be and what is. The nomological or empirical sciences study what is in its various empirical manifestations.

The sciences have a certain hierarchy of rational government so that one science gives the other its leading principles (1906, CP 7.52). Peirce's classification stresses the hierarchy of the most general and abstract leading principles serving as the regulative principles for the less general and abstract disciplines, for example, the manner in which the logic ought to draw upon the leading principles of mathematics, and how the leading principles in phenomenology can serve to classify sign types in semiotic, or the way in which the formal principles in metaphysics should serve as the leading principles in the empirical sciences (1896, CP 3.427). Indeed, it could be argued that mathematics provides the concepts necessary for esthetics, such as unity, equality, balance, symmetry, proportion, repetition and the like. To the extent that harmony can be explained mathematically, that too appeals to mathematical principles. Phenomenology, in turn, supplies the categories by which all phenomena of esthetic experience are organized. Esthetics, in turn, supplies the leading principles of good design or organization. As Peirce expresses this in reference to August Comte's classificatory scheme:

> the sciences may be arranged in a series with reference to the abstractness of their objects; and that each science draws regulating principles from those superior to it in abstractness. . . . So far as the sciences can be arranged in such a scale, these relationships must hold good. (1896, CP 3.427)

Within each science, there are related subdivisions. In semiotic, grammar lays the foundation for critic and critic for rhetoric. The idioscopic, empirical sciences, are subdivided into nomological, which study the general laws of the relevant empirical domain; classificatory sciences, which study the various kinds of objects pertinent to the science and explains them by means of those general laws; and, descriptive sciences, which study particular objects, based on the finding of the nomological and classificatory subdivisions (Kent, 1987, p. 134).

Peirce describes the classification of the sciences as a fractal, and uses the metaphor of a mounting ladder to describe it: "where each rung is itself a ladder of rungs, so that the whole is more like a succession of waves each of which carries other waves and so on, until we should come to single investigations (c. 1905, R 328, p. 20; Kent, 1987, pp. 135–136).

There is also a vertical organization among the main division of the sciences into heuretic, review and practical. Through the heuretic sciences, the sciences of discovery, things come to be known. Through the sciences of review those discoveries are communicated, and through the practical sciences, they are realized in the practices of living, by which means they act upon the world (1903, HL, p. 209). Indeed, the forgotten science of pragmatics, sketched in 1896 by Peirce, may have been meant to fulfill this role. Recall that it is defined as "the study of how we ought to behave in the light of the truths of empirics" (1896, R 1345, p. 1). Thus, it takes from the sciences of mathematics, logic, metaphysics and the nomological sciences of psychology and physics, and uses these to study "the processes by which the outer world is to be brought into accordance with our wishes" (1896, R 1345, p. 2), that is, the ends that are to be pursued. Recall that it includes the general principles of conduct, policies regarding special problems, the study of what pleasures ought to pursued, social ethics, polity and a plethora of practical ends, such as health, food, clothing, shelter, light, warmth, transportation and all of the technical arts and sciences (1896, R 1345, pp. 5–24).

In this way, the sciences have an order, a design of parts that best functions to produce its end, knowledge, and a path that can adapt it to the practical world. It is *to kalon* in Plato's sense of a design best suited to its function and is well-ordered to the ends of some good, the good of knowledge. To use the language of Schiller, the system of sciences is a living shape. Its shape is the design of parts and wholes as Peirce has so characterized it, but its *living* shape is found in the communities of scientific practice. Scientists cluster around the "animating purpose" of "real truth." They pursue it by means of a "well-considered method." Scientists seek "cooperation in the hope that truth may be found" (c. 1902, CP 7.54). They have acquired the key sentiment of "love of truth" (1902, CP 1.576), and they have aspired to an intergenerational altruism (1893, CP 6.289). They have acquired the virtues most conducive to good inquiry: honesty, humility, probity and industry (1902, CP 1.576; 1902, CP 2.82). The basic norms of inquiry are appropriate to its end. The practice of science is "public." It is public in the sense that the investigations and their results "must be something open to anybody to observe" (1902, CP 7.87). Claims are to be "determined in a public and methodical manner," as opposed to privately (1893, CP 5.380n1).

It is interesting that Peirce prefers the term "public" to Kant and Plato's "cosmic" in describing architectonic and sees its cognate—architecture—as the symbol of architectonic. Works of sculpture and painting are usually by a single artist and represent a fragment of a larger whole. They are locked up in special venues and seen by a few. "A great building," on the other hand, "is meant for the whole people, and is erected by the exertions of an army representative of the whole people. It is the message with which an age is charged, and which it delivers to posterity" (c. 1896, CP 1.176). Peirce repeats this sentiment a few years later in a report to George Morison on the Hudson River bridge project, on which he worked as a consulting engineer:

> For whoever, in allowing his eye of a morning to rest a moment for refreshment on that splendid scene, should catch sight of that bridge and should reflect upon how calmly and simply it performed a great duty, conforming in every detail to the principles of good sense and of sound reason, would certainly receive a moral lesson which would have its effect upon his conduct for all that day.
>
> (c. 1888, R 1357, p. 9)

As Peirce explains the idea of an architectonic in reference to his own theory of pragmatism, a system is constructed,

> just as a civil engineer, before erecting a bridge, s ship, or a house, will think of the different properties of all materials and will use no iron, stone, or cement, that has not been subjected to tests; and will put them together in ways minutely considered, so, in constructing the doctrine of pragmatism the properties of all indecomposable concepts were examined and the ways in which they could be compounded. Then the purpose of the proposed doctrine having been analyzed, it was constructed out of the appropriate concepts so as to fulfill that purpose.
>
> (c. 1905, CP 5.5)

In other words, much like the notion of *to kalon*, an architectonic is a well-ordered relation of parts to wholes that is so designed as to achieve its purpose.

If science is illustrative of learning, then the system of sciences also exemplifies what Peirce means by growth. In science one has a continuous diversification of studies, physics, geology, biology, chemistry, psychology, sociology, each of which also has its subbranches. Yet, despite the diversity, they can be organized architectonically, where principles of the more fundamental sciences serve as foundations for other sciences, but where individual sciences may provide outcomes that inform or modify existing principles, as well as other sciences. In general, as more knowledge is acquired, its organization grows more systematically over time. Growth is exemplified by this sort of architectonic of learning.

The sense of architectonic as a public, living shape suggests that it could be applied to any worthy end, for example, the ends of justice, good government, economies, health systems and other institutions and practices. The use of this sense of "public" by Peirce echoes John Rawls' notion of a "well-ordered" society. For John Rawls, a well-ordered society involves a public conception of justice in which all members of the society believe that its institutions and practices advance their good, and in which everyone accepts and knows that the others accept the same principles of justice (1971, pp. 454–453). It is "publicly known by those engaged in it to satisfy the appropriate principles of justice" (1971, p. 457). In this way, a just society, it might be said, is visible to all, and erected by the hands of many rather than the few. Well-ordered societies are not the work of a sculptor, as the way in which Plato designs *The Republic*, but should be modeled after a great building.

It is clear that Peirce sees science and scientific practice as models for proper community, and communities of inquiry could be considered well-ordered, *to kalon*, in this respect. Not only are the different branches of science systematically well-ordered, but the practice of science itself is so in Rawls's sense. Recall that Peirce favors science as a way of justifying beliefs precisely because its ways are public, communal and dialogic, and not capricious like authority-based societies. For this reason, it produces more stability since it is more likely to self-correct, fix beliefs and, through that, to fix conduct. Stability is also a feature of the well-ordered society according to Rawls, who characterizes it in terms of resilience. Well-ordered societies are so such structured that perturbations or disturbances are not sufficient to send the system into disequilibrium (1971, p. 457), and changes that occur to institutions and practices are such that they remain just (1971, p. 458).

If architectonic is the model, then any candidate for the highest end should be like an edifice that can be seen, felt, conceived and lived-in so that it is sufficiently public to comprehend its effects. It is constituted by the habits of sentiment and conduct of fellow citizens, and the arrangement of practices and institutions that made up the economic, social and political life of society. As such its totality would leave a certain esthetic impression, surely a bad one if people living under its design felt contempt, fear, anxiety and resentment, its ugliness and baseness. On the other hand, it would surely be a good sign of right direction, if it evoked feelings of admiration, loyalty and contentment.

Peirce's Science of Esthetics

There appears to be a family resemblance among Schiller's notion of *living shape*, Plato's concept of *to kalon* and Kant's idea of the *architectonic*. But at the same time, each of these thinkers bring out different aspects of the esthetic. They all share the idea of form or design as essential to esthetic quality or goodness. Plato and Kant especially emphasize the importance of how the form or design is a matter of a certain interrelation of parts and wholes. For Plato, there is an emphasis on the harmony, measure and proportion of that relation. For Schiller, the emphasis is the harmony of form and matter, reason and sensuousness in the living shape. Kant sees architectonic as a concrete manifestation of reason playing out in the world, a well-ordered system of knowledge. Schiller is more concerned with how reason and sentiment might be balanced in the living shape of a person's conduct, the harmony of duty and sentiment. Plato is concerned not just with design but how the design fits its function and the goodness of the function, and how fit, goodness and pleasure are integrated in *to kalon*. If the allusions and references to these thinkers on these matters are any indication, they are likely to have been formative for Peirce's own thinking about esthetics. All of this must have been swirling in Peirce's head, but comes out in the form of some very fundamental questions to be answered. If truth is the end of logic, why should people seek it? If the truth is good, why should people seek the good? If it is because these ends are admirable, beautiful and lovable, what makes them so that people should pursue them?

There are four principal textual sources of Peirce's account of esthetics. The first is in drafts to his *Minute* Logic—the second and fourth chapters in particular. The second is the first and fifth Harvard Lectures of 1903. The third is the first of the Lowell Lectures, also in 1903. The last is "The Basis of Pragmaticism," written in 1906. Of the four, the Harvard Lectures provide the most characterization of the science, as sketchy as it is.

In *The Minute Logic*, Peirce is concerned with determining the aim of logic since, without a definitive end, it can be used instrumentally for good or ill. This is a matter of ethics, and he assigns the task of the discovery of ends to "pure ethics" (1902, CP 1.575; 1901, CP 7.201). He reaffirms this duty of ethics a few years later in 1906 in "The Basis of Pragmatism." There he divides ethics into a general ethics and *practics*. Although he complains about how it has been traditionally practiced, ethics, more generally, studies the nature of the *summum bonum*." *Practics* is defined here as "the theory of the control of conduct, and of action in general, so as to conform to an ideal" (1906, EP2, p. 377). It sorts out those actions which are beneficial from those that are "pernicious" (1906, EP2, p. 179). This division of labor within ethics is repeated in the Harvard Lectures, where he defines ethics as "the study of what ends of action we are deliberately prepared to adopt," but also the study of "right action which is in conformity to ends which we are prepared deliberately to adopt" (1903, HL, p. 212). After the introduction of pure ethics in *The Minute Logic*, he says

> what I propose now to do is to pass in review every one of the general classes of objects which anybody could suppose to be an ultimate

> good, and to question . . . as to whether it can be considered to be in itself a good at all, irrespective of its effects. I shall arrange my list so as to commence with the most particular satisfactions and proceed step by step to the most general.
>
> (1902, CP 1.581)

He notes that there are 28 such candidate goods (1902, R 434 Draft B, p. 28). He starts this review but only manages to get to the first few, becoming occupied with the dialogues of Plato (1902, CP 1.582-CP 1.584). He is most likely referring to the 28 he developed in his classifications associated with the review of Karl Pearson's *Grammar of Science* a year earlier (1901, R 1434, Draft C, p. 7ff). In the diagrams of these classifications there are exactly 28 candidates of ends or "motives." These are discussed in detail in Appendix I.

But ethics is not the end of matter. Esthetics is introduced in *The Minute Logic* as a third normative science which concerns the matter of the highest ends, but in a different respect than ethics. It is all fine and good to determine which end people *ought* to pursue as the highest end, but what would *attract* people to that end, what would make it lovable and worthy of pursuit? Is it a respect (*Achtung*) for the law, as Kant suggests—a sense of duty—or is it as Schiller imagines, an end whose living shape is one of inspired beauty? Peirce poses the question rather mundanely:

> Ethics asks to what end all effort *shall* be directed. That question obviously depends upon the question what it would be that, independently of the effort, we should *like* to experience.
>
> (emphasis added) (1902, CP 2.199)

The latter is the job of esthetics. Here the difference between the task of ethics and the task of esthetics seems to hinge on the use of *shall* and *like*. Ethics is concerned with what people's efforts *shall* be directed toward, that is, what end people *should* or *ought* to be committed to seek. On the other hand, esthetics is concerned with what people would *like* to experience as this ultimate end.

Certainly, it would be odd if the ultimate end that people ought to seek is something they would not like to experience or find repulsive and base. On the other hand, it would be odd if the ultimate end they *ought* to seek was simply a matter of what people would *like* in the sense of what they would *prefer*. Such subjectivism could lead to all sorts of moral mischief, and Peirce was concerned in the Lowell Lectures to refute such subjectivism both in reasoning and in morals (1903, R 451, pp. 3–4). Subjectivism essentially leads to the denial of a distinction between good and bad conduct since each individual is the final word, making whatever each desires or finds satisfactory, right. Therefore, anything desired is right, so nothing desired is wrong (1903, R 448, p. 9).

Instead, Peirce uses what is to become his standard language of *admiration* in association with the highest ends in his two public lectures—the Harvard and Lowell Lectures (1903, HL, p. 212; 1903, HL, p. 119; 1903, CP 1.613; 1903, CP 1.615). As Peirce writes, "but we cannot get any clue to the secret of Ethics . . . until we have first made up our formula for what it is that we are prepared to admire" (1903, HL, p. 118). Admiration connotes something that is more objectively noble than "like," something truly worthy and good, rather than something that's just a matter of personal preference. It doesn't have the sense of obedience of Kant's *Achtung* (respect), and it has a tinge of feeling or sentiment attached to it, more akin to feelings associated with Schiller's notion of grace and beauty. It also ties in with Aristotle's noble person. Recall, that for Aristotle, the person who is *kalos k'agathos* is a noble, virtuous persons worthy of praise and admiration, someone who adopts the interests of the community above self-interest (*Rhetoric*, 1366a33–1367a33). When people admire certain public or historical figures, they find them lovable and aspire to be like them, to emulate them, but that is because there is something objectively identifiable about their conduct, character, accomplishments, or ideas.

If esthetics is concerned with what ends may prove attractive or admirable, people are naturally attracted to the beautiful. This has been the traditional subject of esthetics. But, as noted, Peirce thinks that beauty doesn't quite get at the matter and, in fact, characterizing esthetics as the study of beauty has hurt the science (1902, CP 2.199). It is at this point in *The Minute Logic* that Peirce adopts the term *to kalon* as a substitute for *beauty*, the subject of esthetics. No doubt the term has come to mind given his preoccupation in Chapter 4 with the study of Plato. Peirce, as discussed, interprets Plato's sense of *to kalon*, with three characteristics: it is identified as the good (1902, R 434, p. 30); it is constituted by measure, proportion, harmony (1902, R434, p. 156); and it is lovable and pleasing (1902, R 434, pp. 57–58). *To kalon* connotes something more than beautiful appearance for Peirce. It is something noble, good, admirable and lovable. Indeed, As Peirce writes in his application to the Carnegie Endowment in the same year, esthetics answers the question of "what it is that we would deliberately pronounce to be *kalon k'agathon*" (1902, R L75, Draft D, p. 232). Now, as Peirce says in *The Minute Logic*, esthetics is concerned with "what is the one quality that is, in its immediate presence, *kalos*" (1902, CP 2.199).

Peirce gives his first public introduction of esthetics in the Harvard Lectures of 1903. He begins the lectures with reaffirming the hierarchy among the three normative sciences. Logic, which is how people ought to think is dependent on ethics, which determines what people ought to do. Esthetics, on the other hand, sets up a "formula for what it is that we are prepared to admire. I don't care what doctrine of ethics be embraced," Peirce says, it will still have to pass the test of what is admirable (1903,

HL, p. 118). He also reaffirms the division of labor between ethics and esthetics on the matter of ends.

> In short, ethics must rest upon a doctrine which without at all considering what our conduct is to be, divides ideally possible states of things into two classes, those that would be admirable and those that would [be] unadmirable and undertakes to define precisely what it is that constitutes the admirableness of an ideal.
>
> (1903, HL, p. 119)

Esthetics is what defines that doctrine of what would count as an admirable end. "*Ethics*," on the other hand, as he says in Lecture Five, "*is the study of what ends of action we are deliberately prepared to adopt*" (1903, HL, p. 212). Esthetics determines which ends are admirable and ethics determines, among admirable ends, which ought to be adopted.

However, this clear division of labor articulated in Lecture One is muddled in Lecture Five. There are three drafts of the lecture (1903, R 310-R 312). Of the three, an audience might consider the second draft the best, but Peirce chose to deliver the third. As promised in his drafts of *The Minute Logic*, Peirce seems to have more questions than answers, more puzzles than solutions to the matter of esthetics (1902, CP 2.197; 1902, R 432-R 434). He presents a number of enigmatic claims and somewhat obscure statements in the lecture. As he warns his audience, "Now I am going to make a series of assertions which will sound wild" (1903, HL, p. 208).

The first enigma makes four claims. First, an admirable end is marked by "esthetic goodness" (1903, HL, p. 213). Second, esthetic goodness is to be defined as follows:

> an object to be esthetically good must have a multitude of parts so related to one another as to impart a positive immediate quality to their totality; and whatever does this is, in so far, esthetically good, no matter what the particular quality of the total may be.
>
> (1903, HL, p. 213)

Third, "the morally good will be the esthetically good specially determined by a peculiar superadded element" (1903, HL, p. 213). This would suggest, as in Lecture One, that ethics would determine among the *esthetically good* ends, which would be *morally good* to pursue.

However, directly after this definition of esthetic goodness, he seems to refute this chain of reasoning by claiming, fourthly, there can be "no such thing as esthetic goodness" (1903, HL, p. 213). "I am seriously inclined to doubt," he says, "there being any distinction of pure esthetic betterness and worseness. My notion would be that there are innumerable varieties of esthetic quality, but no purely esthetic grade of excellence" (1903, HL, p. 214). Given the definition of esthetic goodness, anything can be esthetically good so long as its totality produces some immediate quality. The nauseating or frightening can be esthetically good for that reason. As he says, "vulgarity and pretension, themselves, may appear quite delicious in their perfection, if we can once conquer our squeamishness about them" (1903, HL, p. 211).

"This is better than that," Peirce says, is the result of an ethical judgment. The esthetic makes no such distinction (1903, R 310, p. 12). If there is no possibility of judgment between the admirable and the repugnant, then what purpose does esthetics serve? It would seem to make esthetics useless as a normative science. To resolve the enigma, either Peirce needs a different definition of esthetic goodness, or he needs to make some distinctions here that could get him out of this conceptual quandary.

Peirce must have recognized his mistake in thinking that there cannot be a distinction between esthetic goodness and badness since he corrects this claim in "The Basis of Pragmaticism" a few years later in 1906. As if scolding himself, he writes, "it would be the height of stupidity to say that esthetics knows no good and bad" (1906, CP 5.551). He emphasizes the "emphatic dualism of the three normative sciences," logic as the science of "the conditions of truth and falsity," ethics, as "wise and foolish conduct," and esthetics as "attractive and repulsive ideas" (1906, EP2, p. 378). Jeffrey Barnouw notes the transition around 1905 of Peirce's view of esthetics as non-dualistic, dealing with firstness as mere quality and immediacy, to this "emphatic dualism" (1988, p. 612). Now that Peirce recognizes esthetics as a truly critical normative science, he proclaims that "it is evident that it is in esthetics that we ought to seek for the deepest characteristics of normative science, since esthetics, in dealing with the very ideal itself, whose mere materialization engrosses the attention of practics and logic, must contain the heart, soul, and spirit of normative science" (1906, EP 2, p. 379).

This is perhaps where a better understanding of Plato's and Aristotle's sense of *to kalon* may have been helpful to Peirce. If the interpretations of Plato's and Aristotle's notions of *to kalon* discussed earlier are fairly done, then Peirce should have defined esthetic goodness as a question of form *and* function. Something is *kalos* if it meets two conditions, first, that its form fits its end and, second, that its end is good. The first, in Peirce's language, would be a determination of what is esthetically good, while the second is a determination of what is ethically good. What Peirce left out of his definition of esthetically good is how the totality of parts and wholes relates to some end. After all, esthetics is about ends. Peirce seems to have forgotten how he defined the normative sciences earlier in the fifth lecture. "For normative science in general being the science of the laws of conformity of things to ends, esthetics considers those things *whose ends* are to embody qualities of feeling" (emphasis added) (1903, HL, p. 212). True, an interrelation of parts and wholes are such that its totality will produce a quality that evokes a feeling of some sort, but the form or design should also be considered in relation to some end or purpose. Something is esthetically good, in this sense, if its form, the design of its parts and wholes, fits its end, purpose, or function; it is esthetically bad if its form does not fit its function. As such, they would produce two different qualities associated with different types of feelings. Peirce says something like that in one of the Harvard Lecture drafts: The repugnant is "the unsuitability of the object for some purpose" (1903, R 310, p. 6). Just as for Plato, the ugly (*aischron*) is the unsuitability of the design of something for its purpose.

This distinction also provides a way to explain what counts as esthetically good and bad, no matter what the end may be. For example, a playwright who writes a tragedy with the intent of evoking "pity and terror" in the audience but, instead, evokes laughter and frivolity, has made something esthetically bad since its design did not fit its purported end. By the same token, the playwright who has succeeded in horrifying and nauseating the audience—with that end in mind—has produced something esthetically good. Van Gogh's *Starry Night* may evoke wonder, awe and delight in the viewer, and Francis Bacon's *Painting 1946* may evoke disgust and nausea in the viewer, but both are esthetically good in Peirce's terms for that reason. But this would not only apply to art but to anything. The fig-wood soupspoon is esthetically good since its design best fits its function to stir and flavor the soup. Picasso's *Guernica* is esthetically good since its design conveys the horror and suffering of the bombing of Guernica by the Nazis. Both result in a certain feeling, but with different qualities of feeling.

Peirce provides some hints about this in "The Basis of Pragmaticism." There he tends to emphasize esthetics as a matter of feeling and defines it as "the formation of habits of feeling" (1906, EP 2, p. 378), as he does in the opening of the fifth Harvard Lecture (1903, HL, p. 212). In the 1906 work, Peirce asserts that "esthetic good and evil are closely akin to pleasure and pain." As Peirce characterizes pleasure and pain, the feeling of pain is a "symptom of a feeling which repels us; the feeling of pleasure is the symptom of an attractive feeling." A toothache has a distinct quality of feeling, such that pain accompanies it, and that is why people are not attracted to it (1906, EP 2, p. 379). In turn, attraction and repulsion are a kind of action, hence a connection between feeling and motivation. In general, "the good is attractive" and evil is "repulsive."

Peirce hints at this way to solve the enigma of Lecture Five in the lectures that follow. In Lecture Six he claims that "any kind of goodness consists in the adaptation of its subject to its *end* (1903, HL, p. 224). In explaining abductive reasoning, he writes, "the question of the goodness of anything is whether that thing *fulfills* its end" (emphasis added). As an example, he argues that the end of a hypothesis is to avoid surprise and to establish "a habit of positive expectation that shall not be disappointed" (1903, CP 5.197). Thus, a good hypothesis would fulfill that end; a bad hypothesis is one that does not, that is, does not predict what it claims will be so. At the same time, at the end of Lecture Five, he discusses the matter of logical goodness. There he claims that the very design of the hypothesis *in terms of its suitability to fulfill its end* is an esthetic matter. "Esthetic goodness, or *expressiveness*, may be possessed, and in some degree must be possessed, by any kind of representamen—rhema, proposition, or argument" (1903, CP 5.140). It can be supposed that a hypothesis is well-expressed, that is, esthetically good, if it follows the dictates of the pragmatic maxim, and achieves the third grade of clarity in terms of the practical consequences it would predict. A claim that is not designed so that it can be tested in such a manner is esthetically bad. On the other hand, a proposition or an argument is *morally* good, Peirce says, if it has "veracity" (1903, CP 5.141). In other words, if it fulfills its function as being accurate, and its function—truth-telling—is good, then that makes it morally good.

This suggests a modification to the division of labor between esthetics and ethics as proposed in the first lecture. Just as for Plato, something is *kalos* when it is suited to its purpose *and* the purpose is good, something is admirable, when it is suited to its end and its end is good. This would suggest that what is admirable is a product of *both* esthetic *and* moral goodness. Rather than saying "The morally good will be the esthetically good specially determined by a peculiar superadded element" (1903, CP 5.131), Peirce should have said that the *admirable* would be the esthetically good, specially determined by the "peculiar superadded element" of the morally good. For example, when Peirce explains to his audience in Lecture Five that the vulgar is esthetically good, the "squeamishness" people feel, "that is a *moral* and not an *esthetic* way of considering them" (1903, HL, p. 211).

Thus, the function of esthetics and ethics work together to determine what is admirable, *to kalon*, that is, what is so designed as to be *suitable* to its end *and best fulfills* that end, but also that the *end is good to fulfill*. This would seem to clarify the division of labor between ethics and esthetics. As Peirce says in the outline of his classification of the sciences handed out to the audience for his 1903 Lowell Lectures, esthetics is to *aid* ethics in the determination of the *summum bonum*, which suggests that the determination of the highest end is a function of both ethics and esthetics (1903, CP 1.191). This is a somewhat different model than the one presented in Lecture One of the Harvard Lectures, where the functions are more linear and sequential: esthetics determines which ends are admirable and ethics determine which are good.

In drafts to the first of the Lowell Lectures, delivered a few months after the Harvard ones, Peirce describes the process by which "ideals of conduct" are typically formed by individuals that may serve as a model of this division of labor between esthetics and ethics. There is no reason to think that it does not also describe the process at a larger, collective scale.

It is explained in the context of his interest in refuting the claim by some German thinkers that logical validity rests on "the reasoner's feeling of logicality" (1903, R 448, p. 7). Peirce thinks that this claim would infer that "there is no distinction of good and bad reasoning" (1903, R 448, p. 6). This sort of subjectivism would make the validity of logical reasoning rest on each individual's feeling that it is so, thus there would be no basis for adjudicating between anyone's feeling of logicality. To avoid this sort of subjectivism, there must be an appeal to norms or ideals of reasoning. Peirce wants to show that the feeling of logicality is not the cause of the validity, but the effect of satisfactorily conforming to an ideal.

To make his point he wants to show his audience that this is "parallel" to the argument that there is no moral right or wrong (1903, R 448, p. 9). To refute it, he illustrates how norms or ideals are formed. At first, people form an initial ideal based on "esthetic quality," such that they think it is "fine." As such it is "coarse and sentimental" and based on their "taste for the time being." But then, they attempt "to shape . . . ideals into consistency with each other" (1903, R 448, p. 13). This is also noted in the Harvard Lectures. One requisite of a candidate end is that it can be "consistently" pursued. "An aim which *cannot* be adopted and consistently pursued is a bad aim. It cannot properly be called an ultimate aim at all" (1903, HL, p. 214).

"In the third place," they imagine "what the consequence of fully carrying out . . . ideals would be," and they ask themselves "what the esthetic quality of those consequences would be" (1903, R 448, p. 13). Peirce says something similar in the Harvard Lectures: "it is incumbent upon us to inquire what an ultimate aim, capable of being pursued in an indefinitely prolonged course of action, can be" (1903, HL, p. 214).

As Peirce continues in the Lowell Lectures, he claims the initial ideals may have been "imbibed in childhood," but through this process, they have "gradually been shaped" by "a continuous process of growth." Upon reflection they develop into rules, and "reflection upon these rules, as well as the general ideals behind them," shape their habits and dispositions of conduct. In this review of ideals, "the experience of life is continually contributing instances more or less illuminative," so that over time people "will tend to do better than . . . before" (1903, R 448, p. 20). In other words, it is a process of self-correction.

This perhaps clarifies Peirce's rather obscure remarks in the Harvard Lectures, where the ultimate aim "should accord with a free development of the agent's own esthetic quality." There has to be a harmony between "the esthetic quality toward which the agent's free development tends and that of the ultimate action of experience upon him," such that they become "parts of one esthetic total" (1903, HL, p. 215). As he says in the Lowell Lectures, this process illustrates "controlled action," and through such a process "the man *can*, or if you please is *compelled to make his life more reasonable*" (1903, R 448, p. 22), that is, to self-correct to the proper end. One might say in Schiller's language, that through this process a *living shape* is developed as exemplified in the person's character and habits of action and constrained by experiments of living. It can be supposed that there is a parallel in process between the individual and the collective, so that not only do individuals but practices and institutions become reasonable to the extent that they engage in revision of norms and ideals in light of the "illuminations" of experience.

Here a clearer account of reasonableness emerges. *Reasonableness is the very process of correcting and improving norms and ideals* in light of experience, that is, living experiments with whatever norms and ideals they initially devise. *Reasonableness is self-correction.* The reasonable individual is one who is willing to correct ostensibly erroneous beliefs and adopt those that are less erroneous in their place. To be unreasonable is to refuse to improve, to grow when the "illuminations" of experience warrant it. The unreasonable are those, illustrated in the "Fixation of Belief," who tenaciously cling to their beliefs, or who accept authoritative beliefs without evidence or contrary to evidence; it is the cognitively dissonant and those that cherry-pick evidence to support what they want to believe, that is unreasonable. The fallibilists are reasonable in the sense that they believe what is believable until there are reasons not to believe it. It is only by being reasonable in this sense that inquirers can converge toward true beliefs and true norms and ideals. To be reasonable is to go where truth leads. Just as this applies to individuals, it would also suppose that the same can be said of practices and institutions. Science, certainly, would be heralded by Peirce as the exemplar of a reasonable practice in this regard, since its methodology is so designed as to master the detection of error and processes of self-correction.

This account of the development of ideals may also help to explain another, rather obscure passage in the fifth Harvard Lecture. Peirce makes an interesting but puzzling distinction between two types of goodness:

> I hardly need remind you that goodness, whether esthetic, moral, or logical, may either be negative—consisting in freedom from fault—or quantitative—consisting in the degree to which it attains.
>
> (1903, CP 5.127)

The audience undoubtedly does need reminding, since it's most certain that they have no idea what he's talking about. He notes at this point that "in an inquiry, such as we are now engaged upon, negative goodness is the important thing" (1903, CP 5.127).

It's rather difficult to sort out this distinction on the basis of such a thin description. In Lecture Four he thinks "goodness is a colorless quality, a mere absence of badness" (1903, HL, p. 199), a sense that aligns with negative goodness as defined above. This might be interpreted in light of his claim that scientific progress is made through the detection of erroneous hypotheses. Similarly, negative goodness in ethics and esthetics is a process by which faulty norms and ideals are detected over time and replaced by ones that correct the fault. This would align somewhat with the process of the correction of ideals and norms, Peirce describes in the Lowell Lectures, but a more collective level.

It is easier to recognize error than it is truth. To say that something is true, Peirce says, "means simply that it never can be found out to be false" (1903, CP 5.142). Scientific reasoning proceeds through the recognition of error and correcting that error. Peirce says that "one of the most wonderful features of reasoning and one of the most important philosophemes in the doctrine of science, of which, however, you will search in vain for any mention in any book I can think of; namely, that reasoning tends to correct itself, and the more so, the more wisely its plan is laid." (1898, CP 5.575). This would seem to apply to any type of inquiry, including ethical and esthetic ones. Peirce claims "that inquiry of every type, fully carried out, has the vital power of self-correction and of growth. "This," as Peirce writes, is a "property . . . deeply saturating its inmost nature." Peirce argues that "no matter how erroneous your ideas of the method may be at first, you will be forced at length to correct them so long as your activity is moved by that sincere desire [for truth] (1898, CP 5.591). Growth and improvement is through the correction of error.

At the end of Lecture Five, Peirce gives another bit of description to negative and positive goodness as it pertains to logic. The negative sense is the "more fundamental," its "soundness and weight, its really having the force that it pretends to have that force being great." On the other hand, its positive, "quantitative goodness consists in the degree in which it advances our knowledge." Peirce then asks, in regard to the question of negative goodness—"In what then does the soundness of argument consist?" (1903, HL, p. 217). Peirce goes on to explain the three types of argument—deduction, induction and abduction. In explaining the "justification" of induction, that is, the soundness, he argues that "although the conclusion at any stage of the investigation may be more or less erroneous, yet the further application of the same method must correct the error" (1903, HL, p. 218). He says the same thing elsewhere: "the true guarantee of the validity of induction is that it is a method of reaching conclusions which, if it is persisted in long enough, will assuredly correct any error concerning future experience into which it may temporarily lead us" (c. 1905, CP 2.769). Abduction formulates new hypotheses in light of problems with existing ones, deduction draws out the testable consequences of those hypotheses and induction detects any error in the proposed hypothesis. Together they work to progress science away from hypotheses that stand in error (1903, HL, p. 218). Thus the "soundness," the negative logical goodness of such reasoning, is found in its ability to self-correct. Positive goodness, it would be assumed, is the measure of how much gain in knowledge such corrections made.

The architectonic of the sciences may serve as a model for this sense of negative and positive goodness in the esthetic, ethical and logical sense. The classification of the sciences as Peirce organizes it has an esthetic quality, as Peirce defines it here in the Harvard Lectures: a "multitude of parts so related to one another as to impart a positive immediate quality to their totality." As Peirce says, "a good classification is a diagram usefully expressive of significant interrelations of the objects classified." As noted, he visualizes the classification of the sciences fractally as a "ladder-like scheme where each rung is itself a ladder of rungs." The whole is "like a succession of waves, each of which carries other waves" (c. 1905, R 328, pp. 18–19; Kent, 1987, pp. 136–137). The sciences are well-ordered by type and function, they have a certain hierarchy of leading principles and a relation of dependency that characterizes its systemic character. The result is a coherent body of knowledge that continues to grow and improve, correcting itself on its way to becoming more and more well-ordered. Peirce would likely agree that, if one were to characterize the quality that is the impression of its totality, it would be one of reasonableness. For Peirce, "knowledge is reasonableness," that is, as he says an "embodiment" of reasonableness. The design of the sciences is such as to be most conducive to knowledge (1903, CP 1.615).

Not only is the design of the system of sciences conducive to knowledge, the aim of science—truth, knowledge—is good. Additionally, it is logically good in both the negative and positive senses. It is negatively good in that the methods by which it pursues knowledge are valid on a whole. It has the capability of self-correcting. It is positively good in the sense that self-correction leads to a growing accumulation of knowledge. The architectonic of the sciences embodies reasonableness, the result of the workings of the communities of inquiry. It is a community occupied by those who are dedicated to truth, and who have an ethos that is conducive to truth, and who work cooperatively with others in the spirit of an intergenerational altruism, to pass on what is known so that others may improve the body of knowledge even more. The practice of science is a living shape a harmony of form and experience, and the system of sciences, the demonstration of that harmony is *to kalon*, meeting both conditions of a design fitted to its end and an end fit to pursue.

By analogy, then, as applied to inquiry into the ultimate ends or ideals, a negative sense of goodness would also be thought in terms of self-correction. As ends, ideals and norms are proposed in the course of living experiments, the ability to detect the erroneous ones could be thought of as a movement away from something worse to something better—amelioration. As Peirce defines meliorism in the Century Dictionary, it is "the doctrine that the world is neither the worst nor the best possible, but that it is capable of improvement: a mean between theoretical pessimism and optimism" (cited in Bergman, 2012, p. 127). If a negative goodness is a matter of "freedom from fault," then the direction is to move from more error to less error. The ultimate good is revealed through the disclosure of error by trial, rather than through the attainment of a preconceived end.

9 Ends

If esthetics and ethics work together to determine what would count as an admirable end, the task is to determine what that end would be. Peirce became interested in cataloging and classifying ends around 1900–1901 as a starting point. This seems to have been prompted by a review of Frank Thilly's *Introduction to Ethics* (1900, CN 2, pp. 249–250). Thilly presented a classification based on Wilhelm Wundt's scheme as Peirce believed. Peirce summarizes it in the following way:

A. The Moral law is externally imposed.
B. The Moral Law is rational:

    I. Its end is happiness:

        a. That of the agent
        b. That of the community.

    II. Its tendency is improvement:

        a. Of the agent
        b. Of the community.

Peirce lists a number of defects in the Thilly/Wundt classification of ends (1900, CN, p. 250), prompting Peirce to devise three variants of his own classification as a corrective in drafts of the review (1900, R 1429). However, he does not include any of them in the published review.

The next attempt at a classification of ends comes a year later in a review of Karl Pearson's *The Grammar of Science* (1901, CP 8.132). What motivates Peirce in this case was his unhappiness with the way Pearson had characterized the ends of science: "to promote the welfare of human society, to increase social happiness, or to strengthen social stability." Peirce was also unhappy with Pearson's ethical guidepost—Darwinism (1901, CP 8.133; Anderson and Rovine, 2012, p. 143). Some years earlier, in "Evolutionary Love," Peirce had railed against the Social Darwinism of his day and, in his Cambridge Lectures of 1898, Peirce had defended the end of science as pure theory, truth for the sake of truth, and setting cautions about its practical and instrumental application. By this time, Peirce had understood that his pragmatic maxim could lead to an instrumental view of science and, given the way in which capitalist America had exploited science for its own instrumental ends, he was keen to defend a nobler purpose for science and protect theoretical science from corruption as he saw it. As he writes in the review:

> The worst feature of the present state of things is that the great majority of the members of many scientific societies, and a large part of others, are men whose chief interest in science is as a means of gaining money, and who have a contempt, or half-contempt, for pure science. Now, to declare that the sole reason for scientific research is the good of society is to encourage those pseudo-scientists to claim, and the general public to admit, that they, who deal with the application of knowledge, are the true men of science, and that the theoreticians are little better than idlers.
>
> (1901, CP 8.142)

Peirce also seemed offended by Pearson's imperious tone implying the superiority of British society and suggesting that its stability was most important for civilization as a whole (1901, CP 8.134; 1901, CP 8.141; Anderson and Rovine, 2012, p. 137).

There are three variants of the classification associated with the Pearson review. One, similar to the classification from the Thilly review, is found in Draft A of the Pearson review (1901, R 1434 Draft A, pp. 4–6; 1901, CP 8.136n3). The second is the classification published in the review itself, which greatly expands the Thilly review variant (1901, CP 8.138). There is a nearly identical version of this in R 1434 (1901, R 1434, Draft D, pp. 5–6). The third variant is in a draft started after Draft B (call it Draft C). It presents the published classification in a more systematic way with some variation (1901, Draft C, pp. 5–7). This is accompanied by three different diagrams of that classification. in pages inserted in the draft. (An analysis of these diagrams and Peirce's attempt at systematizing his list of ends is discussed in Appendix 1.)

Peirce picks up the matter of the classification of ends a few years later in 1903. It is similar to the ones published in the Pearson review and Draft C of the review. It is an attempt to give a systematic rendering of the list as in Draft C, but it is left unfinished (c. 1903, R 1134; c.1903, CP 1.585–1.588).

To avoid confusion, the five classifications will be called in chronological order, the Thilly Classification (1900), the Pearson Draft A Classification (1901), the Pearson Draft C Classification (1901), the Published Classification (1901) and the 1903 Classification. The reader will also need patience in following the divisions and subdivisions of these classifications in their development.

As mentioned, the Thilly Classification is found in a draft of the review of Thilly's book. There are three variants, the second of which seems the most cogent and understandable (1900, R 1429, p. 14). Peirce crosses out the third (1900, R 1429, p. 15). He titles the second classification, "Rational Theories of the End of Action."

Peirce organizes ends in the Thilly classification into three general types that appear to follow his three phenomenological categories of firstness, secondness and thirdness. They are also subdivided in accord with one of his principles of classification, as exemplified in his sign classifications, where firsts have no division, seconds have two and thirds have three (c. 1909, CP 6.331).

An end that would be a simple first would be the end of pleasure, a "purely subjective end" (1900, R 1429, p. 7). An end that would be a simple second would be the continued existence, either (a) of a person or (b) the human race as such. The third sort of end "is to realize a general ideal" in terms of feeling, action and thought (1900, R 1429, p. 14), which is subdivided into three as will shortly be explained.

These three major divisions are reiterated in the Pearson Draft A Classification (1901, R 1434, p. 4). They seem to follow what Peirce says are the "three grand classes of rationalistic moralists," who are divided as to the nature of ends. There are those who see it either as pleasure, others, the continuation of the race, and those who identify it as "law" or "the rationalization of the universe" (1900, R 1429, p. 7)

Peirce directly subdivides this third grand division—"to realize a general ideal"—into three:

i. "to bring about some general state of feeling, such as the greatest pleasure of the greatest number of persons."
ii. to realize certain "inward" characters (a) in individuals of a community, "such as an altruistic sentiment." But also "outward" characters (b) in communities, such as "peace and prosperity."
iii. "to further the realization of an ideal not definable in advance, otherwise than as that which tends to realize itself in the long run, or in some such way."

(1900, R 1429, p. 14)

The three general ideals together paint a pretty picture of ends that ought to be pursued and would be hard to reject. In such a world, if it could be attained, there would be communities that are peaceful and prosperous, whose members are predominantly altruistic and cooperative, and whose lives are comforted by the utilitarian principle, such that there is the greatest amount of pleasure for the greatest number, relative to alternatives. Most importantly, it is a community that is always on the hunt for improvement, relative to the most reasonable ideals. But Peirce seems intent on identifying what is to count as the highest end, even if this might count as a very welcoming end for humankind.

There's more of a sense of what the highest good might be in classifications associated with the Pearson review. This last general ideal listed in the Thilly Classification—"the further realization of an ideal not definable in advance, otherwise than as that which tends to realize itself in the long run, or in some such way"—is expressed somewhat differently and further elaborated in the Pearson Draft A Classification. Here, "the ideal is one whose character cannot be known in advance, so that it can only be defined as the result, whatever it may be, of a *process* recognized as productive of the good" (emphasis added) (1901, R 1434, p. 6).

This introduction of the word *process* gives a better clue as to what Peirce means. It is similarly stated in the Published Classification: It is "hastening some result not otherwise known in advance . . . whatever it may turn out to be, to which some process seeming . . . . good must inevitably lead" (1901, CP 8.138). In other words, the ideal in this sense is not a static, but a dynamic, ongoing process of some sort. If it aligns at all with the Wundt classification in the Thilly review, it would also characterize this process as an effort at "improvement" (1900, CN2, p. 250). Indeed, in drafts to the Lowell Lectures, he writes:

> when these ideas of progress and growth have themselves grown up so as to occupy our minds as they now do, how can we be expected to allow the assumption pass that the admirable in itself is any stationary result? The explanation of the circumstance that the only result that is satisfied with itself is a quality of feeling is that reason always looks forward to an endless future and expects endlessly to improve its results.
>
> (1903, CP 1.614)

As Beverley Kent notes about Peirce's account of this general ideal, "It is the refusal to grant that the esthetic ideal must be a static result. By admitting process, Peirce is no longer limited to a self-satisfied ideal. He can now adopt an end that will always anticipate an improvement in its results" (1976, p. 270). In this view of things, Peirce seems to think that, rather than developing a pre-formed notion of the ideal, such an ideal will be developed through some ongoing process (Aydin, 2009, p. 431).

In the Pearson Draft A Classification, he further subdivides the general ideal of process into the following three types:

(1) "the natural development of feeling may be recognized as good and its ultimate dictum as the ideal. This is sentimentalism "(1901, R 1434, p. 6). The Published Classification adds, "whatever dictates of the human heart may approve" (1901, CP 8.138).
(2) it may be a case where "a developmental process of the world of experience may be recognized as good and its ultimate limit as the

ideal" (1901, R 1434, p. 6). The Published Classification lists two possibilities in this last category: "historicism," or "whatever the historical evolution of public sentiment may decree," or, "evolutionism," as "whatever the operation of cosmical causes may be destined to bring about" (1901, CP 8.138).

(3) it may be the case where "*reasoning may be recognized as good, and the reasonable as the ideal*" (emphasis added) (1901, R 1434, p. 6). In the Published Classification this is filled in by several possible processes:

a. ("rationalism"), "to do nothing not pronounced reasonable by . . . [a person's] own cogitations," or
b. ("dialecticism"), "by public discussion," or
c. (experimentalism, for lack of a title), "by crucial experiment," or
d. ("educationalism"), by "assimilating" truth in such a way that people can "ultimately recognize" their "veritable aim," or
e. ("pancratism"), that which is "destined to gain universal sway," or finally,
f. ("religionism"), "the living reason for the sake of which the psychical and physical universe is in process of creation."

(1901, CP 8.138)

Shortly after the presentation of this classification in the published Pearson review, Peirce declares his candidate for the highest good is this last subdivision of the general ideals, "the reasonable as the ideal": "*The only desirable object which is quite satisfactory in itself without any ulterior reason for desiring it, is the reasonable itself* (emphasis added)." He rejects pleasure or self-satisfaction as candidates for the highest end, and any end "involving dependence on some other" (1901, CP 8.140). It can be inferred, then, that he rejects the first two major divisions of his classification of general ideals as the *summum bonum*: the greatest pleasure for the greatest number, and altruistic sentiment and peace and prosperity of communities—although it is unclear whether he rejects these as ends in some lesser sense.

At the very point at which he nominates reasonableness as the candidate for the highest good, he excuses any demonstration why it is so: "I do not mean to put this forward as a demonstration; because, like all demonstrations about such matters, it would be a mere quibble, a sheaf of fallacies. I maintain simply that it is an experiential truth" (1901, CP 8.140). It's an odd statement from someone who has argued that any assertion commits the assertor to its defense.

This is not the first time he has publicly declared reasonableness as the ultimate end. Earlier in 1899, in a review of *the Many-Sided Franklin* by Paul Ford for *The Nation*, he also calls reasonableness the *summum bonum* (1899, CN 2, pp. 220–221). It is something that he declares consistently afterwards as well. In 1902, in the entry on *pragmatic and pragmatism* for the *Baldwin Dictionary*, he writes that

> a still higher grade of clearness of thought can be attained by remembering that the only ultimate good which the practical factors to which it directs attention can subserve is to further the development of concrete reasonableness; so that the meaning of the concept does not lie in any individual reactions at all, but in the manner in which those reactions contribute to that development.
>
> (1902, CP 5.3)

In the Lowell Lectures of 1903, he makes the declaration outright: "I do not see how one can have a more satisfying ideal of the admirable than the development of Reason so understood. The one thing whose admirableness is not due to an ulterior reason is Reason itself comprehended in all its fullness" (1903, CP 1.615).

In "What Pragmatism Is," published in *The Monist* in 1905, Peirce stresses what is already clear in the Pearson review, that reasonableness is a *process*:

> Accordingly, the pragmaticist does not make the *summum bonum* to consist in action, but makes it to consist in that process of evolution whereby the existent comes more and more to embody those generals which were just now said to be *destined*, which is what we strive to express in calling them *reasonable*.
>
> (1905, CP 5.433)

This is also emphasized earlier in the *Baldwin Dictionary*. There he argues that "almost everybody will now agree that the ultimate good lies in the evolutionary process in some way." As such it is something that is "general or continuous" and, as such, related to his synechism, "founded on the notion that the coalescence, the becoming continuous, the becoming governed by laws, the becoming instinct with general ideas, are but phases of one and the same process of the growth of reasonableness" (1902, CP 5.4). He repeats this claim in 1904, where the *summum bonum* consists in a "process of evolution whereby the existent comes more and more to embody a certain class of generals which in the course of the development show themselves to be reasonable" (c. 1904, R 329, p. 20). Again, he says the same thing a year later in his Monist article, "What Pragmatism Is" (1905, CP 5.433). "Reason," as Peirce remarks, is never "completely perfected," but "always must be in a state of incipiency, of growth" (1903, CP 1.615).

It is also in the Baldwin dictionary that Peirce indicates reasonableness as an ultimate good must be a "*concrete* reasonableness" (1902, CP 5.3). In the Lowell Lectures he stresses that "this development of reason consists . . . in embodiment, that is, in manifestation" (1903, CP 1.615). By concrete reasonableness, Peirce implies that the reasonable is actually operative in the world, like the edifice of a building, presumably in the habit-taking of the natural world, but also the habits of feeling, actions, practices and institutions of the human community. It is not just a formal principle, as it might be expressed in Kant, but it is a living shape in Schiller's sense, a form that shapes the lived experience (Ibri, 2016, p. 606). This is how John Dewey interprets Peirce: "in his later doctrine, concrete rationality means a change in existence brought about through action, and through action which embodies conceptions whose own specific existence consists in habitual attitudes of response" (Dewey, 1916, p. 714).

Although Peirce claims in the Pearson review that he does not have a demonstration of reasonableness as the highest end, Peirce does in fact have a strong argument, if only he had put together all the lessons of his normative science. As articulated in the Lowell Lectures, reasonableness is self-correction toward improvement in beliefs and the conduct that follows from it, self-correction at both the individual and collective levels. It can be an "inward type" in individuals, but also an "outward type" of institutions and practices, such as science. Self-correction is a form of self-control, the core feature of rational, purposive agency. Goal-directed conduct is about paths to a goal, and attainment of that goal requires correcting away from wrong paths. In the character of a person, it is the disposition of detecting and correcting error on the way to an end; in the organization of a practice, it is the process by which error is corrected to achieve the end of a practice. In the person, it is manifested as a willingness to give up beliefs or habits of conduct shown to be false and wrong, and to adopt ones less prone to error, rather than remaining obstinate in one's beliefs regardless of evidence or maintaining blind obedience to authority. At the social level, it is the adoption of truth as the guide, wherever it may lead, rather than imposing self-interested false beliefs through force and coercion. In both cases, people and practices experience growth and improvement through this process of self-correction. One only has to look to science as the model, the most successful practice in fixing belief.

As people and practices self-correct, they tend in the long run to converge toward certain claims or standards of conduct if those claims are true and the conduct good, as the convergence theory of truth asserts. This holds too for claims about good ends and certainly the highest ends. If the highest end selected is reasonableness, understood as self-correction, then there is a guarantee, in the long run, that the highest good will be disclosed, if there is such a highest good. It would certainly not be disclosed if inquirers did not self-correct.

Since self-correction is a process that fits its end of determining what is true and good and reasonableness is a process of self-correction, reasonableness is esthetically good. Since self-correction leads to good ends in the long run, self-correction is ethically good. Since it is both esthetically and ethically good, then it counts as *to kalon*, something admirable. To be reasonable, in the sense of self-correction, has no ulterior motive since it is a disinterested process. The process of self-correction is unclear as to what conclusions such a process will lead. It does not determine ahead of the process what is good and true. For that reason, people engaged in such a process cannot be self-interested, except if one's interest is the truth. In that case, it is pursued with no "ulterior motive," another mark of the highest good.

In establishing reasonableness as the highest end, Peirce has his answer to the fundamental question asked in *The Minute Logic*—why study logic? Logical reasoning, including scientific reasoning—especially induction—is most conducive to self-correction, which is the end of logic, but also the highest end. "In logic, it will be observed that knowledge is reasonableness; and the ideal of reasoning will be to follow such methods as must develop knowledge the most speedily" (1903, CP 1.615). Peirce cautions his readers that "logic came about for the sake of reasonableness, not reasonableness for the sake of logic." Let us never lose sight of that truth, forgotten though it is" (1902, CP 2.195).

The classification of ends associated with the Pearson review still raises a few other questions. First, it is not clear in counting reasonableness as the highest end, whether just one of the processes listed—rationalism, dialecticism, experimentalism, educationalism, pancratism, or religionism—is to be counted as the exemplar of reasonableness or whether all of these are in some sense part of that process.

The latter proposal is inviting. It would suggest that self-correction is a process realized in several ways that are complementary and, at its best, coordinate. It would seem that for some of the outward processes listed to work, the inward process of individuals would also have to be present. Even if experimentalism in the form of induction is a method that detects error and abduction is the reasoning process that proposes a correction to that error, scientists themselves have to be willing to forego erroneous hypotheses in favor of ones that better explain the anomalies of the former.

Peirce seems to favor each of these processes in various places in his writings. Peirce emphasizes the connection between reasonableness and rationalism, as he describes it—"to do nothing not pronounced reasonable" (1901, CP 8.138). In the Lowell Lectures after pronouncing reasonableness as the admirable ideal, he says "under this conception, the ideal of conduct will be to execute our little function in the operation of the creation by giving a hand toward rendering the world more reasonable whenever, as the slang is, it is "up to us" to do so" (1903, CP 1.615). He writes elsewhere: "But the saving truth is that there is a Thirdness in experience, an element of Reasonableness to which we can train our own reason to conform more and more. If this were not the case, there could be no such thing as logical goodness or badness" (1903, CP 5.160). Peirce thinks that it is "by the indefinite replication of self-control upon self-control" that a person "grows an esthetic ideal" (1906, CP 5.402n3).

Peirce also seems to advocate a "dialecticism" in places, understood as reasonableness by "public discussion" (1901, CP 8.138). Peirce notes that there is a growing demand that claims should be publicly vetted and determined in a "methodical manner." The best forms of inquiry are public in nature, so that what one proves can be proven by others (1893, CP 5.380n1). Assertions have a dialogic and public character, such that those who assert have obligations to defend what they assert and entails the right of others to criticize those assertions (1896, CP 3.433; c.1902, CP 5.546; c.1902, CP 5.543; c.1902, CP 2.315; c.1908, CP 5.546). After all, inquiries involve *communities* of inquiry.

In the case of the process of experimentalism, science is the master of self-correction. It is the exemplar of reasonableness in this sense. For Peirce, science exemplifies reasoning, so that "one of the most important philosophemes in the doctrine of science . . . [is] that reasoning tends to correct itself" (1898, CP 5.575). "The true guarantee of the validity of induction," as he writes, "is that it is a method of reaching conclusions which, if it be persisted in long enough, will assuredly correct any error concerning future experience into which it may temporarily lead us" (c. 1905, CP 2.769).

"Educationism" is essentially a process of learning, "assimilating" truths (1901, CP 8.138). Learning, which is a feature of Lamarckian processes of evolution, is a process of self-correction, of growth, as Peirce says (1893, CP 6.301). For Peirce, Lamarckian evolution is one of three types present in the world and explains certain processes of evolution better than Darwinism.

"Pancratism," as a process that results in "universal sway" or consensus, seems to be expressed by Peirce's convergence theory of truth. Inquiries, persisted in, and done rightly over time, will tend to converge opinion to the truth (1878, CP 5.407; 1902, CP 2.781).

"Religionism" enjoins Peirce's theological speculations, that there is an order to the cosmos that is also in the process of growth, as articulated in "Evolutionary Love," and "A Neglected Argument for the Reality of God." As Jaime Nubiola has pointed out, reasonableness also has a cosmic character for Peirce, that is, the tendency of the very order of things to take on a law-like character (Nubiola, 2009, p. 129). Indeed, reality itself is reasonableness. "Reality consists in regularity. Real regularity is active law. Active law is efficient reasonableness, or in other words is truly reasonable reasonableness. Reasonable reasonableness is Thirdness as Thirdness." (c. 1905, CP 5.12). In its most general sense, "reasonableness consists in association, assimilation, generalization, the bringing of items together into an organic whole" (cited in Nubiola, 2009, p. 133). Consistent with his objective idealism, Peirce argues that reasonableness of the human mind and the reasonableness of nature "are essentially the same" (1903, CP 7.687). "The creation of the universe, which did not take place during a certain busy week, in the year 4004 B.C., but is going on today and never will be done, is this very developement of Reason" (1903, CP 1.615).

Peirce's classification in the Pearson review also raises a second question concerning the other two general ideals of the greatest pleasure for the greatest number, and a community constituted by norms of altruism, resulting in peace and prosperity. Even if these are not counted as ultimate ends, are they ends that subserve the ultimate end? That is to say, could they fit into a system of ends—an architectonic of ends—with reasonableness the highest—the mixed ends of Plato. Peirce does say that the "development of Reason requires . . . all qualities of feeling, including pleasure in its proper place among the rest" (1903, CP 1.615). The development of reasonableness would certainly require a community. If there is to be inquiry, public discussion, learning, scientific experimentation, and the like, do these not have to take place within some community? For inquiry, hence, self-correction to occur, communities have to have certain norms and inquirers certain virtues and sentiments, an intergenerational altruism above all, as discussed.

Rather than thinking just in terms of the ultimate good itself, it would appear best to think of a system of ends, with relations of dependence, subserving the highest end. Just as there is an architectonic of knowledge, exemplified in the system of science, one would think that Peirce would also advocate an architectonic of ends in the same sense. Ends would be organized in terms of hierarchies and dependencies, much in the way which leading principles of higher sciences guide the lower ones, and the results of one science feed into the advancement of others. Although there are certain key features to a community of inquiry, necessary for self-correction of beliefs and conduct, it would also be a good to have such a community peaceable and prosperous, and its members living a relatively self-satisfying and pleasurable life. As John Stuhr notes, "rendering the world more reasonable involves acting so as to create and sustain community" (1994, p. 13).

Reasonableness is the highest end. It is a process rather than a static end. It is a process of continual self-correction so that what is ostensibly free from error is kept and what is erroneous is discarded. As Peirce says, it is "self-control upon self-control." It is indeterminate in the sense that its outcomes cannot be preordained but leads wherever it leads. On the way, it creates a living shape, candidate habits of feeling in the form of sentiments, habits of thought, such as beliefs and practical hypotheses, and action, in the form of rules of conduct and norms in institutions and practices that persist and endure or change with correction over time. Peirce suggests that it involves multiple but complementary processes: the use of good reasoning by individuals; public discussion and civic discourse; scientific experimentalism with the best methods for detecting error and correcting it; learning and the accumulation of knowledge that can be passed on to the next generation; and free and open inquiry that has the best chance of leading to consensus. This is all framed by faith in a cosmic order that itself is reasonable.

Imagine, Peirce says, that a fairy can make you dream any dream you like. You can't remember any detail of the dream, but you are left with an "impression of its totality." He asks his audience what they would like to dream about. Peirce's choice would not be one of some pleasurable, blissful event, but something of the following:

> a dream of extreme variety and must seem to embrace an eventful history extending through millions of years. It shall be a drama in which numberless living caprices shall jostle and work themselves out in larger and stronger harmonies and antagonisms, and ultimately execute intelligent reasonablenesses of existence more and more intellectually stupendous and bring forth new designs still more admirable and prolific.
>
> (1903, R 310, pp. 7–8)

Conclusion

The Lessons of the Normative Sciences

Like much of Peirce's work, his study of ethics and esthetics is incomplete. Peirce says of himself: "I am a mere table of contents, so abstract, a very snarl of twine" (c. 1911, CP 6.184). But, typical of his thought, he raises the deeper questions and points to tantalizing answers. His work is more like setting down signposts than providing solutions. As Hilary Putnam thought, "Peirce's great contribution lies in his perception of the depth of individual problems, even if he did not succeed in building a unified system out of all those wonderful perceptions" (1987, p. 80). The attempt here has been to read the signposts concerning the normative sciences and fill in the paths as far as possible.

Peirce characterized moral agency as goal-seeking. People and practices, as Aristotle says, all aim at some end. In that regard, there are two fundamental questions to ask: what ends should be sought and how best should those ends be attained?

Peirce's answer to the first is that whatever ends people seek, the highest end should be reasonableness. He understood reasonableness as a process of self-correction toward what was true and good. Whatever was true and good could only be found by correcting error. What was opposed to reasonableness was obstinacy in belief despite contrary evidence; the imposition of authority rather than reason; blocking the road of inquiry; the denial of evidence contrary to one's belief; the adoption of beliefs that one wants to believe rather than what is true; self-interested and corrupt inquiry. Reasonableness meets the traditional criteria of an ultimate end. It is done for its own sake since it is pursued for no ulterior reason. Since it is not clear where the pursuit of truth and goodness will lead, interests cannot inform the process. All other goods and ends depend upon it, since they cannot be acquired unless the erroneous paths toward those ends are corrected.

Peirce also answers the second fundamental question—what are the best ways to attain those ends? Peirce argued that if reasonableness is the highest end, self-correction requires inquiry and inquiry requires a community of inquiry. Communities of inquiry must engender a certain solidarity among its members in terms of common ends and a consensus about the best means to attain them. To be successful at the task of inquiry, communities of inquiry must be populated by reasonable inquirers, inquirers who are disinterested in that they do not bring an agenda to the inquiry or aim at a predetermined outcome. They must have an altruistic spirit that is intergenerational in outlook, building on what has preceded them and contributing to future work. They must have certain virtues. If inquiry is to be genuine, they must be honest. Inquiries must abide by certain norms. They must be open, transparent and public. All claims must be defended with evidence or reasons. There must be opportunities for inquiries to question, criticize, raise questions and propose alternative claims.

If any claims were true, any ends worthy of pursuit or any norms of conduct righteous, these would be found out if inquiries were structured in this way, and inquirers kept to the reasonable paths. If a claim were true a norm right, an end good, no matter what paths toward these things were initially taken, they would converge in the long run toward the right one, or right ones, so long as inquirers stayed true to correcting what was in error. There could be no higher end since all ends require self-correction toward truth and goodness.

Peirce saw the practice of science as the ideal of inquiry and the leader in the cause of reasonableness. Peirce saw the power of science growing in the 19th century, thanks primarily to its reliable methods of inquiry. But, at the same time, he began to see how that very same power was being exploited for self-interested ends, uses that could corrupt the practice of science unless precautions were taken. The Gilded Age and industrial capitalism, combined with the conjoining of science and technology, were transforming societies in a way not conducive to the nobler aims of science. The use of the Darwinian theory to develop a social ethic threatened to undermine those very norms that were needed for good inquiry and aligned itself with norms of the Gilded Age.

Peirce's pragmatic maxim presaged these things to come. Peirce's motivation for the maxim was to bring the methods of science to bear on the fundamental philosophical questions of meaning and truth. The pragmatic maxim translated the armature of experimental science in such a way so that meaning of concepts could be clarified. If the meaning of a concept was understood in terms of its practical, observable consequences, then it was also set up to have its truth tested experimentally. Thus, there was a way to truth through the clarification of meaning. But, at the same time, the maxim showed that theoretical claims could be translated to practical ones. If diamonds are scratch-hard because they scratch glass then, if one's aim was to cut glass, then diamonds are best friends. The pragmatic maxim showed how scientific, theoretical hypotheses could be conjoined with practical ones by means of the experimental method.

Peirce eventually recognized that the pragmatic maxim was amoral, instrumental, used for any purpose, good or ill. To save science, Peirce thought now that its true aim had to be shown. To figure this out rigorously and persuasively, Peirce thought that the normative sciences had to be developed. There had to be a science of ends and a science of righteous means. Ethics and esthetics were to be these sciences. He set the bones for these disciplines—and they are good bones—but he never could flesh them out. But, in the process, he could see that reasonableness was the aim of science. It was also the highest end since it was through reasonableness that people would be led to what was true and good. If the right path is where truth leads, then reasonableness was the right path.

Although Peirce was speaking against the harms of the Gilded Age, his message resonates today. In an age where public discourse has devolved into deliberate misinformation, assertions made without evidence, bald-faced lies touted as truths, the dismissal of science, strange conspiracy theories and inquiries made on the basis of self-interested results, Peirce stands as a reminder of a nobler aim of discourse, to return inquiry to the pursuit of truth, wherever it may lead.

Appendix 1
Peirce's Classification of Ends

Peirce attempted a systematic classification of "ethical motives" in 1901, in drafts to the review of Karl Pearson's *Grammar of Science* (1901, R 1434). These are likely the 28 candidates for the ultimate good that he notes a year later in drafts of *The Minute Logic* for his chapter on ethics (1902, R 434 Draft B, p. 28). Peirce intended to review each of the 28 to assess whether they could qualify as ultimate goods, but never completed that task (1902, CP 1.581).

In the Pearson review and its associated drafts, Peirce calls this a classification of "ethical motives," not ends (1901, CP 8.137). There is an obvious difference between motives and ends. Motive is a *mens rea*, an end is some event, product, or result of people's actions. People may have several different motives for doing an action that results in the same end. The end may be to reduce hunger in a community. However, one person may want to do that from a motive of social injustice, another from sympathy for the hungry, some from guilt or shame for not helping others in need, and others because they are among the hungry. It can be supposed that a motive correlates with an end. If people are motivated by the injustice of hunger in their community, it can be supposed that their end is to alleviate hunger in the community. People may choose different actions, depending on their motivation. A person acting out of sympathy might donate to the food bank or volunteer in a soup kitchen, whereas those motivated by injustice may work to change laws.

He corrects this mistake in a revision of this classification composed a few years later in 1903: "I enumerated a number of ethical classes of motives, meaning by a motive, not a spring of action, but an aim or end appearing ultimate to the agent" (c. 1903, 1.585). But, in fact, he does seem to mix up motives and ends in the Pearson drafts. For example, if as Peirce says people act out of a motive "from dread of blame," then the corresponding end is to avoid blame or shaming (1901, CP 8.138).

It is likely that a reader's impression of the list of "motives" in the Pearson review is one of a mishmash of odd and arbitrary items. However, there is a system to Peirce's thinking. This becomes clear in the diagrams that accompany the drafts of the review. There are three diagrams intended to represent the classification (these are inserted in 1901, R 1434, Draft C, after page 7). It appears that the third classification was not completed, and much of it illegible. The first two are completed and have many similarities but some differences. Given the state of the third diagram, the focus here will be on the first and second ones.

The first diagram (Figure 1) is presented as follows:

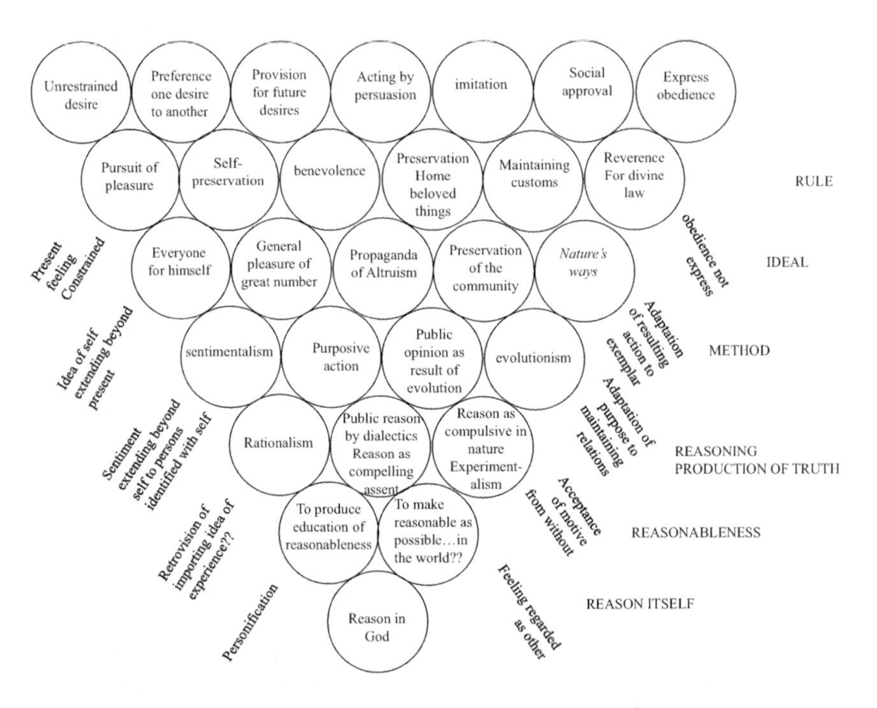

Figure 1 Peirce's Classification of Ends (1901, R 1434, Draft C).

Source: Diagram 1.

The second diagram is represented in Figure 2.

The second diagram comes closest to representing the classification that was published in the Pearson review but there are still some differences (1901, CP 8.138). It should also be noted that these diagrams have some family resemblance to the inverted triangular diagrams Peirce made of his 1903 and 1908 classifications of signs (1903, CP 2.264; 1908, EP 2, p. 481; 1908, EP 2, p. 491), and they follow the same leading principles of phenomenology. How and why are the diagrams organized the way they are?

The second diagram provides more clues to the organization of the motives or ends than the first. There are two overarching variables that characterize the *direction* of the triangle from top down, as indicated by the label on the far right ("depth or freedom") and the far

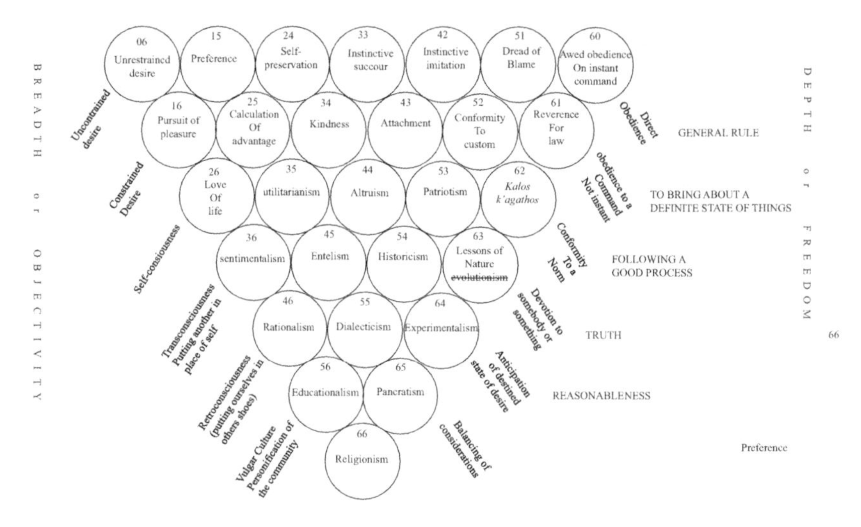

Figure 2 Peirce's Classification of Ends (1901, R 1434, Draft C).

Source: Diagram 2.

left label ("breadth or objectivity"). In terms of breadth, the diagram moves downward from individual and subjective considerations to more collective ones, to experience, to the cosmic order of things. If Peirce defines freedom primarily in terms of the degree of self-control in the action, then there is a similar downward movement in the diagram from complete lack of self-control in unrestrained and instinctive conduct, to deliberate adoption of rules and ideals of conduct, to reasonableness itself as the epitome of freedom. As Peirce writes, "true liberty" for any person "is to make his life more reasonable" (1902, CP 1.602).

The next set of labels inward on the right characterize the *rows* of motives or ends in the diagram. The labels in descending order in the diagram are listed as follows, with the alternative labels in the second diagram in parentheses, and Peirce's neologisms for them in the second diagram in brackets:

Row 1: no label
Row 2: rule (general rule) [ethic, tactic]
Row 3: ideal (to bring about a definite state of things) [teleotic, hyperbolic]
Row 4: method (following a good process) [hyphegetic, methodic]
Row 5: reasoning (truth) [phanerotic]
Row 6: reasonableness (reasonableness) [chresmodotic]
Row 7: reason itself [psychocratic].

The next set of labels characterize the oblique left diagonals of the triangle. These are starting at the top right with the alternatives in the second diagram in parentheses. Most have a number associated with them for reasons to be explained:

Diagonal 0: (direct obedience)
Diagonal 1: obedience not express (obedience to a command not instant)
Diagonal 2: adaptation of resulting action to exemplar (conformity to a norm)
Diagonal 3: adaptation of purpose to maintaining relations (devotion to somebody or something)
Diagonal 4: acceptance of motive from without (anticipation of destined state of desire)
Diagonal 5: feeling regarded as other (balancing of considerations)
Diagonal 6: unlabeled.

The next labels on the left of the diagrams characterize the oblique right diagonals of the triangle, with the second diagram alternatives in parentheses and specific numbers associated with them:

Diagonal 0: unlabeled
Diagonal 1: present feeling constrained (constrained desire)
Diagonal 2: idea of self, extending beyond present (self-consciousness)
Diagonal 3: sentiment, extending beyond self to persons identified with self (transconsciousness, putting another in place of self)
Diagonal 4: retrovision of importing idea of experience (illegible) (ultraconsciousness, retroconsiousness, putting ourselves in others' shoes).
Diagonal 5: personification (vulgar culture, personification of the community)
Diagonal 6: unlabeled.

The next set of markers of the organization of the diagrams is found in the numbering of each entry in the triangle in the second diagram. They are indicated by a duplet, the first being from 0 to 6 as well as the second, as indicated above. The duplets appear to represent the intersection of the two sets of diagonal labels. For example, "conformity to custom" (52) is at the intersection of "personification of the community" (5) and "conformity to a norm" (2). The "calculation of advantage" (25) is at the intersection of "self-consciousness" (self-interest) (2) and "balancing of considerations" (5) and so forth.

This leaves the question as to the content of the specific motives and why there are 28 in the diagrams. In all of Peirce's classifications, he starts with three main divisions that follow the three phenomenological categories: (A) a first, usually pleasure or desire; (B) a second, continued existence or some sort of constraint; (C) a third, something general. He then proceeds, as in the Draft C version of the Pearson review, to subdivide these further (1901, R 1434, Draft C, pp. 5–7). Since, as in the sign classifications, firsts cannot determine seconds or thirds and seconds cannot determine thirds, then this allows for seven possible types in the first subdivision: A, B, BA, BB, C, CA, CB, CC. For example, A could be construed as "unrestrained desire" (06) in the diagram and BA some sort of constrained desire, such as "preference" (15). Since the pursuit of pleasure (16) is a more general aim, this could be the CA type. If these 7 types are combined again by the same phenomenological principle, one ends up the following additional 9. The rule can be formalized such that B cannot follow A, and C cannot follow either A or B in sequence: BA(A), BB(A), BB(B), CA(A), CB(A), CB(B), CC(A), CC(B), CC(C). And if these are subdivided again by the phenomenological principle, one ends up with the following 12: BAA(A), BBA(A), BBB(A), BBB(B), CAA(A), CBA(A), CBB(A), CBB(B), CCA(A), CCB(A), CCB(B), CCC(C). This yields the 28 classes of motives or ends. It would take some imagination and some tweaking to design the content to fit the form, as Peirce does in Draft C of the Pearson review (1901, R 1434, pp. 5–7), but it does explain the list that's delivered in the published Pearson review. For example, CBB(A) is, in general terms, a general constraint of a constraint on pleasure. This might be one way to characterize utilitarianism as the greatest pleasure for the greatest number. One supposes that there could be further subdivisions, but Peirce stops at the third round of combinations.

References

Notes on References: References are APA style. However, some references are dated with the original publication or composition of the author, where appropriate and indicated in parenthesis (date). The date of the edition or translation of the work from which the material is cited, if different, is indicated by brackets [date]. The original date of the publication of some ancient authors is not listed. Ancient authors, such as Plato and Aristotle, are referenced by title and the date of translation, in brackets.

American Law Institute (1962). *Model Penal Code.* https://archive.org/details/ModelPenalCode_ALI

Anderson, Douglas and Rovine, Michael (2012). Peirce and Pearson: The aims of inquiry. In Douglas Anderson and Carl Hausman (Eds.), *Conversations on Peirce: Reals and ideals* (132–148). Fordham University Press.

Annas, Julia (2006). Virtue ethics. In David Copp (Ed.), *The Oxford handbook of ethical theory* (515–536). Oxford University Press.

Anscombe, G.E.M. (1963). *Intention.* Cornell University Press.

Apel, Karl-Otto (1980). The a priori of the communication community and the foundation of ethics. In *Towards a transformation of philosophy* (Glyn Adey and David Frisby, Trans.) (225–300). Routledge and Kegan Paul.

Apel, Karl-Otto (1996). *Karl-Otto Apel: Selected essays: Ethics and the theory of rationality* (Eduardo Mendieta, Ed.). Humanities Press.

Appiah, Kwame (1989). The conservation of 'race'. *Black American Literature Forum*, 23(1), 37–60.

Aquinas, Thomas (1265–1274) [1947]. *Summa theologica.* (Fathers of the English Dominican Province, Trans.) (Vols. 1–3). Benziger Brothers.

Aristotle [1941a]. *Politics* (W. Roberts, Trans.). In R. McKeon (Ed.), *The basic works of Aristotle* (1127–1324). Random House.

Aristotle [1941b]. *Rhetoric* (W. Roberts, Trans.). In R. McKeon (Ed.), *The basic works of Aristotle* (1325–1454). Random House.

Aristotle [1984]. *Nicomachean ethics* (Hippocrates Apostle, Trans.). The Peripatetic Press.

Atkins, Richard (2008). The pleasures of goodness: Peircean aesthetics in light of Kant's *Critique of the power of judgment. Cognition*, 9(1), 13–25.

Atkins, Richard (2018). *Peirce and the conduct of life.* Cambridge University Press.

Atkinson, J.W. (1957). Motivational determinants of risk-taking behavior. *Psychological Review*, 64, 359–372.

Audi, Robert (2001). Kantian intuitionism. *Mind*, 110(439), 601–635.

Audi, Robert (2004). *The good in the right. A theory of intuition and intrinsic value.* Princeton University Press.

Audi, Robert (2006). *Practical reasoning and ethical decision*. Routledge.

Ayala, F.J. (2010). The difference of being human: Morality. *Proceedings of the National Academy of Sciences*, 107(Suppl 2), 9015–9022.

Aydin, Ciano (2009). On the significance of ideals: Charles S. Peirce and the good life. *Transactions of the Charles S. Peirce Society*, 45(3), 422–443.

Ayer, A.J. (1936). *Language, truth and logic*. Gollancz.

Bacon, Francis (1605) [1892]. *The advancement of learning* (G.T. Bettany, Ed.). Ward, Lock, Bowden, and Co.

Baier, Annette (1987). Hume, the women's moral theorist? In E. Kittay and D. Meyers (Eds.), *Women and moral theory.* Owman and Littlefield.

Bain, Alexander (1865). *The emotions and the will* (2nd ed.). Longmans, Green.

Bain, Alexander (1869). Comments. In James Mill (Ed.), *Analysis of the phenomena of the human mind*. www.gutenberg.org/files/56441/56441-h/56441-h.htm

Bain, Alexander (1889). *Logic: Deductive and inductive*. Appleton and Co.

Bandura, Albert (1977). *Social learning theory*. Prentice Hall.

Barney, Rachel (2010). Notes on Plato on the *kalon* and the good. *Classical Philology*, 105(4), 363–377.

Barnouw, Jeffrey (1988). "Aesthetic" for Schiller and Peirce: A neglected origin of pragmatism. *Journal of the History of Ideas*, 49(4), 607–632.

Bartlett, Irving (1993). *John C. Calhoun: A biography*. W. W. Norton.

Baumgarten, Alexander (1739) [2005]. *Metaphysik* (Georg Meier, Ed.). Dietrich Scheglmann Reprints.

Bazerman, Charles (1988). *Shaping written knowledge*. University of Wisconsin Press.

Beiser, Frederick (2005). *Schleiermacher's ethics*. In Jacqueline Marina (Ed.), *The Cambridge companion to Schleiermacher* (53–72). Cambridge University Press.

Bellucci, Francesco (2018). *Peirce's speculative grammar*. Routledge.

Berg, Howard (2004). *E. coli in motion*. Springer Verlag.

Bergman, Mats (2012). Improving our habits: Peirce and meliorism. In Cornelis de Waal and Krzysztof Skowronski (Eds.), *The normative thought of Charles S. Peirce* (125–148). Fordham University Press.

Bernoulli, Jakob (1713) [2005]. *The art of conjecturing* (Oscar Sheynin, Trans.). www.sheynin.de/download/bernoulli.pdf

Black, Henry Campbell (1980). *Black's law dictionary* (6th ed.). West.

Blackburn, Simon (1998). *Ruling passions*. Clarendon Press.

Borel, Émile (1909). Les probabilities dénombrables et leurs applications arithmétiques. *Rendiconti del Circolo Matematico di Palermo*, 27, 247–271.

Boyd, Kenneth (2016). Peirce on assertion, speech acts, and taking responsibility. *Transactions of the Charles S. Peirces Society*, 52(1), 21–46.

Brandom, Robert (1994). *Making it explicit: Reasoning, representing, and discursive commitment*. Harvard University Press.

Brandom, Robert (2000). *Articulating reasons: An introduction to inferentialism*. Harvard University Press.

Bratman, Michael (1999). *Intention, plans and practical reason*. CSLI Publications.

Brent, Joseph (1998). *Charles Sanders Peirce: A life* (2nd ed.). Indiana University Press.

Brink, David (1989). *Moral realism and the foundations of ethics*. Cambridge University Press.

Burke, Kenneth (1950). *A rhetoric of motives*. Prentice Hall.

Calhoun, John C. (1837) [1843]. Speech on the reception of abolition petitions. In *Speeches delivered in the congress of the United States from 1811 to the present time* (222–226). Harper.

Campbell, George (1776) [1823]. *The philosophy of rhetoric*. Charles Ewer.

Carter, Stephen (1996). *Integrity*. Basic.

Cicero (c. 87 B.C.E.) [1960]. *De inventio* (H.M. Hubbell, Trans.). Harvard University Press.

Colapietro, Vincent (1989). *Peirce's approach to the self*. State University of New York Press.

Copp, David (2004). Moral naturalism and three grades of normativity. In Peter Schaber (Ed.), *Normativity and naturalism* (7–45). Ontos Verlag.

Copp, David (2012). Normativity and reasons: Five arguments from Parfit against normative naturalism. In Susana Nuccetelli and Gary Seay (Eds.), *Ethical naturalism* (24–57). Cambridge University Press.

Cousin, Victor (1853) [1890]. *Lectures on the true, the beautiful and the good* (O.W. Wright, Trans.). John Chapman.

Cudworth, Ralph (1731) [1996]. *A treatise concerning eternal and immutable morality* (Sarah Hutton, Ed.). Cambridge University Press.

Cumberland, Richard (1672). *A philosophical inquiry into the laws of nature* (John Maxwell, Trans.). R. Phillips.

Cuneo, Terence (2004). Reid's moral philosophy. In Terence Cuneo and René van Woudenberg (Eds.), *The Cambridge companion to Thomas Reid* (243–266). Cambridge University Press.

Curry, Oliver, Mullins, Daniel and Whitehouse, Harvey (2019). Is it good to cooperate? Testing the theory of morality-as-cooperation in 60 societies. *Current Anthropology*, 60(1), 47–69.

Dalcho, Frederick (1823). *Practical considerations founded on the Scriptures, relative to the slave population of South Carolina by a South-Carolinian*. A. E. Miller.

Davidson, Donald (2006). *The essential Davidson*. Oxford University Press.

Davis, David Brion (2014). *The problem of slavery in the age of emancipation*. Knopf.

Dennett, Daniel (1995). *Darwin's dangerous idea*. Touchstone.

DeSilver, Drew (2019, May 14). Despite global concerns about democracy, more than half of countries are democratic. *Pew Research Center*. www.pewresearch.org/fact-tank/2019/05/14/more-than-half-of-countries-are-democratic/

De Waal, Cornelis (2012). Who's afraid of Charles Sanders Peirce? Knocking come critical common sense into moral philosophy. In Cornelis de Waal and Krzysztof Skowronski (Eds.), *The normative thought of Charles S. Peirce* (83–100). Fordham University Press.

Dewey, John (1916). The pragmatism of Peirce. *The Journal of Philosophy, Psychology and Scientific Methods*, 13(26), 709–715.

Eccles, J.S., Adler, T.F., Futterman, R., Goff, S.B., Kaczala, C.M., Meece, J.L. and Midgley, C. (1983). Expectancies, values, and academic behaviors. In

J.T. Spence (Ed.), *Achievement and achievement motivation* (75–146). W. H. Freeman.

Feibleman, James (1943). A systematic presentation of Peirce's ethics. *Ethics*, 53(2), 98–109.

Feibleman, James (1970). *An introduction to the philosophy of Charles S. Peirce*. MIT Press.

Firth, Roderick (1952). Ethical absolutism and the ideal observer. *Philosophy and Phenomenological Research*, 12, 317–345.

Fisch, Max (1954) [1986a]. Alexander Bain and the geneaology of pragmatism. In Kenneth Ketner and Christian Kloesel (Eds.), *Peirce, semeiotic and pragmatism* (79–109). Indiana University Press.

Fisch, Max (1967) [1986b]. Peirce's progress from nominalism to realism. In Kenneth Ketner and Christian Kloesel (Eds.), *Peirce, semeiotic and pragmatism* (184–200). Indiana University Press.

Foot, Philippa (1978) [2002]. *Virtues and vices and other essays in moral philosophy* (2nd ed.). Oxford University Press.

Frankena, William (1955). Hutcheson's moral sense theory. *Journal of the History of Ideas*, 16(3), 356–375.

Frankfurt, Harry (1969). Alternate possibilities and moral responsibility. *The Journal of Philosophy*, 66(23), 829–839.

Freeman, Christopher (1992). *The economics of hope: Essays on technical change, economic growth and the environment*. Pinter.

Gadamer, Hans-Georg (1975). *Truth and method*. Seabury Press.

Gauthier, David (1986). *Morals by agreement*. Oxford University Press.

Gibbard, Allan (1990). *Wise choices, apt feelings: A theory of normative judgement*. Clarendon Press.

Glauser, Richard and Savile, Anthony (2002). Aesthetic experience in Shaftesbury. *Proceedings of the Aristotelian Society, Supplementary Volumes*, 76, 25–74.

Goldman, Alvin (1970). *A theory of human action*. Prentice-Hall.

Goudge, Thomas (1950). *The thought of C. S. Peirce*. University of Toronto Press.

Gould, Stephen (1991). *Bully for brontosaurus*. Norton.

Grant, Jason (2019). How it feels to "tic out". *Tourette Association of America*. https://tourette.org/blogs/about-tourette/how-it-feels-to-tic-out/

Grean, Stanley (1967). *Shaftesbury's philosophy of religion and ethics: A study in enthusiasm*. Ohio University Press.

Grube, Hans (1927). Plato's theory of beauty. *The Monist*, 37(2), 269–288.

Habermas, Jürgen (1990). Discourse ethics: Notes on a program of philosophical justification (Christian Lenhardt and Shierry Nicholsen, Trans.). In Jürgen Habermas (Ed.), *Moral consciousness and communicative action*. MIT Press.

Hacking, Ian (1988). Origins of randomization in experimental design. *Isis*, 79(3), 427–451.

Hacking, Ian (1991). *The taming of chance*. Cambridge University Press.

Haidt, Jonathan (2012). *The righteous mind*. Pantheon.

Hamilton, William (1964). The genetical evolution of social behaviour. *Journal of Theoretical Biology*, 7, 1–52.

Hampton, Jean (1998). *The authority of reason*. Cambridge University Press.

Hare, R.M. (1981). *Moral thinking*. Oxford University Press.

Harman, Gilbert (1996). Moral relativism. In G. Harman and J.J. Thompson (Eds.), *Moral relativism and moral objectivity* (3–64). Blackwell Publishers.

Harman, Gilbert (2012). Naturalism in moral philosophy. In Susana Nuccetelli and Gary Seay (Eds.), *Ethical naturalism* (8–23). Cambridge University Press.

Harris Poll (2013, December 16). *American's belief in God, miracles and heaven declines*. www.theharrispoll.com/health-and life/Americans__Belief_in_God__Miracles_and_Heaven_Declines.html

Hartl, D.L. and Clark, A.G. (2006). *Principles of population genetics* (4th ed.). Sinauer Associations Inc.

Hobbes, Thomas (1641) [1971]. *Citizen* (Bernard Gert, Ed.). Anchor.

Hodgson, Geoffrey (2001). Is social evolution Lamarckian or Darwinian? In John Laurent and John Nightingale (Eds.), *Darwinism and evolutionary economics* (87–118). Edward Elgar.

Hoerber, Robert (1964). Plato's *Greater Hippias*. *Phronesis*, 9(2), 143–155.

Holmes, John Haynes (1915). *Is death the end?* G. P. Putnam and Sons.

Hookway, Christopher (2002). *Truth, rationality and pragmatism*. Clarendon Press.

Houser, Nathan (1998). Introduction. In Nathan Houser, et al. (Eds.), *The essential Peirce* (Vol. 2) (xvii–xxxviii). Indiana University Press.

Houser, Nathan (2010). Introduction. In Nathan Houser, et al. (Eds.), *The writings of Charles S. Peirce* (Vol. 8) (xxv–xcvii). Indiana University Press.

Hume, David (1739) [1978]. *Treatise of human nature* (L.A. Selby-Rigge and P.H. Nidditch, Eds.). Clarendon Press.

Hutcheson, Francis (1725) [1964a]. *An inquiry concerning the original of our ideas of virtue or moral good*. In L.A. Selby-Bigge (Ed.), *British moralists* (69–177). Bobbs-Merrill.

Hutcheson, Francis (1728) [1964b]. *Illustrations upon the moral sense*. In L.A. Selby-Bigge (Ed.), *British moralists* (403–418). Bobbs-Merrill.

Hutcheson, Francis (1730) [1993]. *Inaugural lecture on the social nature of man*. In Thomas Mautner (Ed.), *Francis Hutcheson: On human nature* (124–147). Cambridge University Press.

Ibri, Ivo (2016). Linking the aesthetic and the normative in Peirce's pragmaticism: A heuristic sketch. *Transactions of the Charles. S. Peirce Society*, 52(4), 598–610.

Jackson, Frank (1998). *From metaphysics to ethics*. Oxford University Press.

Jackson, Frank (2012). On ethical naturalism and the philosophy of language. In Susana Nuccetelli and Gary Seay (Eds.), *Ethical naturalism; current debates* (70–88). Cambridge University Press.

James, William (1891) [1992]. The moral philosopher and the moral life. In Gerald Myers (Ed.), *Writings 1878–1899* (595–617). Library of America.

Jonsen, Albert and Toulmin, Stephen (1988). *The abuse of casuistry*. University of California Press.

Jouffroy, Théodor (1838). *Philosophical miscellanies: Translated from the French of Cousin, Jourffroy, and B. Constant. With introductory and critical notices* (George Ripley, Trans.). Hiliard, Gray and Co.

Jouffroy, Théodor (1840). *Introduction to ethics* (W.H. Channing, Trans.) (Vols. 1–2). Hilliard, Gray and Co.

Kahneman, Daniel (2011). *Thinking, fast and slow*. Farrar, Straus and Giroux.

Kant, Immanuel (1781) [1929]. *Critique of pure reason* (Norman Kemp Smith, Trans.). Macmillan.

Kant, Immanuel (1785) [1959]. *Foundations of the metaphysics of morals* (Lewis White Beck, Trans.). Bobbs-Merrill Press.

Kant, Immanuel (1790) [1974]. *The critique of judgment* (J.H. Bernard, Trans.). Hafner Press.

Kant, Immanuel (1795) [1917]. *Perpetual peace* (M. Campbell Smith, Trans.). George Allen and Unwin.

Kant, Immanuel (1798) [1978]. *Anthropology from a pragmatic point of view* (Victor Lyle Dowdell, Trans.). Southern Illinois University Press.

Keeler, Mary (2004). Using Brandom's framework to do Peirce's normative science: Pragmatism as the game of harmonizing assertions? In K.E. Wolff, H.D. Pfeiffer and H.S. Delugach (Eds.), *Conceptual structures at work* (242–260). Springer.

Kent, Beverley (1976). Peirce's esthetics: A new look. *Transactions of the Charles S. Peirce Society*, 12(3), 263–283.

Kent, Beverley (1987). *Charles S. Peirce: Logic and the classification of the sciences*. McGill-Queens University Press.

Ketner, Kenneth and Putnam, Hilary (1992). Introduction: The consequences of mathematics. In Kenneth Ketner (Ed.), *Charles Sanders Peirce, reasoning and the logic of things* (1–54). Harvard University Press.

Kitcher, Philip (2011). *The ethical project*. Harvard University Press.

Kitcher, Philip (2012). *Preludes to pragmatism: Toward a reconstruction of philosophy*. Oxford University Press.

Kleist, Edward (2000). *Judging appearances: A phenomenological study of the Kantian sensus communis*. Springer.

Koren, Marina (2019, July 11). Why men thought women weren't made to vote. *The Atlantic*. www.theatlantic.com/science/archive/2019/07/womens-suffrage-nineteenth-amendment-pseudoscience/593710/

Korsgaard, Christine (1999). *Creating the kingdom of ends*. Cambridge University Press.

Kronfeldner, Maria (2007). Is cultural evolution Larmarckian? *Biology and Philosophy*, 22, 493–512.

Lane, Robert (2009). Persons, signs, animals: A Peircean account of personhood. *Transactions of the Charles S. Peirce Society*, 45(1), 1–26.

Leighton, Walter (1908). *French philosophers and New-England transcendentalism* [Unpublished doctoral dissertation]. University of Virginia.

Liszka, James Jakób (1996). *A general introduction to the semeiotic of Charles Peirce*. Indiana University Press.

Liszka, James Jakób (2000). Peirce's new rhetoric. *Transactions of the Charles S. Peirce Society*, 36(4), 439–477.

Liszka, James Jakób (2009). Rethinking the pragmatic maxim. *Cognitio*, 10(1), 61–81.

Liszka, James Jakób (2010). Peirce's revolutionary rhetoric. In Mats Bergman, Sami Paavola, Ahti-Veikko Pietarinen and Henrik Rydenfelt (Eds.), *Ideas in action: Proceedings of the applying Peirce conference*. Nordic studies in pragmatism (118–133). Helsinki University Press.

Liszka, James Jakób (2012). Charles Peirce on ethics. In Cornelis de Waal and Krzysztof Skowronski (Eds.), *The normative thought of Charles S. Peirce* (44–82). Fordham University Press.

Liszka, James Jakób (2014a). Peirce's evolutionary thought. In Torkild Thellefsen and Bent Sorensen (Eds.), *Charles Sanders Peirce in his own words: 100 years of semiotics, communication and cognition* (145–152). DeGruyter.

Liszka, James Jakób (2014b). Peirce's idea of ethics as a normative science. *Transactions of the Charles S. Peirce Society*, 50(4), 459–479.

Liszka, James Jakób (2018). The problematics of truth and solidarity in Peirce's rhetoric. *Semiotica*, 2018(220), 235–248.

Liszka, James Jakób (2019). Peirce's convergence theory of truth redux. *Cognitio*. 20(1), 91–112.

Liszka, James Jakób and Babb, Genie (2020). Abduction as an explanatory strategy in narrative. In Tony Jappy (Ed.), *The Bloomsbury companion to contemporary Peircean semiotics* (205–234). Bloomsbury.

Lloyd, Alfred (1907). *The will to doubt*. Swan Sonnenschein.

Locke, Alain (1923). The ethics of culture. *Harvard University Record*, 17, 178–185.

Mackie, J.L. (1977). *Ethics: Inventing right and wrong*. Penguin.

Madden, Edward and Manns, James (1987). Jouffroy's contributions to the common sense tradition. *Journal of the History of Philosophy*, 25(4), 573–584.

Mayorga, Rosa (2012). Peirce's moral realicism. In Corenlis de Waal and Piotr Skowronski (Eds.), *The normative thought of Charles S. Peirce* (101–124). Fordham University Press.

Mayr, E. (1974). Teleological and teleonomic, a new analysis. In R.S. Cohen and M.W. Wartofsky (Eds.), *A portrait of twenty-five years: Boston studies in the philosophy of science* (133–159). Springer.

Merton, Robert (1971). *The sociology of science: Theoretical and empirical investigations* (Norman Storer, Ed.). University of Chicago Press.

Metcalfe, J. Stanley (1993). Some Lamarckian themes in the theory of growth and economic selection: A provisional analysis. *Revue Internationale De Systemique*, 7, 487–504.

Misak, Cheryl (1991). *Truth and the end of inquiry: A Peircean account of truth*. Clarendon Press.

Misak, Cheryl (2000). *Truth, politics, morality: Pragmatism and deliberation*. Routledge.

Misak, Cheryl (2004). C. S. Peirce on vital matters. In Cheryl Misak (Ed.), *The Cambridge companion to Peirce* (150–174). Cambridge University Press.

Mischel, Theodore (1970). Wundt and the conceptual foundations of psychology. *Philosophy and Phenomenological Research*, 31(1), 1–26.

Moore, G.E. (1903). *Principia ethica*. Cambridge University Press.

Morillo, Carolyn (1990). The reward event and motivation. *Journal of Philosophy*, 87(4), 169–186.

Mountford, J.F. (1923). The musical scales of Plato's republic. *The Classical Quarterly*, 17(3/4), 125–136.

Murphey, Murray (1993). *The development of Peirce's philosophy*. Hackett.

Nagel, Thomas (1978). *The possibility of altruism*. Princeton University Press.

National Academies of Science (2020). *Evolution resources at the National Academies*. www.nationalacademies.org/evolution/science-and-religion

National Institute on Drug Abuse (2014). *Drugs, brains, and behavior: The science of addiction*. Pub. No. 14–5605. National Institutes of Health.

Nettleship, R. L. (1955). *The theory of education in Plato's Republic*. Oxford University Press.

Nietzsche, Friedrich (1886) [1990]. *Beyond good and evil* (R.J. Hollingdale, Trans.). Penguin.

Nozick, Robert (1974). *Anarchy, state, and utopia*. Basic.
Nubiola, Jaime (2009). What reasonableness really is. *Transactions of the Charles S. Peirce Society*, 45(2), 125–134.
Nussbaum, Martha (1990). *Love's knowledge*. Oxford University Press.
Oxford English Dictionary (2005). (3rd ed.). Oxford University Press.
Parfit, Derek (2011). *On what matters* (Vols. 1–3). Oxford University Press.
Parker, Kelly (2003). Reconstructing the normative sciences. *Cognition*, 4(1), 27–45.
Peirce, Charles (1958). *Values in a universe of chance: Selected writings of Charles S. Peirce* (Philip Wiener, Ed.). Doubleday. [Cited as VC].
Peirce, Charles (1976). *The new elements of mathematics* (Carolyn Eisele, Ed.) (Vols. 1–4). Mouton. [Cited as NEM].
Peirce, Charles (1977). *Semiotic and significs: The correspondence between Charles S. Peirce and Victoria Lady Welby* (Charles Hardwick, Ed.). Indiana University Press. [Cited as LW]
Peirce, Charles (1978a). *Charles S. Peirce: Contributions to the Nation* (Kenneth Ketner and James Cook, Eds.) (Vols. 1–3). Texas Tech University Press. [Cited as CN]
Peirce, Charles (1978b). *The collected papers of Charles S. Peirce* (Charles Hartshorne, Paul Weiss and Arthur Burks, Eds.) (Vols. 1–8). Harvard University Press. [Cited as CP].
Peirce, Charles (1982). *The writings of Charles S. Peirce* (Max Fisch, Edward Moore, Christian Kloesel, Nathan Houser, André De Tienne, et al. Eds.) (Vols. 1–6, 8). Indiana University Press. [Cited as W].
Peirce, Charles (1992a). *Reasoning and the logic of things* (Kenneth Ketner, Ed.). Harvard University Press. [Cited as RLT]
Peirce, Charles (1992b). *The essential Peirce* (Nathan Houser and Christian Kloesel, Eds.) (Vol. 1–2). Indiana University Press. [Cited as EP].
Peirce, Charles (1997). *Pragmatism as a principle and method of right thinking: The 1903 Harvard lectures on pragmatism* (Patricia Turrisi, Ed.). State University of New York Press. [Cited as HL].
Pew Research Center (2015, July 1). *Evolution and perceptions of scientific conw*perceptions-of-scientific-consensus/
Pew Research Center (2019, May 14). *Attitudes on same-sex marriage*. www.pewforum.org/fact-sheet/changing-attitudes-on-gay-marriage/
Plato [1961a]. *Euthydemus* (W.H.D. Rouse, Trans.). In Edith Hamilton and Huntington Cairns (Eds.), *The collected dialogues of Plato*. Princeton University Press.
Plato [1961b]. *Gorgias* (W.D. Woodhead, Trans.). In Edith Hamilton and Huntington Cairns (Eds.), *The collected dialogues of Plato*. Princeton University Press.
Plato [1961c]. *Greater Hippias* (Benjamin Jowett, Trans.). In Edith Hamilton and Huntington Cairns (Eds.), *The collected dialogues of Plato*. Princeton University Press.
Plato [1961d]. *The Philebus* (R. Hackforth, Trans.). In Edith Hamilton and Huntington Cairns (Eds.), *The collected dialogues of Plato*. Princeton University Press.
Plato [1961e]. *The Republic* (Paul Shorey, Trans.). In Edith Hamilton and Huntington Cairns (Eds.), *The collected dialogues of Plato*. Princeton University Press.

Plato [2014]. *The first Alcibiades* (Benjamin Jowett, Trans.). University of Adelaide Press.

Poisson, Siméon (1837). *Probabilité des jugements en matière criminelle et en matière civile, précédées des règles générales du calcul des probabilities*. Bachelier.

Potter, Vincent (1967). *Charles S. Peirce: On norms and ideals*. University of Massachusetts Press.

Prichard, H.A. (1968). *Moral obligation and duty and interest* (W.D. Ross and J.O. Urmson, Eds.). Oxford University Press.

Pritchard, James (Ed.) (1950). *Ancient near-Eastern texts*. Princeton University Press.

Putnam, Hilary (1987). *The many faces of realism*. Open Court.

Putnam, Hilary (1995). Pragmatism and moral objectivity. In M. Nussbaum and J. Glover (Eds.), *Women, culture and development: A study of human capabilities* (199–224). Oxford University Press.

Radcliffe, Elizabeth (1999). Hume on the generation of motives: Why beliefs alone never motivate. *Hume Studies*, 25(1&2), 101–122.

Rawls, John (1971). *A theory of justice*. Harvard University Press.

Rawls, John (1980). Kantian constructivism in moral theory. *Journal of Philosophy*, 77(9), 515–572.

Read, Dwight (2014). Incest taboos and kinship: A biological or cultural story? *Reviews in Anthropology*, 43(2), 150–175.

Reid, Thomas (1785) [1969]. *Essays on the intellectual powers of man*. MIT Press.

Reid, Thomas (1788) [1969]. *Essays on the active powers of the mind*. MIT Press.

Richardson, Henry (1994). *Practical reasoning about final ends*. Cambridge University Press.

Robin, Richard (1964). Peirce's doctrine of the normative sciences. In Edward Moore and Richard Robin (Eds.), *Studies in the philosophy of Charles Sanders Peirce: Second series* (271–288). University of Massachusetts Press.

Robin, Richard (1967). *Annotated catalogue of the papers of Charles S. Peirce*. University of Massachusetts Press.

Ross, W.D. (1930). *The right and the good: Some problems in ethics*. Clarendon Press.

Russell, Daniel (2005). *Plato on pleasure and the good life*. Oxford University Press.

Sanford, J.B. (1911). *Argument against women's suffrage*. https://sfpl.org/pdf/libraries/main/sfhistory/suffrageagainst.pdf

Santayana, George (1896) [1955]. *The sense of beauty*. Dover.

Scanlon, T.M. (2000). *What we owe each other*. Harvard University Press.

Schiller, Friedrich (1793a) [2005]. On Grace and Dignity (Jane Curran, Trans.). In Jane Curran and Christophe Fricker (Eds.), *Schiller's "On Grace and Dignity" in its cultural context: Essays and a new translation*. Camden House.

Schiller, Friedrich (1793b) [2003]. Kallias or concerning beauty: Letters to Gottfried Körner (Stefan Bird-Polan, Trans.). In J.M. Bernstein (Ed.), *Classic and romantic German aesthetics*. Cambridge University Press.

Schiller, Friedrich (1795) [1965]. *The aesthetic education of man* (Reginald Snell, Trans.). Frederick Ungar.

Schroeder, Mark (2007). The Humean theory of reasons. In Russ Schafer-Landau (Ed.), *Oxford studies in metaethics* (195–219). Oxford University Press.

Schroeder, Mark (2013). *Slaves of the passions*. Oxford University Press.
Schroeder, Mark (2014). *Explaining the reasons we share*. Oxford University Press.
Shafer-Landau, Russ (2003). *Moral realism: A defence*. Clarendon Press.
Shaftesbury, Anthony Ashley Cooper, Third Early of (1711) [1999]. *Characteristics of men, manners, opinions, times* (L.E. Klein, Ed.). Cambridge University Press.
Shaftesbury, Anthony Ashley Cooper, Third Early of (1900). *The life, unpublished letters, and philosophical regimen of Anthony, Earl of Shaftesbury* (Benjamin Rand, Ed.). Swan Sonnenshein.
Short, Thomas (2007). *Peirce's theory of signs*. Cambridge University Press.
Short, Thomas (2012). Normative science? *Transactions of the Charles S. Peirce Society*, 48(3), 310–334.
Simon, Herbert (1956). Rational choice and the structure of the environment. *Psychological Review*, 63(2), 129–138.
Simon, Herbert (1981). *The sciences of the artificial* (2nd ed.). MIT Press.
Sloan, Douglas (1979). The teaching of ethics in the American undergraduate curriculum, 1876–1976. *The Hastings Center Report*, 9(6), 21–41.
Smith, Adam (1759) [1976]. *Theory of the moral sentiments*. Oxford University Press.
Smith, Adam (1776) [1904]. *The wealth of nations* (Edwin Cannan, Ed.). Methuen.
Smith, Michael (1987). The Humean theory of motivation. *Mind*, 96(381), 36–61.
Smith, Michael (2000). *Moral realism*. In Hugh Lafollette (Ed.), *The Blackwell guide to ethical theory* (15–37). Blackwell.
Sørensen, Bent and Thellefsen, Torkild (2004). Making the knowledge profile of C. S. Peirce's concept of esthetics. *Semiotica*, 151(1/4), 1–39.
Stevenson, C.L. (1937). The emotive meaning of ethical terms. *Mind*, 46(181), 14–31.
Stevenson, C.L. (1944). *Ethics and language*. Yale University Press.
Stigler, Stephen (1986). *The history of statistics*. Harvard University Press.
Stuhr, John (1994). Rendering the world more reasonable: The practical significance of Peirce's normative science. In Herman Parret (Ed.), *Peirce and value theory* (3–15). John Benjamins.
Talisse, Robert (2005). *Democracy after liberalism: Pragmatism and deliberative politics*. Routledge.
Trammell, Richard (1973). Charles Sanders Peirce and Henry James the Elder. *Transactions of the Charles S. Peirce Society*, 9(4), 202–220.
Überweg, Friedrich (1857). *System der Logik und Geschichte der logischen Lehren*. Marcus.
Velleman, J. David (1996). The possibility of practical reason. *Ethics*, 106(4), 694–726.
Velleman, J. David (2013). *Foundations for moral relativism*. Open Book Publishers.
Wallace, James (2009). *Norms and practices*. Cornell University Press.
Walzer, Michael (1994). *Thick and thin: Moral argument at home and abroad*. University of Notre Dame Press.
Whewell, William (1846). *Lectures on systematic morality*. John Parker.
Whewell, William (1864). *The elements of morality, including polity* (4th ed.). Cambridge University Press.
Wigfield, Allan and Jacquelynne, S. Eccles (1992). The development of achievement task values: A theoretical analysis. *Developmental Review*, 12(3), 265–310.

Wigfield, Allan and Jacquelynne, S. Eccles (2000). Expectancy-value theory of achievement motivation. *Contemporary Educational Psychology*, 25(1), 68–81.
Wiggins, David (1998). *Needs, values, truth* (3rd ed.). Clarendon Press.
Wiggins, David (2006). *Ethics: Twelve lectures on the philosophy of morality*. Harvard University Press.
Williams, Bernard (1993). *Moral luck*. Cambridge University Press.
Wundt, Wilhelm (1908). *Logik: Eine Untersuchung der Prinzipien der Erkenntnis und der Methoden wissenschaflicher Foruschung* (3rd ed.) (Vols. 1–3). Enke.
Xenophon [1965]. *Memoribilia* (Anna Benjamin, Trans.). Bobbs-Merrill.

Index

Printed in Great Britain
by Amazon